JAMESTOWN  EDUCATION

Literature

An Adapted Reader

Grade 9

Mc Graw Hill **Glencoe**

New York, New York   Columbus, Ohio   Chicago, Illinois   Peoria, Illinois   Woodland Hills, California

JAMESTOWN EDUCATION

 Glencoe

The *McGraw·Hill* Companies

ACKNOWLEDGMENTS
Grateful acknowledgment is given authors, publishers, photographers, museums, and agents for permission to reprint the following copyrighted material. Every effort has been made to determine copyright owners. In case of any omissions, the Publisher will be pleased to make suitable acknowledgments in future editions.
Acknowledgments continued on p. 300.

Send all inquiries to:
Glencoe/McGraw-Hill
8787 Orion Place
Columbus, OH 43240-4027

ISBN-13: 978-0-07-874316-0 (Student Edition)
ISBN-10: 0-07-874316-8 (Student Edition)

ISBN-13: 978-0-07-874329-0 (Annotated Teacher Edition)
ISBN-10: 0-07-874329-X (Annotated Teacher Edition)

Printed in the United States of America
2 3 4 5 6 7 8 9 10 079 11 10 09 08 07

Contents

UNIT ② Short Story......68

UNIT ③ Drama......144

Why Use This Book?

Read a Variety of Texts

The notes and features of *Jamestown Literature* guide you through the process of reading and understanding each literature selection. As you use these notes and features, you practice the skills and strategies that good readers use whenever they read.

UNIT 1

Short Story

What's a Short Story?

Everyone loves a good story. When something exciting happens to you, chances are you can't wait to pick up the phone, find a friend, or send an e-mail to share the experience. Some of the most entertaining stories, however, describe situations and events that never actually happened! These are called short stories.

A **short story** is a brief piece of fiction—writing that is about imaginary people and events. Like most literary forms, a short story can take many shapes. It might be as short as one page or as long as fifty pages. It might be made up mostly of dialogue, or it might have no speech—or even human characters—at all. However, all good stories share a sense of direction. Whether the author wants to teach us, show us, amuse us, or scare us, a good story takes us somewhere, and we are happy to go along for the ride.

What qualities do you think make a good short story?

Why Read Short Stories?

Short stories give us an opportunity to see life through the eyes of others. Everyone's experiences are different. It's only by sharing stories that we gain a clear picture of the world around us. In the next section of this book, you will read four short stories. Each offers a unique view of life.

Your *reason* for reading might affect the way you read a story:

• If you're reading simply for recreation, you might read quickly as you get involved with the characters and events.

• If you're reading for a class, you might take your time, looking for specific details to discuss with your classmates.

How Do I Read Short Stories?

Focus on key **literary elements** and **reading skills** to get the most out of reading the short stories in this unit. Here are two key literary elements and two key reading skills that you will practice in this unit.

Key Literary Elements

• Setting

The **setting** is the time and place of a story. The setting includes the values and beliefs of the time and place. For example, if the setting of a story is New York City in the early 1900s, people will have different values and beliefs than a story that is set in ancient Greece. The setting often helps create a mood or atmosphere.

• Theme

A **theme** is the important message of a story. It tells about life or human nature. To figure out the theme, ask yourself, "What does this story mean?" A story may have more than one theme, but one message will probably be the strongest. For example, if a story tells about two friends who help each other through hard times, the theme is probably the importance of friendship.

Key Reading Skills

• Predict

When you **predict**, you use details from the story and what you know to make a guess about what may happen in a story. As a skillful reader, you become involved in the action of a story and in the behavior of the characters. You wonder what will happen next. How will this character behave when faced with a problem? As you continue reading, you check to see if your predictions are correct. Don't worry if your prediction isn't right. You can change your predictions as you get more information from the story.

• Respond

When you stop and consider your thoughts and feelings about something you've read, you are **responding.** Active readers respond to what they are reading. Think about what you read and how you feel about it. You can ask yourself, "How does this make me feel?" and "What does this mean to me?" You don't have to answer aloud. But thinking about and answering these questions will help you to understand what you have read.

What Is It? Why Read?

The genre, or type of writing, is defined for you at the beginning of the unit. Learn why a particular genre offers important and entertaining reading.

Literary Elements and Reading Skills

New literary elements and reading skills are introduced in each unit opener. Use these elements and skills to get the most out of your reading.

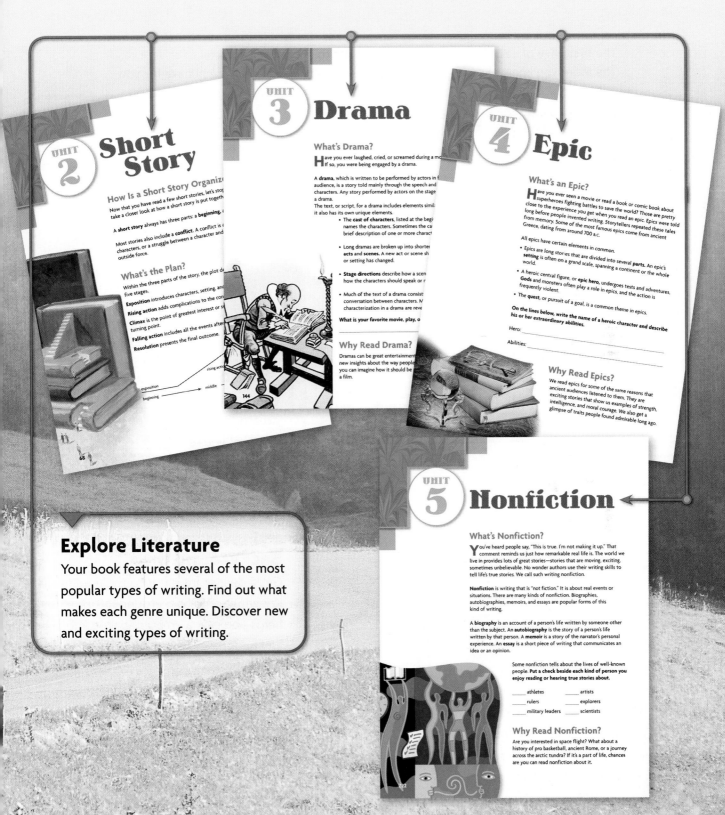

UNIT 2 — Short Story

How Is a Short Story Organized?

Now that you have read a few short stories, let's stop
take a closer look at how a short story is put togeth

A **short story** always has three parts: a **beginning,**

Most stories also include a **conflict.** A conflict is a
characters, or a struggle between a character and
outside force.

What's the Plan?

Within the three parts of the story, the plot d
five stages.

Exposition introduces characters, setting, and

Rising action adds complications to the con

Climax is the point of greatest interest or s
turning point.

Falling action includes all the events after

Resolution presents the final outcome.

68

UNIT 3 — Drama

What's Drama?

Have you ever laughed, cried, or screamed during a mo
If so, you were being engaged by a drama.

A **drama,** which is written to be performed by actors in f
audience, is a story told mainly through the speech and
characters. Any story performed by actors on the stage
a drama.

The text, or script, for a drama includes elements simila
it also has its own unique elements.

• The **cast of characters,** listed at the begi
names the characters. Sometimes the ca
brief description of one or more charact

• Long dramas are broken up into shorter
acts and scenes. A new act or scene sh
or setting has changed.

• **Stage directions** describe how a scen
how the characters should speak or r

• Much of the text of a drama consist
conversation between characters. M
characterization in a drama are reve

What is your favorite movie, play, o

Why Read Drama?

Dramas can be great entertainment
new insights about the way people
you can imagine how it should be
a film.

144

UNIT 4 — Epic

What's an Epic?

Have you ever seen a movie or read a book or comic book about
superheroes fighting battles to save the world? Those are pretty
close to the experience you get when you read an epic. Epics were told
long before people invented writing. Storytellers repeated these tales
from memory. Some of the most famous epics come from ancient
Greece, dating from around 700 B.C.

All epics have certain elements in common.

• Epics are long stories that are divided into several **parts.** An epic's
setting is often on a grand scale, spanning a continent or the whole
world.

• A heroic central figure, or **epic hero,** undergoes tests and adventures.
Gods and monsters often play a role in epics, and the action is
frequently violent.

• The **quest,** or pursuit of a goal, is a common theme in epics.

**On the lines below, write the name of a heroic character and describe
his or her extraordinary abilities.**

Hero: _____

Abilities: _____

Why Read Epics?

We read epics for some of the same reasons that
ancient audiences listened to them. They are
exciting stories that show us examples of strength,
intelligence, and moral courage. We also get a
glimpse of traits people found admirable long ago.

Explore Literature

Your book features several of the most
popular types of writing. Find out what
makes each genre unique. Discover new
and exciting types of writing.

UNIT 5 — Nonfiction

What's Nonfiction?

You've heard people say, "This is true. I'm not making it up." That
comment reminds us just how remarkable real life is. The world we
live in provides lots of great stories—stories that are moving, exciting,
sometimes unbelievable. No wonder authors use their writing skills to
tell life's true stories. We call such writing nonfiction.

Nonfiction is writing that is "not fiction." It is about real events or
situations. There are many kinds of nonfiction. Biographies,
autobiographies, memoirs, and essays are popular forms of this
kind of writing.

A **biography** is an account of a person's life written by someone other
than the subject. An **autobiography** is the story of a person's life
written by that person. A **memoir** is a story of the narrator's personal
experience. An **essay** is a short piece of writing that communicates an
idea or an opinion.

Some nonfiction tells about the lives of well-known
people. **Put a check beside each kind of person you
enjoy reading or hearing true stories about.**

_____ athletes   _____ artists

_____ rulers   _____ explorers

_____ military leaders _____ scientists

Why Read Nonfiction?

Are you interested in space flight? What about a
history of pro basketball, ancient Rome, or a journey
across the arctic tundra? If it's a part of life, chances
are you can read nonfiction about it.

Get Set!

The first page of each lesson helps you get ready to read. It sets the stage for your reading. The more you know about the reading up front, the more meaning it will have for you.

Get Ready to Read!
Sweet Potato Pie

Meet
Eugenia Collier

Eugenia Collier was born in 1928. She went to segregated schools before college. She became a college teacher and an award-winning writer. Of her career, Collier stated, "The fact of my blackness is the core and center of my creativity. . . . I discovered the richness, the diversity, the beauty of my black heritage." "Sweet Potato Pie" was first published in 1972.

What You Know
Sometimes people make judgments about others based on visual clues, such as the style of their clothes or the kind of backpacks they carry. Do you think it's fair to make judgments based on visual clues? Discuss your opinions with other classmates.

Reason to Read
Read to see how two brothers view symbols of social standing or importance.

Background Info
Sharecropping was a farming system common in the South in the years between the Civil War and World War II. Sharecroppers, who were mostly African Americans, farmed land that belonged to someone else. The landowner allowed the sharecroppers to live on the land in exchange for a large portion of the crop. Sharecroppers worked very hard but almost never had enough money to meet their basic needs. In the 1940s, machines ended the need for sharecroppers. Hundreds of thousands of African Americans headed north to find work in cities.

What You Know
Think about your own experience and share your knowledge and opinions. Then, build on what you know as you read the lesson.

Reason to Read
Set a purpose for reading. Having a reason to read helps you get involved in what you read.

Background Info
Get a deeper insight into the reading. Knowing some background information helps you gain a greater appreciation and understanding of what you read.

Meet the Author
Meet the authors to get to know where they come from, what or who inspires them, and why they write.

Build Vocabulary

Each lesson introduces you to words that help build your vocabulary. You'll find these words in the reading. Understanding these words before you read makes reading easier.

Word Power

In an after-reading activity, you practice the vocabulary words you learned in the lesson.

Word Power (card, top left)

elated (i lā´ tid) *adj.* filled with joy; p. 251
I was *elated* when I got the lead part in the school play.

imposing (im pōz´ ing) *adj.* impressive in appearance or manner; p. 254
King Kong was *imposing*, standing over three stories tall.

exhilarated (ig zil´ a rāt´ id) *adj.* cheerful, lively, or excited; refreshed; p. 255
I was *exhilarated* when I found out our family was taking a camping trip.

collateral (ka lat´ ar al) *n.* money or property that is given to a lender as a pledge that a loan will be repaid; p. 255
When I lent my friend money, he gave me his video game as *collateral*.

eloquence (el´ a kwans) *n.* an expressive or strong way of speaking; p. 257
If you want to make the debate team, you must learn to speak with *eloquence*.

Answer the following questions that contain the new words above. Write your answers in the spaces provided.

1. If you are feeling *exhilarated*, are you excited or bored? _____

2. If something is *imposing*, is it remarkable or dull? _____

3. If you give someone *collateral*, are you likely or unlikely to repay the loan?

4. If you are *elated*, are you miserable or extremely happy? _____

5. If someone speaks with *eloquence*, does he or she speak well or poorly?

(Reading passage, center)

My father worked with Mr. Shimada for ten years, becoming first the buyer for his Seattle store and later, manager of the Portland branch. During this time Mr. Shimada continued on a course of **exhilarated** expansion. He established two Japanese banks in Seattle, bought a fifteen-room house outside the dreary confines of the Japanese community and dressed his wife and daughter in velvets and ostrich feathers. When his daughter became eighteen, he sent her to study in Paris, and the party he gave on the eve of her departure, with musicians, as well as caterers to serve roast turkey, venison, baked ham and champagne, seemed to verify rumors that he had become one of the first Japanese millionaires of America.

In spite of his phenomenal success, however, Mr. Shimada never forgot his early friends nor lost any of his generosity, and this, ironically enough, was his undoing. Many of the women for whom he had once sewn dresses were now well established, and they came to him requesting loans with which they and their husbands might open grocery stores and laundries and shoe repair shops. Mr. Shimada helped them all and never demanded any **collateral**. He operated his banks on faith and trust and gave no thought to such common prudence as maintaining a reserve.

When my father was called to a new position with a large Japanese firm in San Francisco, Mr. Shimada came down to Portland to extend personally his good wishes. He took Father to a Chinese dinner and told him over the peanut duck and chow mein that he would like always to be considered a friend.

"If I can ever be of assistance to you," he said, "don't ever hesitate to call." And with a firm shake of the hand, he wished father well.

Word Power

exhilarated (ig zil´ a rāt´ id) *adj.* cheerful, lively, or excited; refreshed
collateral (ka lat´ ar al) *n.* money or property that is given to a lender as a pledge that a loan will be repaid

C Word Power (card, right)

Complete each sentence below, using one of the words in the box.

> elated imposing exhilarated
> collateral eloquence

1. The court house is a grand, _____ building, with wide steps and huge columns in the front.

2. Taylor felt _____ after her refreshing swim in the cold lake.

3. My little sister was _____ when she got the dollhouse she wanted for her birthday.

4. People may not lend you money unless you give them _____

5. The speaker spoke with _____ at our graduation ceremony.

Circle the word that best completes each sentence.

6. Jamal's **(eloquence, imposing)** brought tears to the eyes of the audience.

7. Sadao was **(elated, collateral)** at the happy news.

8. Sarah was **(imposing, exhilarated)** by the climb up the mountain and greatly enjoyed the view.

9. Nate was reluctant to use his house as **(eloquence, collateral)** for the loan.

10. The tall woman wearing the long robe was very **(elated, imposing)**.

260

Word Power

Before you read, you learn key vocabulary words and their definitions. The definitions and sample sentences help you complete the questions that follow.

Word Power Footnotes

Look for pronunciations and definitions of vocabulary words at the bottom of pages throughout the reading. Vocabulary words appear in dark type in the text.

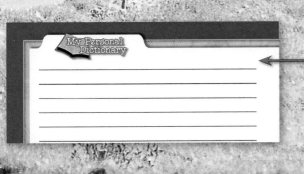

My Personal Dictionary

As you read, jot down words in your personal dictionary that you want to learn more about. Later, ask a classmate or your teacher what they mean, or look them up in a dictionary.

Read, Respond, Interact

Notes in "My Workspace" support and guide you through the reading process. Interact with and respond to the text by answering the questions or following the directions in the workspace notes.

Literary Element

notes help you understand important features of literature. Whenever you read text that is highlighted in blue, look for a Literary Element note in your workspace.

English Coach notes

explain difficult or unusual words and cultural references. Whenever you read text that is highlighted in red, look for an English Coach note in your workspace.

Reading Skill notes let

you practice active reading strategies that help good readers think as they read. Whenever you read text that is highlighted in green, look for a Reading Skill note in your workspace.

Use the **Did You Know?** feature to get a clear picture of something interesting in the text.

Adapted from

American History

Judith Ortiz Cofer

Literary Element

Setting El Building is one setting in the story. Underline details on this page that help describe El Building. Three details have already been highlighted for you.

English Coach

Viragos (vi rä´ gōs) in Spanish means "bad-tempered women." In this story, these women use harsh language. Check the three words below that also mean "bad-tempered."
- [ ] cranky
- [ ] irritable
- [ ] cheerful
- [ ] crabby

Word Power

profound (pra found´) *adj.* significant; deep; intense

I once read in a *Ripley's Believe it or Not* column that Paterson, New Jersey, is the place where the Straight and Narrow (streets) intersect. The Puerto Rican tenement known as El Building was one block up from Straight. It was, in fact, the corner of Straight and Market; not "at" the corner, but *the corner*.

At almost any hour of the day, El Building was like a monstrous jukebox, blasting out *salsas* from open windows as the residents, mostly new immigrants just up from the island, tried to drown out whatever they were currently enduring with loud music. But the day President Kennedy was shot, there was a **profound** silence in El Building; even the abusive tongues of *viragos*, the cursing of the unemployed, and the screeching of small children had been somehow muted. President Kennedy was a saint to these people. In fact, soon his photograph would be hung alongside the Sacred Heart and over the spiritist altars that many women kept in their apartments.

Did You Know?

John F. Kennedy was shot and killed on November 22, 1963. He was the thirty-fifth president of the United States.

18

My Workspace

Comprehension Check

Reread the boxed text. What makes Doodle always want to try again?

_____

_____

_____

_____

Reading Skill

Sequence Reread the highlighted text. What takes place at the party? Number the events in the order in which they occur.

_____ The narrator waltzes Aunt Nicey around.

_____ Doodle walks across the room.

_____ Mama cries and both parents hug Doodle.

_____ The narrator brings Doodle to the door in the go-cart.

He'd nod his head, and I'd say, "Well, if you don't keep trying, you'll never learn." Then I'd paint for him a picture of us as old men, white-haired, him with a long white beard and me still pulling him around in the go-cart. This never failed to make him try again.

Finally one day, after many weeks of practicing, he stood alone for a few seconds. When he fell, I grabbed him in my arms and hugged him. Now we knew it could be done. "Yes, yes," I cried, and he cried it too.

With success so close, we decided not to tell anyone until he could actually walk. Each day, except when it rained, we sneaked into Old Woman Swamp, and by cotton-picking time Doodle was ready to show what he could do. He still wasn't able to walk far, but we could wait no longer. We chose to reveal all on Doodle's sixth birthday, and for weeks ahead we promised everybody a most spectacular surprise.

On our chosen day, when Mama, Daddy, and Aunt Nicey were in the dining room, I brought Doodle to the door in the go-cart just as usual and had them turn their backs. I helped Doodle up, and when he was standing alone I let them look. There wasn't a sound as Doodle walked slowly across the room and sat down at his place at the table. Then Mama began to cry and ran over to him, hugging him and kissing him. Daddy hugged him too, so I went to Aunt Nicey, and began to waltz her around.

Doodle told them it was I who had taught him to walk, so everyone wanted to hug me, and I began to cry.

"What are you crying for?" asked Daddy, but I couldn't answer. They did not know that I did it for myself, that pride, whose slave I was, spoke to me louder than all their voices, and that Doodle walked only because I was ashamed of having a crippled brother.

90

x

Della finished her cry and attended to her cheeks with the powder rag. She stood by the window and looked out dully at a gray cat walking a gray fence in a gray backyard. Tomorrow would be Christmas Day, and she had only $1.87 with which to buy Jim a present. She had been saving every penny she could for months, with this result. Twenty dollars a week doesn't go far. Expenses had been greater than she had calculated. They always are. Only $1.87 to buy a present for Jim. Her Jim. Many a happy hour she had spent planning for something nice for him. Something fine and rare and silver—something just a little bit near to being worthy of the honor of being owned by Jim.

Suddenly Della whirled from the window and stood before the mirror. Her eyes were shining brilliantly, but her face had lost its color within twenty seconds. Rapidly she pulled down her hair and let it fall to its full length.

Now, there were two possessions of the James Dillingham Youngs in which they both took a mighty pride. One was Jim's gold watch that had been his father's and his grandfather's. The other was Della's hair. Had the Queen of Sheba lived in the next door, Della would have let her hair hang out the window some day to dry just to make Her Majesty jealous.

Had King Solomon been the janitor, with all his treasures piled up in the basement, Jim would have pulled out his watch every time he passed, just to see him pluck at his beard from envy.

So now Della's beautiful hair fell about her, rippling and shining like a cascade of brown waters. It reached below her knee and made itself almost a piece of clothing for her. And then she did it up again nervously and quickly. Once she faltered for a minute and stood still while a tear or two splashed on the worn red carpet.

Connect to the Text

Reread the text boxed in purple. Have you ever wanted to buy a nice gift for someone but were unable to afford it? How did you feel? What are some alternatives to buying a gift?

_____
_____
_____

Comprehension Check

Reread the text boxed in green. Underline the two things that Jim and Della value most.

Connect to the Text

notes help you connect what you're reading to something in your own life. Whenever you read text that is boxed in purple, look for a Connect to the Text note in your workspace.

Comprehension Check notes

help you understand what you're reading. Whenever you read text that is boxed in green, look for a Comprehension Check note in your workspace.

"In the other direction lie two cliffs. One of them nearly touches the sky with its sharp peak. The summit is always in clouds. No man could ever climb this mountain, even if he had twenty hands and feet. The rock is smooth and polished. In the middle of this rock there is a shadowy cave toward the westward. Make for that cave, noble Odysseus. The cave is so high a strong archer could not reach it with his arrow. This is where Scylla lives, shrieking terribly. Her voice is like a newborn puppy's, it's true, but she herself is a huge monster. No one would like to meet her. I tell you, not even a god."

"She has twelve dangling feet and six long necks. On each neck there is a gruesome head, each head with three rows of teeth. She wallows in the middle of her hollow cave and pokes her heads out of the cavern. She fishes there, watching about the rock for dolphins and even whales, if they come by. No one has ever passed her unharmed. She always snatches a man from the ships with each of her heads."

"The other cliff is lower. Here there is a large wild fig-tree. Under this, Charybdis sucks in the black water. Three times a day she sucks it in, and three times a day she spouts it out. Don't be there when she sucks the water in, for then no one could save you, not even Poseidon himself. You'd better sail by Scylla. It's better to lose six of your companions than the whole ship."

"Tell me, O goddess," I said, "can I avoid Charybdis and attack Scylla when she rushes to **seize** my men?"

"Stubborn fool," she replied, "you're asking for trouble. Won't you yield even to the immortal gods? Scylla cannot be killed. She is a deathless evil, terrible and difficult and fierce. You cannot fight with her. There is no defense. Flight is the only course. If you delay for a fight, she'll come back for another round of six men. Make haste through that point and pray that Scylla takes no more men."

Word Power

seize (sēz) v. to grab and hold suddenly

Reading Skill

Visualize Reread the description of Scylla (sil′ə), highlighted in green. Use the details to draw a sketch of Scylla.

Your Sketch

Background Info

Charybdis (kə rib′ dis) is a monster in the form of a whirlpool.

Literary Element

Epic Hero Reread the text highlighted in blue. Circe calls Odysseus a "stubborn fool." Which characteristic of an epic hero does Odysseus's stubbornness display? Check the correct response.

☐ It shows human faults.
☐ It shows he is a larger-than-life figure.
☐ It shows he is doing something that will earn him fame.

The margin notes let you interact with what you're reading in several ways. Some notes ask you to write out your response. Other notes may ask you to draw a picture, underline answers in the text, or interact in some other way.

Background Info notes give

information about a particular event, time, person, or place mentioned in the reading. Whenever you read text that is boxed in orange, look for a Background Info note in your workspace.

Wrap It Up!

The Break Time, Respond to Literature, and Compare and Contrast pages help you focus your understanding of the text. You apply the skills and strategies you've practiced during reading.

Literary Element

In this activity, use the lesson's literary element to help you understand passages from the reading.

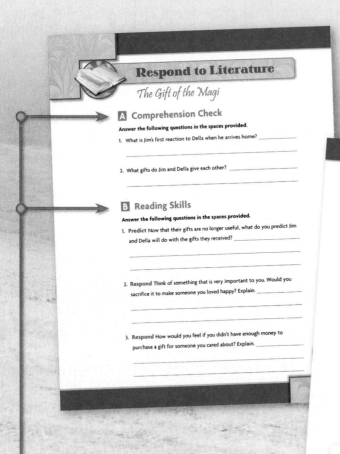

Respond to Literature
The Gift of the Magi

A Comprehension Check

Answer the following questions in the spaces provided.

1. What is Jim's first reaction to Della when he arrives home? _____

2. What gifts do Jim and Della give each other? _____

B Reading Skills

Answer the following questions in the spaces provided.

1. Predict Now that their gifts are no longer useful, what do you predict Jim and Della will do with the gifts they received? _____

2. Respond Think of something that is very important to you. Would you sacrifice it to make someone you loved happy? Explain. _____

3. Respond How would you feel if you didn't have enough money to purchase a gift for someone you cared about? Explain. _____

Respond to Literature

D Literary Element: Epic Hero

The passage below comes from the part of *The Odyssey* you have just read. As you reread it, think about what the sentences reveal about Odysseus's qualities as an epic hero.

Eurycleia hurried in, following Telemachus.[1] She found Odysseus standing among the dead, spattered with blood.[2] He looked like a lion that has devoured an ox.[3] His chest and cheeks were covered with gore.[4] When she saw the dead and all the blood, she began to raise a shout of praise, but Odysseus stopped her on the spot.[5] "Old woman," he said, "rejoice quietly.[6] It is not holy to boast over the slain.[7] The gods have brought these men low because they had no respect for anyone."[8]

1. What details in sentences 1–5 help you understand that Odysseus is the kind of hero who takes action when faced with a conflict? _____

2. In sentences 6–8, what does Odysseus tell Eurycleia to stop doing? What does that show about his character? _____

Comprehension Check and Reading Skills

In the Comprehension Check activity, you recall events and facts from the text. In the Reading Skills activity, you apply the reading skills you practiced while reading.

Break Time

Think about how the narrator and his father relate to Grandma. How do they interact with her when she first arrives? How do they interact with her after she has lived with them for awhile? Complete the chart by adding details about the narrator's and the father's relationships with Grandma. Examples have been provided.

Grandma's relationships with the family		
	when she first arrives	after she's lived with the family for awhile
narrator	The narrator does not understand Grandma at all.	The narrator begins to appreciate Grandma's sense of humor.
father		

GO Turn the page to continue reading.

Break Time

The Break Time page helps you organize your thoughts about the text.

E Comic Strip

Look at the four frames of the comic strip below. Read the speech balloons for Richard's brother and parents. Add words to Richard's thought balloons to show what he might be thinking. Draw more details and color in the frames if you wish.

276

Writing Activity

Develop your writing skills by completing various types of activities. Here's your chance to be creative!

Assessment

Fill in the circle next to each correct answer.

1. How many brothers does the author have?
   - ○ A. four
   - ○ B. five
   - ○ C. six
   - ○ D. seven

2. Based on details from the essay, which statement could you make about the author?
   - ○ A. She thinks her family is too noisy.
   - ○ B. She loves her visits to Mexico City.
   - ○ C. College was not what she hoped it would be.
   - ○ D. Her father's approval makes her happy.

3. At the start of the essay, the author sets out to
   - ○ A. describe her family members in detail so that readers get to know them all.
   - ○ B. persuade readers that a college education is valuable.
   - ○ C. explain why being an only daughter has made her who she is.
   - ○ D. inform readers about a culture they may not know well.

4. In this essay, the author is
   - ○ A. a writer and a college professor.
   - ○ B. a mother and wife.
   - ○ C. a student in high school.

s.

ns a collection of writings?

247

Assessment

The lesson assessment helps you evaluate what you learned in the lesson.

Wrap-up

Compare and Contrast

Black Boy and *Night* are **autobiographical** writings. In each selection, the author writes about a terrible experience he lived through. Although the times and places of their experiences are different, both authors are deeply affected by the events.

Complete the boxes below. In the left box, tell how the stories are alike. In the right box, tell how they are different. Consider the following points in your comparison:

- the settings
- each boy's age
- their relationships with their parents
- their situations
- their feelings

An example in each column has been done for you.

Alike	Different
• Both authors are young boys.	• Richard is very scared of his mother and tries to hide from her. Elie loves his father and is scared he will be killed by the SS.

293

Compare and Contrast

The Compare and Contrast activity helps you see how two texts are alike and different.

The What, Why, and How of Reading

LITERARY ELEMENTS

Each lesson focuses on one literary element. Before you begin a lesson, read carefully the explanations of the literary elements found at the beginning of the unit. You can refer to this chart for an overview. The more familiar you become with these important features, the more you will understand and appreciate each reading.

Unit 1	What Is It?	Example
	Setting The setting is the time and place of a story. The setting can also include the culture, values, and beliefs of the time and place. The setting often helps create a mood or atmosphere.	In "The Pit and the Pendulum," the setting of a dark, gloomy dungeon helps to create an eerie atmosphere.
	Theme A theme is the important message of a story. It tells about life or human nature. A story may have more than one theme, but one message will probably be the strongest.	The theme of "The Horned Toad," that every creature should be left where it belongs, is illustrated by what happens to both the lizard and Grandma.
Unit 2	**Plot** Plot is the story's basic framework. The exposition introduces the characters, the setting, and the conflict. Then the rising action builds to a climax, or emotional high point. The falling action shows the results of the climax. The resolution is the story's end.	In "The Open Window," after characters are introduced, their conversations lead to a surprising climax, followed by a resolution that explains what came before.
	Tone Tone is the writer's attitude toward a subject. A writer's tone may be communicated through words and details that express emotions and evoke an emotional response in the reader.	In "Sweet Potato Pie," the author uses a tone of love and respect when writing about Buddy's relationship with his brother Charley.

Unit 3	What Is It?	Example
	Conflict Conflict is a struggle between two opposing forces. An external conflict is a struggle between a character and an outside force. An internal conflict is a problem within a character's mind.	In *Romeo and Juliet*, an external conflict exists between two families. Romeo and Juliet also face an internal conflict about their relationship.
Unit 4	**Epic Hero** The central character in an epic is an epic hero. Epic heroes are larger-than-life figures with superhuman qualities. They are stronger, smarter, and braver than the average person.	In *The Odyssey*, Odysseus shows great strength, wisdom, and courage when he leads his men in their escape from the Cyclops.
Unit 5	**Author's Purpose** The author's purpose is his or her reason for writing. An author's purpose can be to inform, to persuade, or to entertain—or a combination of several purposes.	In "Of Dry Goods and Black Bow Ties," the author's purpose is to inform the reader of the difficulties an immigrant faces.
	Autobiography In an autobiography, a writer tells his or her life story from the first-person point of view, using the pronouns *I, me, my,* and *mine*.	In *Night* the author describes events from his own life as he tries to survive in a concentration camp during World War II.

READING SKILLS

You will use reading skills to respond to questions in the lessons. Before you begin a lesson, read carefully the explanations of the reading skills found at the beginning of the unit. You can refer to this chart for an overview. The more you practice the skills in the chart, the more these active reading strategies will become a natural part of the way you read.

Unit 1	What Is It?	Why It's Important	How To Do It
	Predict Predicting is making an educated guess about what will happen.	Predicting gives you a reason to read. It helps you get involved in the action of a story and in the behavior of the characters.	Combine what you already know with clues in the text to guess what will happen next.
	Respond You are responding when you stop and consider your thoughts and feelings about something you've read.	When you react in a personal way to what you are reading, you enjoy it more and understand it better.	Consider how you feel about what you read. Also ask yourself, "How would I act in this situation?"
Unit 2	**Sequence** Sequence is the order in which events occur. Stories can be told in the order in which events actually occur or told out of order.	Following the sequence of events helps you see how a text is organized. It also helps you understand how events relate to each other.	As you read, look for clue words like *first*, *then*, and *later*. These words can help you figure out the order in which things happen.
	Infer Inferring is making an educated guess about information that is not directly stated in the text.	Inferring helps you look more deeply into the thoughts and motives of characters and often points you toward the theme of the story.	Connect your own knowledge with details in the story to figure out what the writer is hinting at.

Unit 3	What Is It?	Why It's Important	How To Do It
	Main Idea The main idea is the most important thought in a passage or text.	Finding main ideas helps you discover an author's purpose for writing.	Look for the idea that all the sentences in a passage are about. Some writers directly state a main idea, while others present it through examples and other clues.
	Interpret Interpreting is using your own understanding of the world to decide what the events or ideas in the text mean.	Interpreting can give you a better understanding of a work—as well as a personal connection to it.	Apply what you already know about yourself and the world to what you are reading. Also ask yourself: What's the writer really saying here?
Unit 4	**Visualize** Visualizing is picturing in your mind a person, place, object, or event from the text.	Visualizing is one of the best ways to understand and remember ideas, characters, and other details from the text.	Build on details the writer provides. Pay attention to descriptions of the setting and characters—try to "see" them in your mind.
	Summarize Summarizing is stating the main ideas or important events from the text in your own words.	Summarizing teaches you to rethink what you've read and to separate main ideas from supporting information.	Ask yourself: What is this selection about? Answer *who*, *what*, *where*, *when*, and *how* questions. Put that information in a logical order.
Unit 5	**Draw Conclusions** Drawing conclusions is using information from the text to make a general statement.	Drawing conclusions helps you find connections between ideas and events.	Notice details about people, ideas, and events. Then make a general statement based on these details.
	Evaluate Evaluating is making a judgment about what you are reading and how it is presented.	When you make judgments about what you are reading, you can better understand its purpose and how effective it is.	Think about the writer's words. Evaluate what you read by asking yourself questions: Are the events believable? Is the text interesting?

UNIT 1

Short Story

What's a Short Story?

Everyone loves a good story. When something exciting happens to you, chances are you can't wait to pick up the phone, find a friend, or send an e-mail to share the experience. Some of the most entertaining stories, however, describe situations and events that never actually happened! These are called short stories.

A **short story** is a brief piece of fiction—writing that is about imaginary people and events. Like most literary forms, a short story can take many shapes. It might be as short as one page or as long as fifty pages. It might be made up mostly of dialogue, or it might have no speech—or even human characters—at all. However, all good stories share a sense of direction. Whether the author wants to teach us, show us, amuse us, or scare us, a good story takes us somewhere, and we are happy to go along for the ride.

What qualities do you think make a good short story?

_____

Why Read Short Stories?

Short stories give us an opportunity to see life through the eyes of others. Everyone's experiences are different. It's only by sharing stories that we gain a clear picture of the world around us. In the next section of this book, you will read four short stories. Each offers a unique view of life.

Your _reason_ for reading might affect the way you read a story:

- If you're reading simply for recreation, you might read quickly as you get involved with the characters and events.

- If you're reading for a class, you might take your time, looking for specific details to discuss with your classmates.

How Do I Read Short Stories?

Focus on key **literary elements** and **reading skills** to get the most out of reading the short stories in this unit. Here are two key literary elements and two key reading skills that you will practice in this unit.

Key Literary Elements

• Setting

The **setting** is the time and place of a story. The setting includes the values and beliefs of the time and place. For example, if the setting of a story is New York City in the early 1900s, people will have different values and beliefs than a story that is set in ancient Greece. The setting often helps create a mood or atmosphere.

• Theme

A **theme** is the important message of a story. It tells about life or human nature. To figure out the theme, ask yourself, "What does this story mean?" A story may have more than one theme, but one message will probably be the strongest. For example, if a story tells about two friends who help each other through hard times, the theme is probably the importance of friendship.

Key Reading Skills

• Predict

When you **predict,** you use details from the story and what you know to make a guess about what may happen in a story. As a skillful reader, you become involved in the action of a story and in the behavior of the characters. You wonder what will happen next. How will this character behave when faced with a problem? As you continue reading, you check to see if your predictions are correct. Don't worry if your prediction isn't right. You can change your predictions as you get more information from the story.

• Respond

When you stop and consider your thoughts and feelings about something you've read, you are **responding.** Active readers respond to what they are reading. Think about what you read and how you feel about it. You can ask yourself, "How does this make me feel?" and "What does this mean to me?" You don't have to answer aloud. But thinking about and answering these questions will help you to understand what you have read.

Get Ready to Read!

THE PIT AND THE PENDULUM

Meet Edgar Allan Poe

Edgar Allan Poe was born in Baltimore in 1809. His parents died before he was three years old, so Poe was sent to live with John and Fanny Allan in Virginia. Poe left college after one year, joined the army, and later enrolled at West Point. During this time, he wrote some of his first poems and stories. Poe's writings—full of terror and suspense—deal with the dark or mysterious side of life. Poe was in debt his whole life, and died a poor man in 1849.

What You Know

Everyone experiences difficult situations. In fact, sometimes it seems like things will never get better. Talk with a partner about whether or not you think there is *always* hope, even in the most desperate circumstances.

Reason to Read

Read to learn how a man confronts a life-threatening situation.

Background Info

This story takes place in Spain during the Spanish Inquisition (1478–1834). The Inquisition started in the Middle Ages, and was a strong political and religious force for hundreds of years. During this time, many people accused of not supporting the beliefs of the state or the Catholic Church were arrested, tortured, or sentenced to death.

Word Power

agony (ag′ ə nē) *n.* intense pain or suffering; p. 4
I was in great *agony* after breaking my arm.

merged (murjd) *v.* joined together; p. 4
All of my friends *merged* into one group at the party.

clammy (klam′ ē) *adj.* cold and sticky; sweaty; p. 5
When Julio feels nervous, his hands get *clammy*.

abyss (ə bis′) *n.* an extremely deep pit; p. 5
The scary part of climbing a mountain is looking down into the *abyss*.

resolving (ri zolv′ ing) *v.* making a strong decision; p. 6
I am *resolving* to do better on my next math test.

hideous (hid′ ē əs) *adj.* very ugly; p. 6
Aurora thought the scary painting was the most *hideous* thing she had ever seen.

**Answer the following questions that contain the new words above.
Write your answers in the spaces provided.**

1. Was a company *merged* to make it into one bigger company or two smaller companies? _____

2. Are *clammy* hands wet or dry? _____

3. Does *agony* feel painful or comfortable?_____

4. If something went into an *abyss,* would it drop down or float up?

   _____

5. If you are *resolving* to fix a problem, are you planning on doing something about the problem or hoping it will fix itself?

   _____

6. Would you be more likely to see *hideous* characters in a horror movie or a love story? _____

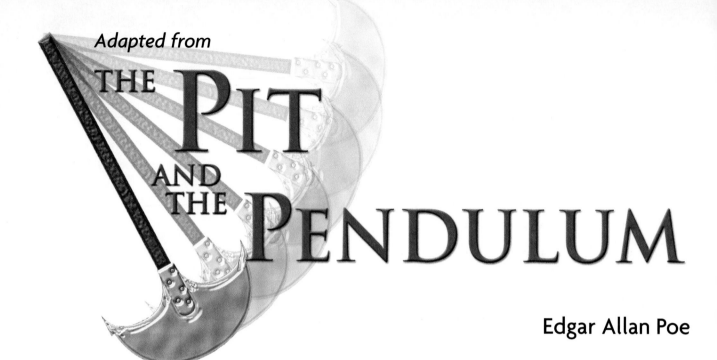

Adapted from
THE PIT AND THE PENDULUM

Edgar Allan Poe

English Coach

Here, the word *sentence* means "the punishment for a crime." What is another meaning of *sentence*?

_____

_____

_____

Comprehension Check

Reread the boxed text. When the narrator first opens his eyes in the prison cell, what does he see? Check the correct response.

☐ a deep pit
☐ skeletons on the wall
☐ the Judges
☐ nothing but blackness

I was sick—deathly sick—from my long **agony.** And when they finally untied me, and I was allowed to sit, I felt that my senses were leaving me. And the sentence—the dread sentence of death—was the last thing I remember hearing. After that the sound of the Judges' voices **merged** together into one dreamy hum.

I had fainted. And now, although my senses had begun to return, I had not yet opened my eyes. But I felt that I lay upon my back, unbound. Reaching out my hand, I felt something damp and hard. Not daring to move, I remained still for many minutes trying to imagine where I was.

At length, I opened my eyes. There was nothing to see! The blackness of night surrounded me. I struggled for breath, for the air was stuffy and humid. Where was I?

Trembling, I stood up and thrust my arms wildly above and around me in all directions. I felt nothing. I cautiously moved forward with my arms outstretched. My eyes were bursting from their sockets in the hope of catching some faint ray of light.

Word Power
agony (ag′ ə nē) *n.* intense pain or suffering
merged (murjd) *v.* joined together

Taking a few cautious steps forward, I felt my hands against something solid. It was a stone wall—very smooth, slimy and cold. I decided to follow the wall to see if I could determine the size of my cell. To mark the place where I started, I tore a piece of my shirt and stuffed it into the crack in the wall.

Then, I staggered onward, feeling my way along the wall until I finally returned to the piece of cloth. There were a hundred paces in all. I figured the dungeon to be fifty yards around.

I decided to walk across the cell. The floor was very slippery so I walked cautiously. I had walked about twelve paces when the hem of my garment got tangled between my legs and I fell violently on my face.

As I lay there in a confused state, I noticed something strange. My chin rested upon the floor, but my lips and the upper portion of my head touched nothing, even though they were lower than my chin. My forehead seemed bathed in a **clammy** vapor and the odd smell of decayed fungus rose to my nostrils.

I put my arm out and shuddered to find that I had fallen at the very edge of a circular pit. I took a stone and let it fall into the **abyss.** It took awhile for it to hit the water, because the pit was very deep.

At the same moment I heard what sounded like the quick opening and closing of a door overhead. A faint gleam of light flashed suddenly through the gloom, then faded away just as quickly. I now saw the doom which had been prepared for me. One more step and the world would have seen me no more. To the victims of the Inquisition, there was the choice of a quick, painful death or a slow, torturous one. And I had been reserved for the slow, torturous one.

Word Power

clammy (klam′ē) *adj.* cold and sticky; sweaty
abyss (ə bis′) *n.* an extremely deep pit

Literary Element

Setting Reread the text highlighted in blue. Write down words or phrases that describe the cell.

_____
_____
_____
_____
_____
_____

Reading Skill

Predict Reread the text highlighted in green. The narrator has been sentenced to a slow death instead of a quick one. What do you predict the narrator will do with the extra time he's been given?

_____
_____
_____
_____
_____
_____

Shaking in every limb, I groped my way back to the wall, **resolving** to die rather than risk the terrors of the well. Crouching by the wall, I was kept awake by fear for many long hours until finally I fell asleep from exhaustion.

When I awoke, I found by my side a loaf of bread and a pitcher. With a burning thirst, I emptied the pitcher quickly. It must have been drugged, for a deep sleep soon fell upon me. How long it lasted, I know not, but when I opened my eyes, the room was visible. I had been greatly mistaken about the size of the room; it did not exceed twenty-five yards.

The walls which I had thought were stone now seemed to be of iron in huge plates with joints between them. The entire surface of this metal cell was crudely painted with **hideous** pictures of torture devices and skeletons. In the center of the floor was the circular pit from whose jaws I had so narrowly escaped.

Literary Element

Setting Reread the highlighted text. Describe the setting of the cell.

_____

_____

_____

_____

_____

_____

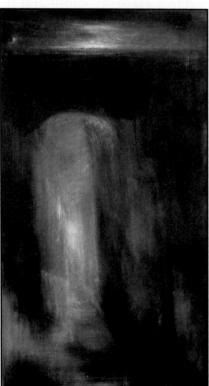

Brücke, 1987. Christa Näher. Oil on canvas, 90 x 50 cm. Private collection.

How might you feel if you were isolated, as the narrator is, in a place like the one shown in this painting?

Word Power

resolving (ri zolv´ ing) *v.* making a strong decision

hideous (hid´ ē əs) *adj.* very ugly

Suddenly I realized that my condition had changed greatly during my sleep. I was now on my back, tied to a low wooden frame.

Only my head and my left arm were free—just enough to feed myself from an earthen dish on the floor beside me. The pitcher was gone and the meat in the dish was salted to make me more thirsty.

As I looked up at the ceiling of my prison, which was about thirty feet overhead, I saw there the painted figure of Time as he is often represented. But in place of his scythe, I noticed the image of a huge pendulum, such as we see on antique clocks.

While I gazed at it, I thought I saw it move. Its sweep was brief and slow. I watched it for a while, but soon got tired and turned my eyes upon other objects in the cell. A slight noise had caught my attention, and looking to the floor, I saw several large rats coming from the pit. And even as I gazed, more came. They crossed the room in troops, with hungry eyes, driven by the scent of the greasy meat on my plate.

Did You Know?

A *scythe* (sĭth) is a long, curved blade used for mowing or cutting grass. Father Time is often shown with a scythe to symbolize the mowing down of life.

. . . .

After an hour of struggling to frighten off the rats, I again cast my eyes upward. What I saw shocked and amazed me. The sweep of the pendulum had increased by nearly a yard. But what mainly disturbed me was that it had also *descended*.

Now I saw—with what horror I need not describe—that the bottom of the pendulum was a crescent of glittering steel. Its under edge was sharp as a razor, and the whole thing *hissed* as it swung through the air.

Inch by inch—for what seemed to be ages—down and still down it came! Days passed, and soon it swung close enough to fan me with its bitter breath.

Comprehension Check

Reread the boxed text. How has the narrator's condition changed since he first found himself in the cell?

_____

_____

_____

_____

Reading Skill

Respond Reread the highlighted text. How would you feel in this situation?

_____

_____

_____

_____

My Workspace

Reading Skill

Respond Reread the highlighted text. Imagine you are the narrator. Do you think you would react the same way he does here? Why or why not?

_____

_____

_____

_____

_____

_____

Comprehension Check

Reread the boxed text. Why does the narrator put food on the ropes?

_____

_____

_____

_____

_____

_____

The odor of sharp steel forced itself into my nostrils. Oh mad demon! Steadily down it came, stalking me like a tiger. To the right—to the left—far and wide with the hiss of Evil! I cried, I laughed, I grew madder with each swing. I prayed for its speedy descent. And then, I fell suddenly calm.

At that moment, there rushed to my mind a half-formed thought of hope. With the nervous energy of despair, I began to piece together a plan of escape. For many hours the area around the low frame upon which I lay had been swarming with rats. They were wild, bold, starving—their red eyes glaring at me. I took the food from my plate and rubbed it into the ropes which bound me. Then, I lay breathlessly still.

Seeing that I was motionless, two of the boldest rats leaped upon the frame. This seemed a signal for the general rush. They clung to the wood, overran it and leaped in hundreds upon me. They began gnawing at my ropes. The killer pendulum was only ten swings away from slashing my chest. But the rats were not disturbed by it at all. They busied themselves with gnawing at the ropes. They wriggled at my throat, their cold lips touched my own. I was half suffocated by their weight, yet I resolved to lie perfectly still.

Soon, as I had hoped, I felt I was free, for the ropes hung loosely from my body. But the stroke of the pendulum had already pressed close to my chest. It had cut the cloth of my shirt. Twice again it swung and a sharp pain shot through my body.

But the moment of escape had arrived. With a steady movement—cautious, sidelong, shrinking and slow—I slid from the ropes and beyond the reach of the pendulum. I was free!

Free!—and right into the grasp of the Inquisition. No sooner had I slipped from the wooden bed of horror when the motion of the hellish machine stopped. Then it was drawn up, by some invisible force, through the ceiling. Without doubt, my every motion was being watched.

With that thought I nervously rolled my eyes around the walls of iron. Something unusual was happening, but I couldn't tell exactly what. I noticed that the outlines of the figures on the walls had become brilliantly colored. Demon eyes, wild and staring, gleamed like fire.

Unreal! The walls of my cell were aglow with a ghastly heat! Even while I breathed, I smelled the vapor of heated iron. A suffocating odor filled the prison. Panting and gasping for breath, I shrank from the glowing metal walls to the center of the cell. With the thoughts of the fiery destruction to come, the idea of the coolness of the pit came over my soul. I rushed to its deadly edge.

I looked below. The glare from the fiery roof lit up the pit. Oh horror! Oh most evil of tortures! With a shriek I rushed from the pit's edge and buried my face in my hands—weeping bitterly.

Once again I looked up. There had been a second change in the cell—the room which had been square was now oblong. The walls were closing in on me! Smaller and smaller grew the room as the walls pressed me onward—closer to the pit. "Death," I said, "any death but that of the pit!"

Reading Skill

Respond Reread the text highlighted in green. How would you feel if you just escaped and then realized you were being watched the whole time?

_____

_____

_____

_____

_____

Literary Element

Setting Reread the text highlighted in blue. How has the cell changed since the beginning of the story?

_____

_____

_____

_____

Connect to the Text

Write about a time when you had to make a choice between two unpleasant courses of action. How did you feel? What did you do?

_____

_____

_____

_____

_____

_____

Reading Skill

Predict Earlier you made a prediction about what the narrator would do with the extra time his sentence to a "slow death" gave him. How is your prediction similar to or different from what happens in the story?

_____

_____

_____

_____

_____

Closer and closer came the burning walls. There was no longer an inch to stand on the firm floor. I struggled no more, but the agony of my soul released one loud, long and final scream of despair.

And then I heard a distant hum of voices, and then a loud blast of trumpets! The fiery walls rushed back! An outstretched hand caught my own as I fell fainting into the pit. It was that of General Lasalle. The French army had entered Toledo. The Inquisition was in the hands of its enemies, and I was saved.

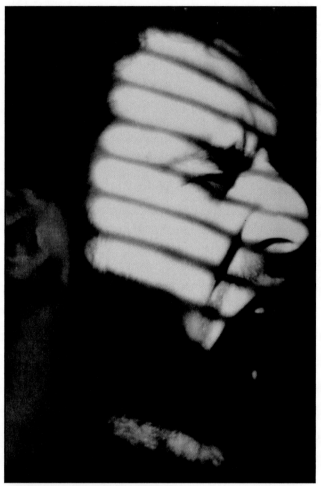

How might this photograph reflect the pain and distress of the narrator?

_____

Respond to Literature

THE PIT AND THE PENDULUM

A Comprehension Check

Answer the following questions in the spaces provided.

1. How does the narrator escape from the razor-sharp pendulum?

   _____

   _____

2. What happens to the narrator at the end of the story?

   _____

   _____

B Reading Skills

Answer the following questions in the spaces provided.

1. **Respond** How did you feel when the narrator got rescued at the end? Why? _____

   _____

   _____

2. **Predict** The narrator goes through a terrifying experience at the hands of the people holding him captive. Predict what you think would happen if the narrator were given a chance for revenge. Would he take it? Why or why not? _____

   _____

   _____

C Word Power

Complete each sentence below, using one of the words in the box.

agony	merged	clammy
abyss	resolving	hideous

1. My feet feel _____ in these heavy boots.

2. What are you _____ to improve in your life?

3. Le Ly could not stand to look at the _____ dress she was supposed to wear.

4. The two lines _____ into one.

5. He dropped a rock into the _____.

6. He was really in _____ after burning his fingers.

D Literary Element: Setting

Read the passages below from "The Pit and the Pendulum." As you read, think about the setting of the story. Then answer the questions that follow.

At length, I opened my eyes.[1] There was nothing to see![2] The blackness of night surrounded me.[3] I struggled for breath, for the air was stuffy and humid.[4] Where was I?[5]

Unreal! The walls of my cell were aglow with a ghastly heat![6] Even while I breathed, I smelled the vapor of heated iron.[7] A suffocating odor filled the prison.[8] Panting and gasping for breath, I shrank from the glowing metal walls to the center of the cell.[9]

1. Even though the narrator cannot see anything in sentences 1–5, what details help you imagine where the narrator is?

   _____

   _____

2. In sentences 6–9, how does the setting create an intense and ominous

   atmosphere? _____

   _____

   _____

   _____

E Court Testimony

Imagine that you are the narrator. The people who tortured you have been put on trial. Tell the court your story.

Your Honors,

I was cruelly tortured by these men. First, I was sentenced to death. I was placed in a cell. There was no light. I explored the cell and discovered

_____

_____

I drank some water and fell into a deep sleep. When I awoke, I was tied to a wooden frame and above me I saw _____

_____

I came up with a plan to escape. I _____

_____

_____

But then, _____

_____

Just as I was about to die, _____

Your Honors, I believe these men should be punished for what they did. Their sentence should be _____

_____

Assessment

Fill in the circle next to each correct answer.

1. What does the narrator do immediately after he is sentenced?
   - ○ A. He escapes.
   - ○ B. He shrieks.
   - ○ C. He falls asleep.
   - ○ D. He faints.

2. How does the narrator first figure out that there is a pit in his cell?
   - ○ A. He sees it.
   - ○ B. He knows that rats always live near pits.
   - ○ C. He falls and his head doesn't hit the ground.
   - ○ D. The guards tell him.

3. Which sentence from the story **best** supports a prediction that the narrator will be rescued?
   - ○ A. "And then I heard a distant hum of voices, and then a loud blast of trumpets!"
   - ○ B. "The walls were closing in on me!"
   - ○ C. "Steadily down it came, stalking me like a tiger."
   - ○ D. "A slight noise had caught my attention, and looking to the floor, I saw several large rats coming from the pit."

4. This story takes place
   - ○ A. in a person's home.
   - ○ B. during the American Revolution.
   - ○ C. in a prison cell.
   - ○ D. on board a ship.

5. Which word means the same as *merged?*
   - ○ A. split
   - ○ B. joined
   - ○ C. ran
   - ○ D. entered

Get Ready to Read!

American History

Meet Judith Ortiz Cofer

Judith Ortiz Cofer was born in 1952 in Puerto Rico. She spent the first part of her childhood in Puerto Rico, where she spoke Spanish. Then she moved to the United States where she had problems in school because she spoke very little English. However, Ortiz Cofer says that she learned the language by reading lots of books. Today she is an award-winning author of poems, essays, novels, and short stories.

What You Know

Have you ever met a person whom you liked right away, but something prevented the friendship from growing? Discuss your experience with a partner. Write a list of some reasons that a friendship may fail to develop. Together, present your conclusions to the class.

Reason to Read

Read to learn about a special friendship. Look for the forces that prevented the friendship from growing.

Background Info

Most Americans who were alive in 1963 can still remember exactly what they were doing when they learned of President Kennedy's death. Throughout the country, people reacted to the news with disbelief and deep sorrow. Kennedy—the youngest man to be elected President of the United States—was a popular leader who gave the American people hope for the future. During his brief term, Kennedy urged Congress to pass sweeping civil rights laws, saying, ". . . race has no place in American life or law." His campaign slogan was "A Time for Greatness," and many Americans believed Kennedy fulfilled this promise once he took office.

Word Power

profound (prə found´) *adj.* significant; deep; intense; p. 18
She said something very meaningful and *profound*.

discreet (dis krēt´) *adj.* showing good judgment; cautious; p. 21
It is important to be *discreet* when you help someone with a problem.

infatuated (in fach´ o͞o ā´ təd) *adj.* in love or attracted in a foolish way; p. 22
Manny is so *infatuated* with Kim that he cannot study.

vigilant (vij´ ə lənt) *adj.* careful and looking out for trouble; p. 22
A *vigilant* police officer will keep the town safe.

enthralled (en thrôld´) *adj.* spellbound; fascinated; p. 23
I was *enthralled* by the beautiful music.

elation (i lā´ shən) *n.* a feeling of great joy; p. 25
We felt *elation* when we all passed the test.

distraught (dis trôt´) *adj.* very upset; p. 26
Koria is *distraught* because she lost her dog.

solace (sol´ is) *n.* relief from sorrow or disappointment; comfort; p. 27
Friends can give us *solace* during sad times.

**Answer the following questions that contain the new words above.
Write your answers in the spaces provided.**

1. Is a *profound* speech filled with important ideas or foolish ideas? _____

2. Would a *discreet* person tell a secret or keep it private? _____

3. If you are *infatuated*, is your attraction foolish or reasonable? _____

4. Would a *vigilant* person pay attention or daydream in class? _____

5. If you are *enthralled* by a painting, are you fascinated or bored by it? _____

6. If you are feeling *elation*, are you happy or sad? _____

7. Would a *distraught* person feel tense or relaxed? _____

8. If you needed *solace*, would you be feeling sad or cheerful? _____

American History

Judith Ortiz Cofer

Literary Element

Setting El Building is one setting in the story. Underline details on this page that help describe El Building. Three details have already been highlighted for you.

English Coach

Viragos (vi rä′ gōs) in Spanish means "bad-tempered women." In this story, these women use harsh language. Check the three words below that also mean "bad-tempered."

- ☐ cranky
- ☐ irritable
- ☐ cheerful
- ☐ crabby

I once read in a *Ripley's Believe it or Not* column that Paterson, New Jersey, is the place where the Straight and Narrow (streets) intersect. The Puerto Rican tenement known as El Building was one block up from Straight. It was, in fact, the corner of Straight and Market; not "at" the corner, but *the corner*.

At almost any hour of the day, El Building was like a monstrous jukebox, blasting out *salsas* from open windows as the residents, mostly new immigrants just up from the island, tried to drown out whatever they were currently enduring with loud music. But the day President Kennedy was shot, there was a **profound** silence in El Building; even the abusive tongues of *viragos*, the cursing of the unemployed, and the screeching of small children had been somehow muted. President Kennedy was a saint to these people. In fact, soon his photograph would be hung alongside the Sacred Heart and over the spiritist altars that many women kept in their apartments.

Did You Know?
John F. Kennedy was shot and killed on November 22, 1963. He was the thirty-fifth president of the United States.

Word Power

profound (prə found′) *adj.* significant; deep; intense

On the day that President Kennedy was shot, my ninth grade class had been out in the fenced playground of the Public School Number 13. We had been given "free" exercise time and had been ordered by our P.E. teacher, Mr. DePalma, to "keep moving." That meant that the girls should jump rope and the boys toss basketballs through a hoop at the far end of the yard. He in the meantime would "keep an eye" on us from just inside the building.

It was a cold gray day in Paterson. The kind that warns of early snow. I was miserable, since I had forgotten my gloves and my knuckles were turning red and raw from the jump rope. I was also taking a lot of abuse from the black girls for not turning the rope hard and fast enough for them.

"Hey, Skinny Bones, pump it, girl. Ain't you got no energy today?" Gail, the biggest of the black girls who had the other end of the rope yelled, "Didn't you eat your rice and beans and pork chops for breakfast today?"

There was only one source of beauty and light for me that school year. The only thing I had anticipated at the start of the semester. That was seeing Eugene. In August, Eugene and his family had moved into the only house on the block that had a yard and trees. I could see his place from my window in El Building. In fact, if I sat on the fire escape I was literally suspended above Eugene's backyard. It was my favorite spot to read my library books in the summer. Until that August the house had been occupied by an old Jewish couple. I had a view of their kitchen and their backyard, and though I could not hear what they said, I knew when they were arguing, when one of them was sick, and many other things.

Did You Know?
A *fire escape* is a fireproof stairway attached to an outside wall of a building.

Connect to the Text
Reread the boxed paragraph. Some students are making fun of the narrator. How would you feel in this situation?

Comprehension Check
Reread the boxed text. Who moves into the only house on the block that has a yard and trees? Check the correct response.
- [ ] Gail
- [ ] Eugene and his family
- [ ] Mr. DePalma
- [ ] an old Jewish couple

Literary Element

Setting How does this picture help you imagine the setting of El Building as described in the beginning of the story?

_____

_____

_____

_____

_____

_____

Harlem, 1942. Jacob Lawrence. Gouache on composition board, 21¾ x 29¾ in. Private collection, New York.

The old man had died in June. The last week of school I had not seen him at the table at all. Then one day I saw that there was a crowd in the kitchen. The old woman had finally emerged from the house on the arm of a stocky middle-aged woman whom I had seen there a few times before, maybe her daughter. Then a man had carried out suitcases. The house had stood empty for weeks. I had had to resist the temptation to climb down into the yard and water the flowers the old lady had taken such good care of.

By the time Eugene's family moved in, the yard was a tangled mass of weeds. The father had spent several days mowing, and when he finished, I didn't see the red, yellow, and purple clusters that meant flowers to me from where I sat. I didn't see this family sit down at the kitchen table together. It was just the mother, a red-headed tall woman who wore a white uniform—a nurse's, I guessed it was; the father was gone before I got up in the morning and was never there at dinner time. I only saw him on weekends when they sometimes sat on lawn chairs under the oak tree, each hidden behind a section of the newspaper; and there was Eugene. He was tall and blond, and he wore glasses. I liked him right away because he sat at the kitchen table and read books for hours. That summer, before we had even spoken one word to each other, I kept him company on my fire escape.

Once school started I looked for him in all my classes, but P.S. 13 was a huge, overpopulated place and it took me days and many **discreet** questions to discover that Eugene was in honors classes for all his subjects; classes that were not open to me because English was not my first language, though I was a straight A student. After much maneuvering I managed "to run into him" in the hallway where his locker was—on the other side of the building from mine—and in study hall at the library, where he first seemed to notice me but did not speak; and finally, on the way home after school one day when I decided to approach him directly, though my stomach was doing somersaults.

Word Power

discreet (dis krēt´) *adj.* showing good judgment; cautious

Comprehension Check

Reread the boxed text. Underline words or phrases that describe Eugene and his family.

Reading Skill

Predict Reread the highlighted text. Do you think the narrator and Eugene will become friends? Why or why not?

_____

_____

_____

_____

_____

Background Info

Here, P.S. stands for "public school."

Reading Skill

Predict Reread the paragraph beginning with the highlighted sentence. Earlier, you made a prediction about the narrator and Eugene's relationship. Did you make an accurate prediction? Underline words or phrases in the paragraph that show the two are becoming friends.

English Coach

Acting *"moony"* refers to someone who acts dreamily, or is lost in a romantic fantasy. What are some other words for acting "moony"?

_____

_____

I was ready for rejection, snobbery, the worst. But when I came up to him, practically panting in my nervousness, and blurted out: "You're Eugene. Right?" He smiled, pushed his glasses up on his nose, and nodded. I saw then that he was blushing deeply. Eugene liked me, but he was shy. I did most of the talking that day. He nodded and smiled a lot. In the weeks that followed, we walked home together. He would linger at the corner of El Building for a few minutes then walk down to his two-story house. It was not until Eugene moved into that house that I noticed that El Building blocked most of the sun and that the only spot that got a little sunlight during the day was the tiny square of earth the old woman had planted with flowers.

I did not tell Eugene that I could see inside his kitchen from my bedroom. I felt dishonest, but I liked my secret sharing of his evenings, especially now that I knew what he was reading, since we chose our books together at the school library.

One day my mother came into my room as I was sitting on the windowsill staring out. In her abrupt way she said: "Elena, you are acting 'moony.'" *Enamorada* was what she really said—that is, like a girl stupidly **infatuated.** Since I had turned fourteen my mother had been more **vigilant** than ever. She acted as if I was going to go crazy or explode or something if she didn't watch me and nag me all the time about being a *señorita* now. She kept talking about virtue, morality and other subjects that did not interest me in the least. My mother was unhappy in Paterson, but my father had a good job at the blue jeans factory in Passaic, and soon, he kept assuring us, we would be moving to our own house there. I had learned to listen to my parents' dreams, which were spoken in Spanish, as fairy tales, like the stories about life in the island paradise of Puerto Rico before I was born.

Word Power

infatuated (in fach′ oo ā ′ təd) *adj.* in love or attracted in a foolish way
vigilant (vij′ ə lənt) *adj.* careful and looking out for trouble

I had been to the Island once as a little girl, to grandmother's funeral, and all I remembered was wailing women in black, my mother becoming hysterical and being given a pill that made her sleep two days, and me feeling lost in a crowd of strangers all claiming to be my aunts, uncles, and cousins. I had actually been glad to return to the city. We had not been back there since then, though my parents talked constantly about buying a house on the beach someday, retiring on the island—that was a common topic among the residents of El Building. As for me, I was going to go to college and become a teacher.

But after meeting Eugene I began to think of the present more than of the future. What I wanted now was to enter that house I had watched for so many years. I wanted to see the other rooms where the old people had lived and where the boy I liked spent his time. Most of all, I wanted to sit at the kitchen table with Eugene like two adults, like the old man and his wife had done, maybe drink some coffee and talk about books. I had started reading *Gone with the Wind*. I was **enthralled** by it, with the daring and the passion of the beautiful girl living in a mansion, and with her devoted parents and the slaves who did everything for them. I didn't believe such a world had ever really existed, and I wanted to ask Eugene some questions, since he and his parents, he had told me, had come up from Georgia, the same place where the novel was set. His father worked for a company that had transferred him to Paterson. His mother was very unhappy, Eugene said, in his beautiful voice that rose and fell over words in a strange, lilting way. The kids at school called him the Hick and made fun of the way he talked. I knew I was his only friend so far, and I liked that, though I felt sad for him sometimes. Skinny Bones and the Hick, was what they called us at school when we were seen together.

Word Power

enthralled (en thrôld´) *adj.* spellbound; fascinated

Reading Skill
Predict The highlighted lines show that the narrator is fascinated with Eugene's house. Predict whether she will eventually go inside his house.

_____

_____

_____

_____

Background Info
Gone with the Wind is a romantic novel about the South during and after the Civil War.

Connect to the Text
Reread the text boxed in purple. The kids at school are making fun of Eugene and Elena. Have you ever had trouble fitting in? Write about your experience below.

_____

_____

_____

23

Connect to the Text

Reread the boxed text. Put yourself in Elena's shoes. How would you feel about Mr. DePalma's crying?

_____

_____

_____

_____

_____

Reading Skill

Respond Reread the highlighted lines and think about how Mr. DePalma is speaking to the students. Do you think he is acting in an appropriate way? How do you think he should have acted?

_____

_____

_____

_____

_____

_____

_____

The day Mr. DePalma came out into the cold and asked us to line up in front of him was the day that President Kennedy was shot. Mr. DePalma, a short, muscular man with slicked-down black hair, was the science teacher, P.E. coach, and disciplinarian at P.S. 13. He was the teacher to whose homeroom you got assigned if you were a troublemaker, and the man called out to break up playground fights, and to escort violently angry teenagers to the office. And Mr. DePalma was the man who called your parents in for "a conference."

That day, he stood in front of two rows of mostly black and Puerto Rican kids, brittle from their efforts to "keep moving" on a November day that was turning bitter cold. Mr. DePalma, to our complete shock, was crying. Not just silent adult tears, but really sobbing. There were a few titters from the back of the line where I stood, shivering.

"Listen," Mr. DePalma raised his arms over his head as if he were about to conduct an orchestra. His voice broke, and he covered his face with his hands. His barrel chest was heaving. Someone giggled behind me.

"Listen," he repeated, "something awful has happened." A strange gurgling came from his throat, and he turned around and spit on the cement behind him.

"Gross," someone said, and there was a lot of laughter.

"The president is dead, you idiots. I should have known that wouldn't mean anything to a bunch of losers like you kids. Go home." He was shrieking now. No one moved for a minute or two, but then a big girl let out a "yeah!" and ran to get her books piled up with the others against the brick wall of the school building. The others followed in a mad scramble to get to their things before somebody caught on. It was still an hour to the dismissal bell.

A little scared, I headed for El Building. There was an eerie feeling on the streets. At El Building, the usual little group of unemployed men were not hanging out on the front stoop, making it difficult for women to enter the front door. No music spilled out from open doors in the hallway. When I walked into our apartment, I found my mother sitting in front of the grainy picture of the television set.

She looked up at me with a tear-streaked face and just said: "*Dios mío*," turning back to the set as if it were pulling at her eyes. I went into my room.

Though I wanted to feel the right thing about President Kennedy's death, I could not fight the feeling of **elation** that stirred in my chest. Today was the day I was to visit Eugene in his house. He had asked me to come over after school to study for an American history test with him. We had also planned to walk to the public library together. I looked down into his yard. The white kitchen table with the lamp hanging just above it looked cozy and inviting. I would soon sit there, across from Eugene, and I would tell him about my perch just above his house. Maybe I would.

In the next thirty minutes I changed clothes, put on a little pink lipstick, and got my books together. Then I went in to tell my mother that I was going to a friend's house to study. I did not expect her reaction.

Literary Element

Setting Reread the highlighted passage. How is El Building different on the day President Kennedy is shot? Check the **best** response below.

☐ Music is blasting from the windows.

☐ It's quiet and people aren't hanging out on the front stoop.

☐ People are arguing and hanging out on the front stoop.

Word Power

elation (i lā´shən) *n.* a feeling of great joy

Reading Skill

Predict Reread the highlighted text. Do you think Elena's mother is being overly protective? Predict whether or not this warning will come true.

_____

_____

_____

_____

_____

_____

Background Info

The Spanish phrase *Verde-Esperanza* (vār´dae es pe rän´ sä) literally translates as Green-Hope.

"You are going out *today*?" The way she said "today" sounded as if a storm warning had been issued. It was said in utter disbelief. Before I could answer, she came toward me and held my elbows as I clutched my books.

"*Hija*, the president has been killed. We must show respect. He was a great man. Come to church with me tonight." She tried to embrace me, but my books were in the way. My first impulse was to comfort her, she seemed so **distraught,** but I had to meet Eugene in fifteen minutes.

"I have a test to study for, Mama. I will be home by eight."

"You are forgetting who you are, *Niña*. I have seen you staring down at that boy's house. You are heading for humiliation and pain." My mother said this in Spanish and in a resigned tone that surprised me, as if she had no intention of stopping me from "heading for humiliation and pain." I started for the door. She sat in front of the TV, holding a white handkerchief to her face.

I walked out to the street and around the chain-link fence that separated El Building from Eugene's house. The yard was neatly edged around the little walk that led to the door. The door was painted a deep green: *verde*, the color of hope. I had heard my mother say it: *Verde-Esperanza*.

I knocked softly. A few suspenseful moments later the door opened just a crack. The red, swollen face of a woman appeared. She had a halo of red hair floating over a delicate ivory face—the face of a doll—with freckles on the nose. Her smudged eye makeup made her look unreal to me, like a mannequin seen through a warped store window.

"What do you want?" Her voice was tiny and sweet-sounding, like a little girl's, but her tone was not friendly.

"I'm Eugene's friend. He asked me over. To study." I thrust out my books, a silly gesture that embarrassed me almost immediately.

Word Power
distraught (dis trôt´) *adj.* very upset

"You live there?" She pointed up to El Building, which looked particularly ugly, like a gray prison with its many dirty windows and rusty fire escapes. The woman had stepped halfway out and I could see that she wore a white nurse's uniform with "St. Joseph's Hospital" on the name tag.

"Yes. I do."

She looked intently at me for a couple of heartbeats, then said as if to herself, "I don't know how you people do it." Then directly to me: "Listen. Honey. Eugene doesn't want to study with you. He is a smart boy. Doesn't need help. You understand me. I am truly sorry if he told you you could come over. He cannot study with you. It's nothing personal. You understand? We won't be in this place much longer, no need for him to get close to people—it'll just make it harder for him later. Run back home now."

I couldn't move. I just stood there in shock at hearing these things said to me in such a honey-drenched voice. I had never heard an accent like hers except for Eugene's softer version. It was as if she were singing me a little song.

"What's wrong? Didn't you hear what I said?" She seemed very angry, and I finally snapped out of my trance. I turned away from the green door and heard her close it gently.

Our apartment was empty when I got home. My mother was in someone else's kitchen, seeking the **solace** she needed. Father would come in from his late shift at midnight. I would hear them talking softly in the kitchen for hours that night. They would not discuss their dreams for the future, or life in Puerto Rico, as they often did; that night they would talk sadly about the young widow and her two children, as if they were family. For the next few days, we would observe luto in our apartment; that is, we would practice restraint and silence—no loud music or laughter. Some of the women of El Building would wear black for weeks.

Word Power

solace (sol´ is) *n.* relief from sorrow or disappointment; comfort

Literary Element

Setting Reread the text highlighted in blue. Underline the words that describe the way El Building looks to Elena at this moment.

Reading Skill

Predict Look at the predictions you made on pages 23 and 26. Retell your predictions and explain whether or not they match what has happened in the text highlighted in green.

_____

_____

_____

_____

_____

_____

Background Info

Luto is Spanish for "mourning." The family was following its customs for mourning.

Reading Skill

Respond Reread the highlighted text. Elena says that although she is trying to "feel the right thing for our dead president," she is mainly crying for herself. How do you feel about Elena crying? How do you think you would have responded to the events of that day?

_____

_____

_____

_____

_____

_____

_____

That night, I lay in my bed, trying to feel the right thing for our dead president. But the tears that came up from a deep source inside me were strictly for me. When my mother came to the door, I pretended to be sleeping. Sometime during the night, I saw from my bed the streetlight come on. It had a pink halo around it. I went to my window and pressed my face to the cool glass. Looking up at the light I could see the white snow falling like a lace veil over its face. I did not look down to see it turning gray as it touched the ground below.

At the Window. William Merritt Chase. Pastel on paper, 18.5 x 11 in. Brooklyn Museum of Art, NY. Gift of Mrs. Henry Wolf, Austin M. Wolf, and Hamilton A. Wolf.

Respond to Literature

American History

A Comprehension Check

Answer the following questions in the spaces provided.

1. What common interests and conditions help to develop a friendship between Elena and Eugene?

   _____

   _____

2. What does Elena feel on the day President Kennedy gets shot? Why is she particularly sorrowful that night?

   _____

   _____

B Reading Skills

Answer the following questions in the spaces provided.

1. **Predict** If Elena and Eugene meet again, what do you think will happen?

   _____

   _____

2. **Respond** Suppose a friend's mother treated you the way that Eugene's mother treated Elena. How would you feel?

   _____

   _____

C Word Power

Complete each sentence below, using one of the words in the box.

profound	discreet	infatuated	vigilant
enthralled	elation	distraught	solace

1. Many people find _____ in spending time with friends.

2. I am careful and _____ about locking the door to my house.

3. The mayor gave a very meaningful and _____ speech.

4. The audience was _____ by the magician's tricks.

5. I only tell secrets to _____ people who will not repeat them.

6. Anne was so _____ during the storm that she broke the dishes.

7. Alberto was so _____ with Isabel that he thought of her constantly and could not study.

8. Rohit felt great _____ after winning the game.

D Literary Element: Setting

Read the passages below from "American History." As you read, think about the setting of the story. Then answer the questions that follow.

It was not until Eugene moved into that house that I noticed that El Building blocked most of the sun and that the only spot that got a little sunlight during the day was the tiny square of earth the old woman had planted with flowers.[1]

"You live there?"[2] She pointed up to El Building, which looked particularly ugly, like a gray prison with its many dirty windows and rusty fire escapes.[3]

1. In sentence 1, how does Elena's awareness of this setting change after Eugene moves in?

   _____

   _____

   _____

2. After reading sentence 3, explain why Elena suddenly thinks El Building looks this way.

   _____

   _____

   _____

E An Instant Message

Imagine that you are either the narrator or Eugene. It is the end of the story. You have not met to study with the other character. Write an instant message to a friend. Tell your friend what has happened and how you feel.

TO: _____

You will not believe what happened to me today.

I am so _____

_____

First, I was supposed to _____

_____

That didn't happen because _____

_____

Then I _____

_____

In the end, _____

_____

I feel _____

_____

Send

Assessment

Fill in the circle next to each correct answer.

1. Which President is killed during the story?
   - ○ A. Kennedy
   - ○ B. Carter
   - ○ C. Roosevelt
   - ○ D. Lincoln

2. In the following sentence, what phrase helps you to **best** predict that Eugene's mother will send the narrator away? "'What do you want?' Her voice was tiny and sweet-sounding, like a little girl's, but her tone was not friendly."
   - ○ A. 'What do you want?'
   - ○ B. Her voice was tiny
   - ○ C. like a little girl's
   - ○ D. her tone was not friendly

3. Who tells Elena that she is "heading for humiliation and pain"?
   - ○ A. Mr. DePalma
   - ○ B. Gail
   - ○ C. Elena's mother
   - ○ D. Eugene's mother

4. This story takes place
   - ○ A. in Puerto Rico.
   - ○ B. in Georgia.
   - ○ C. in 1945.
   - ○ D. in Paterson, New Jersey.

5. Which word can replace *worried* in this sentence?
   I am so worried about the big test tomorrow.
   - ○ A. discreet
   - ○ B. distraught
   - ○ C. enthralled
   - ○ D. vigilant

Get Ready to Read!

The Gift of the Magi

Meet O. Henry

William Sydney Porter, who used the pen name O. Henry, published his first story while he was in jail. He had been convicted of stealing money from the bank where he worked. Some say he took the money in order to pay his dying wife's medical bills. O. Henry became a popular writer of short stories known for their plot twists and surprise endings. He was born in 1862 and died in 1910. This story was first published in 1905.

What You Know

The 19th century novelist George Eliot wrote, "One must be poor to know the luxury of giving." In a small group, discuss Eliot's statement. Begin by restating the quotation in your own words. Talk about whether or not you agree with its message.

Reason to Read

Read to learn how a young married couple discovers the true meaning of gift-giving.

Background Info

This story takes place in New York City. It is the afternoon of Christmas Eve around the year 1900. Christmas is the Christian holiday that celebrates the birth of Jesus. According to the New Testament of the Bible, three wise men came to visit the newborn baby Jesus. These wise men are also called the Magi. The Magi brought precious gifts for the child. Over time, the Magi have come to be associated with the practice of giving gifts.

Word Power

cascade (kas kād´) *n.* a waterfall; a series of small waterfalls; p. 37
It was worth the hike to see this *cascade.*

faltered (fôl´ tərd) *v.* stumbled or paused in an awkward way; p. 37
Joanie *faltered* after she missed the last step on the stairs.

mammoth (mam´ əth) *adj.* extremely large; p. 39
Can you eat that *mammoth* sandwich?

laboriously (lə bôr´ ē əs lē) *adv.* done with hard work or a lot of effort; p. 40
The students *laboriously* cleaned the park.

craved (krāvd) *v.* wanted very badly; p. 42
Max *craved* milk all day long.

**Answer the following questions that contain the new words above.
Write your answers in the spaces provided.**

1. Would a *cascade* have water or fire? _____

2. If she *craved* something, did she desire it or want to avoid it? _____

3. Would people working *laboriously* at a job work really hard or not at all?

   _____

4. Will a *mammoth* homework assignment take you a few minutes or several hours?

   _____

5. If Julio *faltered,* was he graceful or clumsy? _____

Adapted from

The Gift of the Magi

O. Henry

ONE DOLLAR AND EIGHTY-SEVEN CENTS. That was all. And sixty cents of it was in pennies. Pennies saved one and two at a time by bargaining with the grocer and the vegetable man and the butcher. Three times Della counted it. One dollar and eighty-seven cents. And the next day would be Christmas.

There was clearly nothing to do but flop down on the shabby little couch and howl. So Della did it. Which shows, when you think about it, that life is made up of sobs, sniffles, and smiles, with a wealth of sniffles.

While Della is gradually settling down, take a look at the home. A furnished flat at $8 per week.

In the hall below was a letter-box into which no letter would go, and an electric button which no finger could make ring. Also there was a card bearing the name "Mr. James Dillingham Young."

But whenever Mr. James Dillingham Young came home and reached his flat above he was called "Jim" and greatly hugged by Mrs. James Dillingham Young, already introduced to you as Della. Which is all very good.

Della finished her cry and attended to her cheeks with the powder rag. She stood by the window and looked out dully at a gray cat walking a gray fence in a gray backyard. Tomorrow would be Christmas Day, and she had only $1.87 with which to buy Jim a present. She had been saving every penny she could for months, with this result. Twenty dollars a week doesn't go far. Expenses had been greater than she had calculated. They always are. Only $1.87 to buy a present for Jim. Her Jim. Many a happy hour she had spent planning for something nice for him. Something fine and rare and silver—something just a little bit near to being worthy of the honor of being owned by Jim.

Suddenly Della whirled from the window and stood before the mirror. Her eyes were shining brilliantly, but her face had lost its color within twenty seconds. Rapidly she pulled down her hair and let it fall to its full length.

Now, there were two possessions of the James Dillingham Youngs in which they both took a mighty pride. One was Jim's gold watch that had been his father's and his grandfather's. The other was Della's hair. Had the Queen of Sheba lived in the next door, Della would have let her hair hang out the window some day to dry just to make Her Majesty jealous.

Had King Solomon been the janitor, with all his treasures piled up in the basement, Jim would have pulled out his watch every time he passed, just to see him pluck at his beard from envy.

So now Della's beautiful hair fell about her, rippling and shining like a **cascade** of brown waters. It reached below her knee and made itself almost a piece of clothing for her. And then she did it up again nervously and quickly. Once she **faltered** for a minute and stood still while a tear or two splashed on the worn red carpet.

Word Power
cascade (kas kād′) *n.* a waterfall; a series of small waterfalls
faltered (fôl′ tərd) *v.* stumbled or paused in an awkward way

Connect to the Text

Reread the text boxed in purple. Have you ever wanted to buy a nice gift for someone but were unable to afford it? How did you feel? What are some alternatives to buying a gift?

_____

_____

_____

_____

_____

Comprehension Check

Reread the text boxed in green. Underline the two things that Jim and Della value most.

Background Info

Mme. is a French abbreviation for the word *Madame,* which means "Mrs."

English Coach

The author says that the hours "tripped by on rosy wings." This is another way of saying that the time went by quickly. Think of another way to say time went by quickly.

_____

_____

_____

On went her old brown jacket; on went her old brown hat. With a whirl of skirts and with the brilliant sparkle still in her eyes, she fluttered out the door and down the stairs to the street.

Where she stopped the sign read: "Mme. Sofronie. Hair Goods of All Kinds." One flight up Della ran, and collected herself, panting.

"Will you buy my hair?" asked Della.

"I buy hair," said Madame. "Take yer hat off and let's have a sight at the looks of it."

Down rippled the brown cascade.

"Twenty dollars," said Madame, lifting the mass with a practiced hand.

"Give it to me quick," said Della.

Oh, and the next two hours tripped by on rosy wings. She was searching the stores for Jim's present.

Woman at Her Toilet. Edgar Degas (1834–1917). Oil pastel on paper. The Hermitage, St. Petersburg, Russia.

How do you think Della and the woman in this painting feel about having long hair?

_____

She found it at last. It surely had been made for Jim and no one else. There was no other like it in any of the stores, and she had

turned all of them inside out. It was a fob chain simple in design, properly proclaiming its value by substance alone and not by cheap ornamentation—as all good things should do.

It was even worthy of The Watch. As soon as she saw it she knew that it must be Jim's. It was like him. Quietness and value—the description applied to both. Twenty-one dollars they took from her for it, and she hurried home with the 87 cents. With that chain on his watch Jim might be anxious about the time in any company. Grand as the watch was, he sometimes looked at it on the sly on account of the old leather strap that he used in place of a chain.

When Della reached home her excitement gave way a little to reason. She got out her curling irons and lighted the gas and went to work repairing her damaged hair. Which is always a tremendous task, dear friends—a **mammoth** task.

Within forty minutes her head was covered with tiny, close-lying curls that made her look wonderfully like a truant schoolboy. She looked at her reflection in the mirror long, carefully, and critically.

"If Jim doesn't kill me," she said to herself, "before he takes a second look at me, he'll say I look like a Coney Island chorus girl. But what could I do—oh! what could I do with a dollar and eighty-seven cents?"

Did You Know?
A *fob chain* is attached to a pocket watch and worn hanging from a pocket.
. . . .

Word Power
mammoth (mam´ əth) *adj.* extremely large

Literary Element

Theme Remember that theme is the main message in the story.

Reread the text highlighted in blue. Della buys Jim a watch with the money she earns from selling her hair. Check the box with the theme that **best** represents the story.

☐ People make sacrifices for the ones they love.

☐ Giving and receiving gifts is the best part of life.

☐ It is better to save money than to spend it.

Reading Skill

Respond Reread the text highlighted in green. How do you feel about Della and what she has done for Jim?

_____

_____

_____

_____

_____

_____

_____

At 7 o'clock the coffee was made and the frying pan was on the back of the stove hot and ready to cook the chops.

Jim was never late. Della doubled the fob chain in her hand and sat on the corner of the table near the door that he always entered.

Then she heard his step on the stair away down on the first flight, and she turned white for just a moment. She had a habit of saying little silent prayers about the simplest everyday things, and now she whispered: "Please God, make him think I am still pretty."

The door opened and Jim stepped in and closed it. He looked thin and very serious. Poor fellow, he was only twenty-two—and to be burdened with a family! He needed a new overcoat and he was without gloves.

Jim stopped inside the door. His eyes were fixed upon Della, and there was an expression in them that she could not read, and it terrified her. It was not anger, nor surprise, nor disapproval, nor horror, nor any of the sentiments that she had been prepared for. He simply stared at her with a peculiar expression on his face.

Della wriggled off the table and went for him.

"Jim, darling," she cried, "don't look at me that way. I had my hair cut off and sold it because I couldn't have lived through Christmas without giving you a present. It'll grow out again—you won't mind, will you? I just had to do it. My hair grows awfully fast. Say 'Merry Christmas!' Jim, and let's be happy. You don't know what a nice—what a beautiful, nice gift I've got for you."

"You've cut off your hair?" asked Jim, **laboriously,** as if he had not arrived at that obvious fact yet.

"Cut it off and sold it," said Della. "Don't you like me just as well, anyhow? I'm me without my hair, ain't I?"

Jim looked about the room curiously.

"You say your hair is gone?" he said, with an air almost of idiocy.

Reading Skill

Predict Reread the highlighted text. Predict what Jim will say to explain the look on his face.

_____

_____

_____

_____

_____

Word Power

laboriously (lə bôr´ ē əs lē) *adv.* done with hard work or a lot of effort

"You needn't look for it," said Della. "It's sold, I tell you—sold and gone, too. It's Christmas Eve. Be good to me, for it went for you. Maybe the hairs of my head were numbered," she went on with a sudden serious sweetness, "but nobody could ever count my love for you. Shall I put the chops on, Jim?"

Out of his trance Jim seemed quickly to wake. He embraced his Della.

Eight dollars a week or a million a year—what is the difference? A mathematician or a wit would give you the wrong answer. The Magi brought valuable gifts, but that was not among them. This dark statement will be explained later on.

Jim drew a package from his overcoat pocket and threw it upon the table.

"Don't make any mistake, Dell," he said, "about me. I don't think there's anything in the way of a haircut or a shave or a shampoo that could make me like my girl any less. But if you'll unwrap that package you may see why you had me going a while at first."

White fingers and nimble tore at the string and paper. And then a happy scream of joy; and then, alas! a quick feminine change to tears and wails.

Cross Streets of New York, 1899. Everett Shinn. Charcoal, watercolor, pastel, white chalk, and Chinese white on paper, 21½ x 29¼ in. Corcoran Gallery of Art, Washington, D.C.

Look closely at this piece of art. How does the mood of this painting compare with the mood of "The Gift of the Magi"?

_____

Literary Element

Theme Reread the paragraph highlighted in blue. Tell how the theme, "when you love someone, you make sacrifices," becomes apparent in this paragraph.

_____

_____

_____

_____

_____

_____

Reading Skill

Predict Reread the text highlighted in green. What gift do you think Jim has given to Della?

_____

_____

_____

_____

_____

My Workspace

For there lay The Combs—the set of combs, side and back, that Della had worshipped for long in a Broadway window. Beautiful combs, pure tortoise shell, with jeweled rims—just the shade to wear in the beautiful vanished hair. They were expensive combs, she knew, and her heart had simply **craved** and yearned for them. And now, they were hers, but the hair that should have been decorated by them was gone.

But she hugged them to her bosom, and at length she was able to look up with dim eyes and a smile and say: "My hair grows so fast, Jim!"

And then Della leaped up like a little cat and cried, "Oh, oh!"

Jim had not yet seen his beautiful present. She held it out to him eagerly upon her open palm. The dull precious metal seemed to flash with a reflection of her bright spirit.

"Isn't it a dandy, Jim? I hunted all over town to find it. You'll have to look at the time a hundred times a day now. Give me your watch. I want to see how it looks on it."

Instead of obeying, Jim tumbled down on the couch and put his hands under the back of his head and smiled.

"Dell," said he, "let's put our Christmas presents away and keep 'em a while. They're too nice to use just at present. I sold the watch to get the money to buy your combs. And now suppose you put the chops on."

The Magi, as you know, were wise men—wonderfully wise men—who brought gifts to the Babe in the manger. They invented the art of giving Christmas presents. Being wise, their gifts were no doubt wise ones. And here I have lamely related to you the story of two foolish children who most unwisely sacrificed for each other the greatest treasures of their house. But in a last word to the wise of these days let it be said that of all who give gifts these two were the wisest. Of all who give and receive gifts, they are wisest. Everywhere they are wisest. They are the Magi.

Reading Skill

Respond Reread the last paragraph. How would you feel if you were in Jim and Della's situation?

_____

_____

_____

_____

Word Power

craved (krāvd) *v.* wanted very badly

Respond to Literature

The Gift of the Magi

A Comprehension Check

Answer the following questions in the spaces provided.

1. What is Jim's first reaction to Della when he arrives home? _____

   _____

2. What gifts do Jim and Della give each other? _____

   _____

B Reading Skills

Answer the following questions in the spaces provided.

1. **Predict** Now that their gifts are no longer useful, what do you predict Jim
   and Della will do with the gifts they received? _____

   _____

   _____

2. **Respond** Think of something that is very important to you. Would you
   sacrifice it to make someone you loved happy? Explain. _____

   _____

   _____

3. **Respond** How would you feel if you didn't have enough money to
   purchase a gift for someone you cared about? Explain. _____

   _____

   _____

C Word Power

Complete each sentence below, using one of the words in the box.

cascade	faltered	mammoth
laboriously	craved	

1. Have you ever seen such a _____ dog with huge paws?

2. We were so thirsty that we _____ the watermelon at the picnic.

3. Lorraine _____ in her dance steps.

4. The artist _____ worked on the painting all day.

5. A _____ is so beautiful to see from a mountain valley.

Circle the word that best completes each sentence.

6. When she was pregnant, my mother (**laboriously, craved**) pickles and crackers.

7. We watched the (**cascade, faltered**) from our tour guide's boat.

8. During the recital, Latrice (**faltered, mammoth**) on a difficult scale.

9. Demetrius (**cascade, laboriously**) practiced his speech for the debate.

10. The archaeologist found a (**craved, mammoth**) dinosaur bone buried in the ruins.

D Literary Element: Theme

Read the passage below from "The Gift of the Magi." As you read, think about the theme: when you love someone, you make sacrifices. Then answer the questions that follow.

"It's sold, I tell you—sold and gone, too.[1] It's Christmas Eve.[2] Be good to me, for it went for you. Maybe the hairs of my head were numbered," she went on with a sudden serious sweetness, "but nobody could ever count my love for you."[3]

And here I have lamely related to you the story of two foolish children who most unwisely sacrificed for each other the greatest treasures of their house....[4] Of all who give and receive gifts, they are wisest.[5] Everywhere they are wisest.[6]

1. How do sentences 1–3 help illustrate the theme?

2. In sentences 4–6, the narrator calls Jim and Della foolish because they each make an unwise sacrifice. However, in sentence 5, the narrator says that they are the wisest gift-givers. Explain how the gifts could be considered wise and foolish and how they express the theme of the story.

E A Diary Entry

Imagine you are Della or Jim. Write a diary entry telling what happened on the day the story takes place.

Date: December 24

Dear Diary,

Today is Christmas Eve. This morning I had no money to buy a gift. I wanted to buy _____

_____

I thought about how I could pay for this gift. I decided to

_____

_____

On Christmas Eve, we _____

_____

_____

It was the most wonderful Christmas Eve because

_____

_____

Assessment

Fill in the circle next to each correct answer.

1. On which day does the story take place?
   - ○ A. Christmas
   - ○ B. New Year's Eve
   - ○ C. Christmas Eve
   - ○ D. New Year's Day

2. How does Jim get the money to buy Della's present?
   - ○ A. He works extra hours.
   - ○ B. He sells his watch.
   - ○ C. He gets a second job.
   - ○ D. He sells Della's hair.

3. The Magi in the story are
   - ○ A. Jim and Della.
   - ○ B. the shopkeepers who sell the hair comb and fob chain.
   - ○ C. the grocer and the butcher.
   - ○ D. the people everywhere who give nice gifts.

4. Jim comes home on Christmas Eve with a gift and finds Della has cut her hair. Which sentence from the story **best** helps you predict that the gift Jim bought has something to do with Della's hair?
   - ○ A. Jim was never late.
   - ○ B. He simply stared at her with a peculiar expression on his face.
   - ○ C. Say 'Merry Christmas!' Jim, and let's be happy.
   - ○ D. Poor fellow, he was only twenty-two—and to be burdened with a family!

5. Which word **best** replaces laboriously in this sentence?
   We worked *laboriously* all day long.
   - ○ A. quickly
   - ○ B. effortlessly
   - ○ C. hard
   - ○ D. easily

The Horned Toad

Meet
Gerald Haslam

Gerald Haslam was born in 1937. He grew up in Oildale, California. His family is Anglo-Hispanic, just like the family in this story. His stories have themes that deal with issues that all people face. He has said, "no matter what our color or sex, we have more uniting than separating us. What is most important is that we are all members of the human family." This story is fiction but the main characters are based on Gerald Haslam himself, and his *abuelita,* or grandmother.

What You Know

There are many ways to show people that you care about them. For example, you can buy a birthday card for your cousin, visit a sick friend, or help your family with chores at home. How do you show people that you care? Think about your answers and discuss them with a classmate. As a class, list various ways that family members and friends show their support for one another.

Reason to Read

Read to find out what a boy and his family learn about caring when his great-grandmother comes to live with them.

Background Info

The *horned toad* is actually a type of lizard. Horned toads are about 2½ to 4½ inches long. They have large sharp spines that look like horns on their heads. They also have smaller spines on their backs. These spines protect them from predators, or animals that try to kill them for food. Even though horned toads are harmless, they can spurt tiny jets of blood from their eyes to frighten predators.

Word Power

periphery (pə rif´ər ē) *n.* the surrounding area; outskirts; p. 51
We have a fence on the *periphery* of our yard.

complied (kəm plīd´) *v.* obeyed; agreed to do something; p. 51
We *complied* with the rules by not running around the pool.

relented (ri lent´əd) *v.* gave in; p. 52
My parents did not want me to see the movie, but they finally *relented*.

incomprehensible (in´kom pri hen´sə bəl) *adj.* impossible to understand; p. 54
It is *incomprehensible* to think someone could act that way.

gravely (grāv´lē) *adv.* seriously; with a sense of importance; p. 55
We are *gravely* sorry about what has happened.

improvised (im´prə vīzd´) *v.* acted without a plan; made something up along the way; p. 58
Yolonda forgot the lyrics, so she *improvised*.

baffled (baf´əld) *v.* confused; p. 61
I am *baffled* by that riddle.

Answer the following questions, using one of the new words above.
Write your answers in the spaces provided.

1. Which word goes with "followed the rules"? _____

2. Which word goes with "mixed up"? _____

3. Which word goes with "great seriousness"? _____

4. Which word goes with "gave in to someone else's decision"? _____

5. Which word goes with "around the edge"? _____

6. Which word goes with "incapable of being grasped"? _____

7. Which word goes with "made up"? _____

Adapted from

The Horned Toad

Gerald Haslam

English Coach

Tóxicos is similar to the English word "toxic," which also means "poisonous." Name two other things that you know are toxic.

_____

_____

_____

Reading Skill

Predict Reread the text highlighted in green. Predict how the relationship between the narrator and Grandma will continue to develop.

_____

_____

_____

_____

_____

"¡Expectoran su sangre!" exclaimed Great-grandma when I showed her the small horned toad I had removed from my breast pocket. I turned toward my mother, who translated:

"They spit blood."

"De los ojos," Grandma added. "From their eyes," Mother explained, herself uncomfortable in the presence of the small beast.

I grinned, "Awwwwww."

But my great-grandmother did not smile. *"Son muy tóxicos,"* she nodded with finality. Mother moved back an involuntary step, her hands suddenly busy at her breast. "Put that thing down," she ordered.

"His name's John," I said.

"Put John down and not in your pocket, either," my mother nearly shouted. "Those things are very poisonous. Didn't you understand what Grandma said?"

I shook my head.

"Well. . ." Mother looked from one of us to the other and said, "Of course you didn't. Please take him back where you got him, and be careful. We'll all feel better when you do." The tone of her voice told me that the discussion had ended, so I released the little reptile where I'd captured him.

During those years in Oildale, the mid-1940s, I needed only to walk across the street to find a patch of desert. Neighborhood kids called it simply "the vacant lot." Most kids relied on the vacant lot as their primary playground. Even with its bullheads and stinging insects, we played everything from football to kick-the-can on it. We played our games on its sandy center, and conducted such sports as ant fights and lizard hunts on its brushy **periphery.**

That spring, when I discovered the lone horned toad near the back of the lot, had been rough on my family. Earlier, there had been quiet, unpleasant tension between Mom and Daddy. He was a silent man, little given to emotional displays. It was difficult for him to show affection and I guess the openness of Mom's family made him uneasy. Daddy had no kin in California and rarely mentioned any in Texas. He couldn't seem to understand my mother's large, intimate family, their constant noisy concern for one another, and I think he was a little jealous of the time she gave everyone, maybe even me.

I heard her talking on the phone to my various aunts and uncles, usually in Spanish. Even though I couldn't understand— Daddy had warned her not to teach me that foreign tongue because it would hurt me in school, and she'd **complied**—I could sense the stress. I had been afraid they were going to divorce, since she only used Spanish to hide things from me.

Reading Skill

Respond Reread the highlighted text. The narrator's mother agrees with Grandma that the horned toad should be returned. If you were the narrator, what would you do?

_____

_____

_____

_____

_____

Comprehension Check

Reread the boxed text. Underline words or phrases that describe how and why there was tension and stress in the narrator's home. Also underline whom the tension was between.

Word Power

periphery (pə rif´ ər ē) *n.* the surrounding area; outskirts
complied (kəm plīd´) *v.* obeyed; agreed to do something

Comprehension Check

Reread the text boxed in green. Give two reasons why Grandma wants to come live with the narrator's family in Oildale.

_____

_____

_____

_____

Background Info

Loosely translated, *ese gringo* means "that foreigner." A *gringo* is sometimes an impolite word that refers to a person who is foreign-born and does not speak Spanish.

I'd confronted her with my suspicion, but she comforted me, saying, no, that was not the problem. They were merely deciding when it would be our turn to care for Grandma. I didn't really understand, although I was relieved. I later learned that my great-grandmother—whom we simply called "Grandma"—had been moving from house to house within the family, trying to find a place she'd accept. She hated the city, and most of the aunts and uncles lived in Los Angeles. Our house in Oildale was much closer to the open country where she'd dwelled all her life. She had wanted to come to our place right away because she had raised my mother from a baby when my own grandmother died. But the old lady seemed unimpressed with Daddy, whom she called "ese gringo."

In truth, we had more room, and my dad made more money in the oil patch than almost anyone else in the family. Since my mother was the closest to Grandma, our place was the logical one for her, but Ese Gringo didn't see it that way, at least not at first. Finally, after much debate, he **relented.**

In any case, one windy afternoon, my Uncle Manuel and Aunt Toni drove up with four-and-a-half feet of Spanish spitfire: a square, pale face topped by a tightly-curled black wig that hid a bald head—her hair having been lost to typhoid nearly sixty years before.

She walked with a bounce that made her appear half her age, and she barked orders in Spanish from the moment she emerged from Manuel and Toni's car. Later, just before they left, I heard Uncle Manuel tell my dad, "Good luck, Charlie. That old lady's dynamite." Daddy only grunted.

Word Power

relented (ri lent´ əd) *v.* gave in

She had been with us only two days when I tried to impress her with my horned toad. In fact, nothing I did seemed to impress her, and she referred to me as *el malcriado*. Mom explained to me that Grandma was just old and lonely for Grandpa and uncomfortable in town. Mom told me that Grandma had lived over half a century in the country, away from the noise, away from clutter, away from people. She refused to accompany my mother on shopping trips, or anywhere else. She even refused to climb into a car, and I wondered how Uncle Manuel had managed to load her up in order to bring her to us.

She disliked sidewalks and roads, dancing across them when she had to. Things too civilized simply did not please her. Until my great-grandfather died, they lived on a small *rancho* near Arroyo Cantua. Grandpa had bred horses and cattle, scraping together enough of a living to raise eleven children.

He had been a lean, dark-skinned man with wide shoulders, a large nose, and a sweeping handlebar mustache. His Indian blood darkened all his offspring so that not even I was as fair-skinned as my great-grandmother, even though Ese Gringo was my father.

As it turned out, I didn't really understand very much about Grandma at all. She was old, of course, yet in many ways my parents treated her as though she were younger than me, walking her to the bathroom at night and bringing her presents from the store. In other ways—drinking wine at dinner, for example—she was granted adult privileges. Even Daddy didn't drink wine except on special occasions. After Grandma moved in, though, he began to occasionally join her for a glass.

Did You Know?
A *handlebar mustache* has long, curved ends and looks like the handlebars of a bicycle.
. . . .

English Coach

Grandma refers to the narrator as *el malcriado*. This is Spanish for "the rude fellow." In English, as in Spanish, *mal* is a prefix that means "bad." So, if something is malfunctioning, is it working well, or not working well?

_____

Connect to the Text

Reread the boxed text. The narrator is describing how he feels about Grandma and how the family treats her. How do you feel about your own grandma, or another older relative? How does your family treat this person?

_____
_____
_____
_____
_____
_____

Background Info

¡Venga aquí! means *"Come here."¿Qué deseas tomar?* means *"What would you like to have?" Dulce* means *"candy."* In English, the conversation goes like this: "Come here." "What would you like to have?" "Candy." "What did you say?" "I want candy."

Reading Skill

Respond Reread the highlighted sentence. Grandma is both teasing the narrator and showing him she can speak English. How do you feel about Grandma teasing the narrator?

_____

_____

_____

_____

She held court on our front porch, often gazing toward the desert hills east of us or across the street at kids playing on the lot. Occasionally, she would rise, cross the yard and street, sometimes stumbling on the curb, and slowly circle the open lot.

One afternoon I returned from school and saw Grandma perched on the porch as usual, so I started to walk around the house to avoid her sharp, mostly **incomprehensible,** tongue. She had already spotted me. *"¡Venga aquí!"* she ordered, and I understood.

I approached the porch and noticed that Grandma was chewing something. She held a small white bag in one hand. Saying *"¿Qué deseas tomar?"* she withdrew a large orange gumdrop from the bag and began slowly chewing it in her toothless mouth, smacking loudly. I stood below her for a moment trying to remember the word for candy. Then it came to me: *"Dulce,"* I said.

Still chewing, Grandma replied, *"¿Mande?"*

Knowing she wanted a complete sentence, I again struggled, then came up with *"Deseo dulce."*

She measured me for a moment, before answering in nearly perfect English, "Oh, so you wan' some candy. Go to the store an' buy some."

I don't know if it was the shock of hearing her speak English for the first time, or the way she had denied me a piece of candy, but I suddenly felt tears warm my cheeks and I sprinted into the house and found Mom. "Grandma just talked English," I burst between light sobs.

"What's wrong?" she asked as she reached out to stroke my head.

"Grandma can talk English," I repeated.

"Of course she can," Mom answered. "What's wrong?"

Word Power

incomprehensible (in′kom pri hen′sə bəl) *adj.* impossible to understand

54

I wasn't sure what was wrong, but after considering, I told Mom that Grandma had teased me. No sooner had I said that than the old woman appeared at the door and hiked her skirt. Attached to one of her petticoats by safety pins were several small tobacco sacks. She carefully unhooked one and opened it, withdrawing a dollar, then handed the money to me. *"Para su dulce,"* she said. Then, to my mother, she asked, "Why does he bawl like a motherless calf?"

"It's nothing," Mother replied.

"Do not weep, little one," the old lady comforted me, "Jesus and the Virgin love you." She smiled and patted my head. To my mother she said as though just realizing it, "Your baby?"

Somehow that day changed everything. I wasn't afraid of my great-grandmother any longer. Once I began spending time with her on the porch, I realized that my father had also begun paying attention to the old woman. Almost every evening Ese Gringo was sharing wine with Grandma. They talked out there, but I never did hear a real two-way conversation between them. Usually Grandma rattled on and Daddy nodded. She'd chuckle and pat his hand and he might grin, even grunt a word or two, before she'd begin talking again. Once I saw my mother standing by the front window watching them together, smiling.

No more did I sneak around the house to avoid Grandma after school. Instead, she discussed my efforts in class **gravely,** telling Mother that I was a bright boy, *"muy inteligente,"* and that I should be sent to the nuns who would train me. I would make a fine priest. When Ese Gringo heard that, he smiled and said, "He'd make a fair-to-middlin' Holy Roller preacher, too." Even Mom had to chuckle, and my great-grandmother shook her finger at Ese Gringo. "Oh you debil, Sharlie!" she cackled.

Word Power

gravely (grāv′lē) *adv.* seriously; with a sense of importance

Background Info

The Virgin refers to Mary, the mother of Jesus.

Reading Skill

Predict Earlier you made a prediction about how the relationship between the narrator and Grandma would develop. Was your prediction accurate? Describe how their relationship has changed since the beginning of the story.

_____

_____

_____

_____

_____

_____

Literary Element

Theme Remember, a story's theme is its main idea or message. It is often an insight about life or human nature.

Grandma's words relate to one of the story's themes. Reread the text highlighted in blue and think about Grandma's comments. Put a check next to the statement that best summarizes the theme.

- ☐ Always listen to your elders.
- ☐ It's bad luck to capture horned toads.
- ☐ All creatures should be left in their own places.

Reading Skill

Predict Reread the sentence highlighted in green. What do you think happened to the horned toad?

_____

_____

_____

_____

Frequently, I would accompany Grandma to the lot. Grandma greeted even the tiniest new cactus or flowering weed with joy. "Look how beautiful," she would croon. "In all this ugliness, it lives." Oildale was my home and it didn't look especially ugly to me, so I could only grin and wonder.

Because she liked the lot and things that grew there, I showed her the horned toad when I captured it a second time. I was determined to keep it, although I did not discuss my plans with anyone. I also wanted to hear more about the bloody eyes, so I thrust the small animal nearly into her face one afternoon. She did not flinch. *"Hola, señor, sangre de ojos,"* she said with a mischievous grin. *"¿Qué tal?"* It took me a moment to catch on. "You were kidding before," I accused.

"Of course," she acknowledged, still grinning.

"But why?"

"Because the little beast belongs with his own kind in his own place, not in your pocket. Give him his freedom, my son."

I had other plans for the horned toad, but I was clever enough not to cross Grandma. "Yes, Ma'am," I replied. That night I placed the reptile in a flower bed cornered by a brick wall Ese Gringo had built the previous summer. It was a spot rich with insects for the toad to eat, and the little wall, only a foot high, must have seemed massive to so squat an animal.

Nonetheless, the next morning, when I searched for the horned toad it was gone. I had no time to explore the yard for it, so I trudged off to school, my belly troubled. How could it have escaped? Classes meant little to me that day. I thought only of my lost pet—I had changed his name to Juan, the same as my great-grandfather—and where I might find him.

 STOP Stop here for **Break Time** on the next page.

Break Time

Think about how the narrator and his father relate to Grandma. How do they interact with her when she first arrives? How do they interact with her after she has lived with them for awhile? Complete the chart by adding details about the narrator's and the father's relationships with Grandma. Examples have been provided.

	Grandma's relationships with the family	
	when she first arrives	**after she's lived with the family for awhile**
narrator	The narrator does not understand Grandma at all.	The narrator begins to appreciate Grandma's sense of humor.
father		

 Turn the page to continue reading.

Background Info

Praying mantises are insects with long legs. They hold their front legs so that it looks like they are praying.

Reading Skill

Predict Reread the highlighted text. Was your prediction about the horned toad accurate? What clues throughout the story could have helped you to predict the horned toad's death?

_____

_____

_____

_____

_____

_____

_____

I shortened my conversation with Grandma that afternoon so I could search for Juan. "What do you seek?" the old woman asked me as I poked through flower beds beneath the porch. "Praying mantises," I **improvised,** and she merely nodded, surveying me. But I had eyes only for my lost pet, and I continued pushing through branches and brushing aside leaves. No luck.

Finally, I gave in and turned toward the lot. I found my horned toad nearly across the street, crushed. It had been heading for the miniature desert and had almost made it when an automobile's tire had run over it. One notion immediately swept me: if I had left it on its lot, it would still be alive. I stood rooted there in the street, tears slicking my cheeks, and a car honked its horn as it passed, the driver shouting at me.

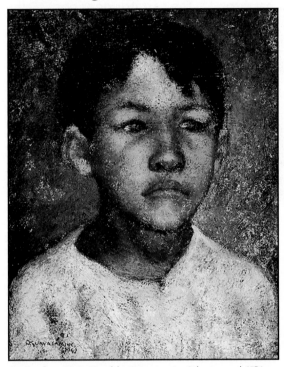

My Brother, 1942. Osvaldo Guayasamin. Oil on wood, 15⅞ x 12¾ in. Museum of Modern Art, New York.

How would you describe the expression of the boy in the painting? At what point in the story might the narrator have worn a similar expression?

_____

Word Power

improvised (im′prə vīzd′) *v.* acted without a plan; made something up along the way

Grandma joined me, and stroked my back. "The poor little beast," was all she said, then she bent slowly and scooped up what remained of the horned toad and led me out of the street. "We must return him to his own place," she explained, and we trooped, my eyes still clouded, toward the back of the vacant lot. Carefully, I dug a hole with a piece of wood.

Grandma placed Juan in it and covered him. We said an Our Father and a Hail Mary, then Grandma walked me back to the house. "Your little Juan is safe with God, my son," she comforted. We kept the horned toad's death a secret, and we visited his small grave frequently.

Grandma fell just before school ended and summer vacation began. As was her habit, she had walked alone to the vacant lot but this time, on her way back, she tripped over the curb and broke her hip. That following week, when Daddy brought her home from the hospital, she seemed to have shrunken. She sat hunched in a wheelchair on the porch, gazing with faded eyes toward the lot, speaking rarely. She still sipped wine every evening with Daddy and even I could tell how concerned he was about her. And if Daddy was home, Grandma always wanted him to push her chair when she needed moving, calling, "Sharlie!" until he arrived.

I was tugged from sleep on the night she died by voices drumming through the walls into darkness. I struggled from bed and walked into the living room just as Daddy closed the front door and a car pulled away.

Mom was sobbing softly on the couch and Daddy walked to her, stroked her head, then noticed me. "Come here, son," he gently ordered.

Literary Element

Theme Reread the highlighted text. As often happens in life, the narrator learns his lesson the hard way. How does the lesson reflect the theme of the story?

_____

_____

_____

_____

_____

_____

_____

Comprehension Check

Reread the boxed paragraph. Why do some family members want to bury Grandma in Bakersfield?

- ☐ It's near the country.
- ☐ The relatives can visit more easily.
- ☐ The relatives think Grandma would like it better.

Literary Element

Theme Reread the highlighted text. Why does the narrator repeat Grandma's message about returning the horned toad to its place?

_____

_____

_____

_____

_____

_____

_____

I walked to him and, uncharacteristically, he put an arm around me. "What's wrong?" I asked, near tears myself. Mom looked up, but before she could speak, Daddy said, "Grandma died." Then he sighed heavily and stood there with his arms around his weeping wife and son.

The next day my Uncle Manuel and Uncle Arnulfo, plus Aunt Chintia, arrived and over food they discussed with my mother where Grandma should be buried. They argued that they could more easily visit her grave if she was buried in Bakersfield. Just when it seemed they had agreed, I could remain silent no longer.

"But Grandma has to go home," I burst. "She has to! It's the only thing she really wanted. We can't leave her in the city."

Uncle Arnulfo, who was on the edge, snapped to Mother that I belonged with the other children, not interrupting adult conversation. My father walked into the room then.

"What's wrong?" he asked.

"They're going to bury Grandma in Bakersfield, Daddy. Don't let 'em, please. When my horny toad got killed and she helped me to bury it, she said we had to return him to his place."

"Your horny toad?" Mother asked.

"He got squished and me and Grandma buried him in the lot. She said we had to take him back to his place. Honest she did."

No one spoke for a moment, then my father, Ese Gringo responded: "That's right ..." he paused, then added, "We'll bury her." I saw a weary smile cross my mother's face. "If she wanted to go back to the ranch then that's where we have to take her," Daddy said.

I hugged him and he, right in front of everyone, hugged back.

No one argued. It seemed, suddenly, as though they had all wanted to do exactly what I had begged for. Grown-ups **baffled** me. Late that week the entire family, hundreds it seemed, gathered at the little Catholic church in Coalinga for mass, then drove out to Arroyo Cantua and buried Grandma next to Grandpa. She rests there today.

My mother, father, and I drove back to Oildale that afternoon across the scorching westside desert, through sand and tumbleweeds and heat shivers. Quiet and sad, we knew we had done our best. Mom, who usually sat next to the door in the front seat, snuggled close to Daddy, and I heard her whisper to him, "Thank you, Charlie," as she kissed his cheek.

Daddy squeezed her, hesitated as if to clear his throat, then answered, "When you're family, you take care of your own."

Connect to the Text

Reread the boxed text. The family supports each other. Write about a time when you and your family members supported each other.

_____

_____

_____

_____

_____

_____

_____

Interior, 1969. Carel Victor Morlais Weight. Oil on canvas. Herbert Art Gallery, Bristol, England.

With what characters in the story might you associate the two women in the picture?

_____

Word Power
baffled (baf ′ əld) *v.* confused

Respond to Literature

The Horned Toad

A Comprehension Check

Answer the following questions in the spaces provided.

1. What happens to the horned toad?

   _____

2. What does the narrator tell his parents to do after Grandma dies?

   _____

B Reading Skills

Answer the following questions in the spaces provided.

1. **Respond** If you were the narrator, how would you feel when your horned toad dies? How would you feel when Grandma dies? Why?

   _____

   _____

   _____

2. **Predict** If this story were to continue after the family returns from burying Grandma, how do you think the relationship between the boy and his father would change?

   _____

   _____

   _____

C Word Power

Complete each sentence below, using one of the words in the box.

periphery	complied	relented	incomprehensible
	gravely	improvised	baffled

1. Esme took the child's toys away but then _____ and gave them back when he cried.

2. The doctor spoke _____ to me about not smoking.

3. I couldn't give a good answer because the question was

   _____.

4. There is a wall around the _____ of the building.

5. Alejandro has _____ with the school's uniform rules by wearing a tie.

6. Even though the problem seemed simple, I was _____ by it.

7. When Shanta ran out of string, she _____ and used a ribbon.

D Literary Element: Theme

Read the passages below from "The Horned Toad." As you read, think about the theme of the story. Then answer the questions that follow.

> "Because the little beast belongs with his own kind in his own place, not in your pocket.[1] Give him his freedom, my son."[2]
>
> "They're going to bury Grandma in Bakersfield, Daddy. Don't let 'em, please.[3] When my horny toad got killed and she helped me to bury it, she said we had to return him to his place."[4]

1. Sentences 1 and 2 state the theme of the story as it applies to the horned toad. What is Grandma trying to tell the narrator?

   _____

   _____

   _____

   _____

2. Reread sentences 3 and 4. Why does the narrator use the example of the toad to persuade his parents not to let the relatives bury Grandma in Bakersfield? Where does he think Grandma should be buried?

   _____

   _____

   _____

   _____

E A Funeral Speech

At a funeral, people often stand up and talk about the person who has died. They tell about the person's life and share some personal memories. Write a speech that the narrator might give at Grandma's funeral.

I loved my Grandma very much. At first, I _____

_____

_____

But then I got to know her better. Soon, she and I _____

_____

_____

Even my father started _____

_____

She taught me an important lesson. I learned that _____

_____

_____

When my family wanted to bury her far from her home, I spoke up and said _____

_____

_____

I will always miss my Grandma, but she will be in my heart forever.

Assessment

Fill in the circle next to each correct answer.

1. Why is there tension between the boy's parents at the beginning of the story?
   - ○ A. They do not want the boy to play with horned toads.
   - ○ B. They do not want Grandma to speak Spanish.
   - ○ C. They are trying to decide where Grandma will live.
   - ○ D. They want the boy to do better in school.

2. Grandma first calls _____ "ese gringo." Later she calls him Sharlie.
   - ○ A. Uncle Manuel
   - ○ B. the boy
   - ○ C. Daddy
   - ○ D. the preacher

3. Read this sentence from the story. "That spring . . . had been rough on my family." What does this sentence make you think the story will be about?
   - ○ A. the death of a lizard
   - ○ B. the school play
   - ○ C. the fun times the family has during the winter
   - ○ D. the challenges the family faces

4. What theme is revealed by Grandma?
   - ○ A. Creatures should be left in their own place.
   - ○ B. Creatures can be kept for only a short time.
   - ○ C. Family members must agree on the pets they choose.
   - ○ D. Pets should always be left alone.

5. Which word means the same as "baffled"?
   - ○ A. confused
   - ○ B. enjoyed
   - ○ C. amused
   - ○ D. helped

UNIT 1

Wrap-up

Compare and Contrast

Theme is an important literary element in "The Gift of the Magi" and "The Horned Toad." Both of these stories have more than one theme. A theme shared by both stories is that people should respect and try to understand what their loved ones value. Think about what the characters in each story value most. Then, think about how other characters respond to these values.

Use the Venn diagram to show the similarities and differences between how this theme is expressed in each story. In the outer parts of the circles list examples of how the theme is shown in each story. In the overlapping part of the circles, list examples of how the theme is shown in similar ways. An example has been done for you in each section.

"The Gift of the Magi"

• Della knows Jim values his watch, so she buys him a chain for it.

Alike

• Characters in both stories are concerned with what is most important to a loved one.

"The Horned Toad"

• The father knows the mother loves Grandma, so he agrees to take her in.

UNIT 2 Short Story

How Is a Short Story Organized?

Now that you have read a few short stories, let's stop for a moment to take a closer look at how a short story is put together.

A **short story** always has three parts: a **beginning,** a **middle,** and an **end.**

Most stories also include a **conflict.** A conflict is a struggle between characters, or a struggle between a character and nature or another outside force.

What's the Plan?

Within the three parts of the story, the plot develops in five stages.

Exposition introduces characters, setting, and conflict.

Rising action adds complications to the conflict.

Climax is the point of greatest interest or suspense. It is the turning point.

Falling action includes all the events after the climax.

Resolution presents the final outcome.

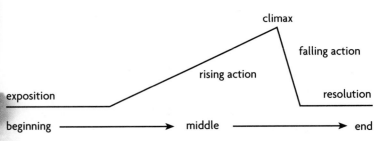

How Do I Read Short Stories?

Focus on key **literary elements** and **reading skills** to get the most out of reading the four short stories in this unit. Here are two key literary elements and two key reading skills that you will practice in this unit.

Key Literary Elements

• Plot

Plot is the sequence of events in a story. It is the story's basic framework. Each event causes or leads to the next. The characters, setting, and conflict are introduced in the **exposition.** Conflict intensifies in the **rising action.** This leads to the **climax**—the emotional point of the story. **Falling action** is the result of the climax. And finally, there is a **resolution,** which is the end of the story.

• Tone

Tone is the writer's attitude toward a subject. A writer's tone may be communicated through particular words and details that express particular emotions and evoke an emotional response in the reader. For example, a good-bye between family members could be expressed in a sad, formal, or angry tone.

Key Reading Skills

• Sequence

The order in which thoughts or actions are arranged is called the **sequence.** In many stories, events often take place in chronological sequence, or in the order in which they actually occur. Sometimes, though, a writer uses flashbacks or other devices to relate a story out of chronological sequence. As you read, look for words like *first, then, meanwhile, eventually,* and *later.* These words can help you figure out when things happen.

• Infer

When you **infer,** you make an educated guess about information you have read. You draw logical conclusions, combining clues from the text with what you already know from experience or other reading. A writer does not always state things directly. For example, instead of telling you that a character is angry, the writer may use details and actions that show the character acting angrily, such as slamming a plate on the floor.

Get Ready to Read!

THE OPEN WINDOW

Meet Saki

The British author H.H. Munro was born in 1870. He used the name Saki (sä′kē) for his writings. He wrote short stories, novels, and plays. He was best known for his short stories, which show great wit and cleverness. Saki's stories often include characters who trick or deceive one another. H.H. Munro joined the army in World War I and was killed in action in 1916. "The Open Window" was first published in 1914.

What You Know

What are some things you can tell about a person you have just met? Has your first impression ever turned out to be wrong? Write about a time when you were mistaken about a first impression. Describe the assumptions you made the first time you met someone, and tell what you learned about him or her later on.

Reason to Read

Read to find out what happens when two characters act on their first impressions of each other.

Background Info

The story takes place at a country house in England more than one hundred years ago. Hunting was a popular sport among the upper classes then. In the story "The Open Window," men are hunting birds. They have brought along a spaniel, which is a dog specially trained to help hunters find and gather birds.

A Spaniel Frightening Ducks, 1821. James Ward. Oil on canvas, 48 x 72 in. Tate Gallery, London.

Word Power

disregarding (dis´ri gärd´ing) *v.* treating without respect or attention; p. 72
The sales clerk was fired for *disregarding* customers' complaints.

conscious (kon´shəs) *adj.* aware; p. 75
It is hard to sleep when you are *conscious* of every little sound.

anniversary (an´ə vur´sə rē) *n.* the yearly date on which a past event happened; p 75
Mama holds a party every June on the *anniversary* of her arrival in this country.

vigorous (vig´ər əs) *adj.* strong and active; p. 75
Riding a bike twenty miles is *vigorous* exercise.

sympathetic (sim´pə thet´ik) *adj.* sharing the feelings of another or expressing pity; p. 76
The nurse's *sympathetic* smile made the patient feel better.

twilight (twī´ līt´) *n.* soft, hazy light reflected from the sun just after sunset; p. 76
We walked home in the *twilight* before darkness came.

**Answer the following questions that contain the new words above.
Write your answers in the spaces provided.**

1. Are *sympathetic* words spoken angrily or gently? _____

2. If you were *disregarding* a rule, would you be following the rule or not following it?

   _____

3. Which is a *vigorous* activity, dancing or napping? _____

4. Does *twilight* occur at the beginning or end of the day? _____

5. If you were *conscious* of a problem, would you know about the problem or not

   know about it? _____

6. Does a wedding *anniversary* happen once a year or once every five years?

   _____

Adapted from

THE OPEN WINDOW

Saki

Reading Skill

Infer Reread the highlighted text. What problem does Framton Nuttel seem to have?

_____

_____

_____

_____

_____

_____

"My aunt will be down presently, Mr. Nuttel," said a very self-confident young lady of fifteen; "in the meantime you must try and put up with me."

Framton Nuttel tried to say something to flatter the niece without **disregarding** the aunt that was to come. Privately he doubted more than ever whether these formal visits of total strangers would help much. He was supposed to be undergoing a cure for his nerves.

"I know how it will be," his sister had said when he was preparing to move to this country area; "you will bury yourself down there and not speak to a living soul, and your nerves will be worse than ever from moping. I shall just give you letters of introduction to all the people I know there. Some of them, as far as I can remember, were quite nice."

Word Power
disregarding (dis´ri gärd´ing) v. treating without respect or attention

72

Framton wondered whether Mrs. Sappleton, the lady to whom he was presenting one of the letters of introduction, was nice or not. "Do you know many of the people round here?" asked the niece, when she judged that they had passed enough time in silence.

"Hardly a soul," said Framton. "My sister was staying here some four years ago, and she gave me letters of introduction to some of the people here."

"Then you know practically nothing about my aunt?" continued the self-confident young lady.

"Only her name and address," admitted the caller. He was wondering whether Mrs. Sappleton was married or widowed. An undefinable something about the room seemed to suggest a male presence.

"Her great tragedy happened just three years ago," said the child; "that would be since your sister's time."

"Her tragedy?" asked Framton; somehow in this restful country spot tragedies seemed out of place.

"You may wonder why we keep that window wide open on an October afternoon," said the niece, indicating a large French window that opened on to a lawn.

"It is quite warm for the time of the year," said Framton; "but has that window got anything to do with the tragedy?"

Did You Know?
A French window is a pair of tall windows that are used as a door.

73

Comprehension Check

Reread the boxed text. Mrs. Sappleton's niece is telling about her aunt's "great tragedy." Underline at least three details that make the story scary or eerie.

Literary Element

Plot: Rising Action

Reread the highlighted text. How do Mrs. Sappleton's comments contribute to the plot complications in the rising action?

_____

_____

_____

_____

_____

"Out through that window, three years ago to a day, her husband and her two young brothers went off for their day's shooting. They never came back. In their favorite shooting ground, they were all three swallowed up in a mucky, muddy bog. It had been that terrible wet summer, you know, and places that were safe in other years gave way suddenly without warning. Their bodies were never recovered. That was the dreadful part of it." Here the child's voice lost its self-confident note and began to break. "Poor aunt always thinks that they will come back some day. She thinks that they and the little brown spaniel that was lost with them will walk in at that window just as they used to do. That is why the window is kept open every evening till it is almost dark. Poor dear aunt, she has often told me how they went out, her husband with his white waterproof coat over his arm, and Ronnie, her youngest brother. He would sing, Bertie, why do you bound? He always did this to tease her, because she said it got on her nerves. Do you know, sometimes on still, quiet evenings like this, I almost get a creepy feeling that they will all walk in through that window—"

She broke off with a little shudder. It was a relief to Framton when the aunt came into the room, apologizing for being late.

"I hope Vera has been amusing you?" she said.

"She has been very interesting," said Framton.

"I hope you don't mind the open window," said Mrs. Sappleton briskly. "My husband and brothers will be home soon from shooting, and they always come in this way. They've been out hunting today, so they'll make a fine mess over my poor carpets. So like you men-folk, isn't it?"

She rattled on cheerfully about the shooting and the lack of birds, and the possibilities for duck in the winter. To Framton it was all purely horrible. He made a desperate but only partly successful effort to turn the talk on to a less terrible topic; he was **conscious** that his hostess was giving him only some of her attention. Her eyes were constantly looking past him to the open window and the lawn beyond. It was certainly unfortunate timing that he paid his visit on this tragic **anniversary.**

"The doctors agree in ordering me complete rest—no mental excitement, and no **vigorous** physical exercise," announced Framton. He assumed that total strangers are hungry for the least detail of one's illnesses. "On the matter of diet they are not so much in agreement," he continued.

"No?" said Mrs. Sappleton, in a voice which only replaced a yawn at the last moment. Then she suddenly brightened into alert attention—but not to what Framton was saying.

Gabrielle Vien as a Young Girl, 1893. Armand Seguin. Oil on canvas, 88 x 115 cm. Musée d'Orsay, Paris.

Word Power

conscious (kon´shəs) *adj.* aware

anniversary (an´ ə vur´sə rē) *n.* the yearly date on which a past event happened

vigorous (vig´ ər əs) *adj.* strong and active

Reading Skill
Infer Reread the highlighted paragraph. What is Framton probably thinking as he hears Mrs. Sappleton's comments?

_____

_____

_____

_____

_____

_____

Literary Element

Plot: Climax Reread the text highlighted in blue and the next three paragraphs. Choose a character and tell how he or she adds to the excitement of the climax. For example: The aunt spots the returning hunters, who are said to have disappeared.

_____

_____

_____

_____

_____

_____

_____

English Coach

The prefix *extra-* in *extraordinary* means "outside or beyond." Think of another word, or find one in the dictionary, with the prefix *extra-*.

_____

_____

_____

"Here they are at last!" she cried. "Just in time for tea, and don't they look as if they were muddy up to the eyes!"

Framton shivered slightly and turned towards the niece. He looked at her with **sympathetic** understanding. The child was staring out through the open window with dazed horror in her eyes. In a chill shock of fear Framton swung round in his seat and looked in the same direction.

In the deepening **twilight** three figures were walking across the lawn towards the window. They all carried guns under their arms, and one of them was also carrying a white coat hung over his shoulders. A tired brown spaniel kept close at their heels. Silently they neared the house, and then a young voice chanted out of the dusk: "I said, Bertie, why do you bound?"

Framton grabbed wildly at his stick and hat. He headed straight for the hall door, the gravel drive, and the front gate. A cyclist coming along the road had to run into the hedge to avoid hitting him.

"Here we are, my dear," said the bearer of the white coat, coming in through the window; "fairly muddy, but most of it's dry. Who was that who bolted out as we came up?"

"A most extraordinary man, a Mr. Nuttel," said Mrs. Sappleton. "He could only talk about his illnesses, and he dashed off without a word of good-bye or apology when you arrived. One would think he had seen a ghost."

"I expect it was the spaniel," said the niece calmly. "He told me he had a horror of dogs. He was once hunted into a cemetery by a pack of dogs. He had to spend the night in a newly dug grave with the creatures snarling and grinning and foaming just above him. Enough to make any one lose their nerve."

Extraordinary tales at short notice was her specialty.

Word Power

sympathetic (sim´pə thet´ik) *adj.* sharing the feelings of another or expressing pity

twilight (twī´ līt´) *n.* soft, hazy light reflected from the sun just after sunset

Respond to Literature

THE OPEN WINDOW

A Comprehension Check

Answer the following questions in the spaces provided.

1. What does Vera learn about Mr. Nuttel before she begins her story?

_____

_____

2. What "tragedy" does Vera describe? _____

_____

_____

B Reading Skills

Complete the following activities in the spaces provided.

1. **Infer** When the aunt spots the hunters returning, she cries, "Here they are at last!" Why does Framton look at the niece with "sympathetic

understanding"? _____

_____

_____

2. **Sequence** Think of three events that occur after Framton Nuttel arrives at the Sappletons' house. List the events in the order in which they happen.

_____

_____

_____

C Word Power

Complete each sentence below, using one of the words in the box.

disregarding	conscious	anniversary
vigorous	sympathetic	twilight

1. Every July my parents celebrate their wedding _____.

2. The heart beats faster with _____ exercise.

3. "Oh, my poor dear," said Grandma in her most _____ voice.

4. The children were giving their new kitten constant attention, but they were _____ their old cat.

5. To change a habit, first try to be _____ of what you are doing.

6. We watched the sun set, and we walked home in the _____.

D Literary Element: Plot

Read the passages below from "The Open Window." As you read, think about the climax. Then answer the questions that follow.

The child was staring out through the open window with dazed horror in her eyes.[1] In a chill shock of fear Framton swung round in his seat and looked in the same direction.[2]

In the deepening twilight three figures were walking across the lawn towards the window.[3] They all carried guns under their arms, and one of them was also carrying a white coat hung over his shoulders.[4] A tired brown spaniel kept close at their heels.[5] Silently they neared the house, and then a young voice chanted out of the dusk: "I said, Bertie, why do you bound?"[6]

Framton grabbed wildly at his stick and hat.[7] He headed straight for the hall door, the gravel drive, and the front gate.[8]

1. How does Vera's reaction in sentences 1–2 add to the excitement of the climax? _____

_____

_____

_____

2. What happens in the climax to cause Mr. Nuttel to react the way he does in sentences 7–8? _____

_____

_____

_____

E Diary Entry

Imagine that you are the character Vera. What will you write in your diary tonight to tell about the events of this evening? Fill in the missing parts of the diary entry with your ideas.

Dear Diary,

This evening, I enjoyed meeting _____

_____

He seemed _____

_____

I decided to have some fun with him. I made up a story

about _____

_____

_____

_____

_____

He believed every word! Then he saw _____

_____

He ran off in a big hurry! My aunt wondered why _____

_____

I told my aunt that he _____

_____

—Vera

Assessment

Fill in the circle next to each correct answer.

1. What makes Mr. Nuttel especially susceptible to Vera's story?
   - ○ A. Framton is coming to visit the aunt's husband.
   - ○ B. Framton is undergoing a "nerve cure."
   - ○ C. Vera is a "young lady of fifteen."
   - ○ D. Framton has "letters of introduction" from his sister.

2. Vera says that the window is left open for
   - ○ A. the dead hunters.
   - ○ B. warmth.
   - ○ C. cooling the room.
   - ○ D. animals.

3. Which of these events is in the climax of the story?
   - ○ A. Framton tells about his health problems.
   - ○ B. Mrs. Sappleton keeps watching the window.
   - ○ C. Mrs. Sappleton talks about hunting.
   - ○ D. The hunters return from their trip.

4. Which sentence below shows events that do **not** occur in the correct order in which they happened in the story?
   - ○ A. Vera meets Framton and then tells him an "extraordinary" tale.
   - ○ B. The aunt meets Framton, and then the hunters return.
   - ○ C. The hunters return, and then Vera tells them Framton is scared of dogs.
   - ○ D. The hunters return, and then Framton tells about his illnesses.

5. Which of these words means "aware"?
   - ○ A. disregarding
   - ○ B. vigorous
   - ○ C. conscious
   - ○ D. anniversary

Get Ready to Read!

The Scarlet Ibis

Meet
James Hurst

James Hurst may have drawn inspiration for the setting of this story from his childhood home in North Carolina. Many of the flowers and plants he describes in the story grew on his family's farm. As a child, he gained firsthand knowledge of hurricanes. This taught him about courage and perseverance, which are things he says this story is about. Although Hurst tried different careers—including opera singing—he spent most of his professional life as a banker in New York City, writing short stories and essays in his spare time. The author was born in 1922. This story was first published in the *Atlantic Monthly* magazine in 1960.

What You Know

Imagine what it might feel like to be embarrassed by or ashamed of someone you care about. How might it feel to know that a close friend or family member felt embarrassed around you?

Reason to Read

Read to learn how a young boy deals with his embarrassment about his brother.

Background Info

The scarlet ibis is a tropical bird with bright red feathers that breeds in the swamps of northern South America. It can occasionally be seen in Florida and along the Gulf Coast of Texas and Louisiana. The bird has long, thin, red legs; a long, slender neck that can curve into an S-shape; a curved beak; and black wing tips. It can reach a total length of about twenty-three inches.

Word Power

invalid (in′ və lid) *n.* a person who is sick or disabled; p. 85
My grandmother became an *invalid* after she had a stroke.

discourage (dis kur′ ij) *v.* to try to persuade someone not to do something; p. 87
I tried to *discourage* my friend from cheating on the test.

careen (kə rēn′) *v.* to tilt or sway while moving, as if out of control; p. 87
We watched the dancers *careen* around the dance floor.

loll (lol) *v.* to act or move in a lazy and relaxed way; p. 88
On hot summer days, my best friend and I *loll* around on the cool grass.

sullenly (sul′ ən lē) *adv.* in a bad-tempered, sulky, or gloomy way; p. 88
When my father ordered me to give my brother half my cookie, I *sullenly* agreed.

precariously (pri kār′ ē əs lē) *adv.* dangerously; insecurely; p. 95
The vase of flowers sat *precariously* on the edge of the table.

mercy (mur′ sē) *n.* compassion or forgiveness; p. 97
My opponent had me pinned down, but finally showed *mercy* by letting me go.

spite (spīt) *n.* a mean feeling toward someone; p. 98
My friend was jealous of my new video game, and I'm sure she broke it out of *spite*.

**Answer the following questions that contain the new words above.
Write your answers in the spaces provided.**

1. If you *loll* about, are you relaxed or agitated? _____

2. Would someone showing *mercy* forgive or punish? _____

3. If you are hanging *precariously*, are you safe or in danger? _____

4. If you act *sullenly,* are you in a good mood or a bad mood? _____

5. If you *discourage* someone from doing something, do you want the person to do it
   or not want the person to do it? _____

6. Is an *invalid* healthy or sick? _____

7. If you see a car *careen* down the street, is the driver most likely in control or
   out of control? _____

8. If Jon feels *spite* towards Juan, does he like him or dislike him? _____

Adapted from

The Scarlet Ibis

James Hurst

It was in the change of seasons, summer was dead but autumn had not yet been born, that the ibis landed in the bleeding tree. The last graveyard flowers were blooming, and their smell drifted through every room of our house, speaking softly the names of our dead.

It's strange that all this is still so clear to me, now that that summer has long since fled and time has had its way. A grindstone stands where the bleeding tree stood, just outside the kitchen door. The flower garden is neatly cut, and the house is gleaming white. But sometimes (like right now), as I sit in the cool, green-draped living room, the grindstone begins to turn, and time with all its changes is ground away—and I remember Doodle.

Did You Know?
A *grindstone* is a tool used for sharpening tools.

Doodle was just about the craziest brother a boy ever had. Of course, he wasn't a crazy crazy like old Miss Leedie, who was in love with President Wilson and wrote him a letter every day. He was a nice crazy, like someone you meet in your dreams. He was born when I was six and was, from the outset, a disappointment. He seemed all head, with a tiny body which was red and shriveled like an old man's. Everybody thought he was going to die— everybody except Aunt Nicey. Daddy had Mr. Heath, the carpenter, build a little mahogany coffin for him. But he didn't die, and when he was three months old Mama and Daddy decided they might as well name him. They named him William Armstrong, which was like tying a big tail on a small kite. Such a name sounds good only on a tombstone.

I thought myself pretty smart at many things, like holding my breath, running, jumping, or climbing the vines in Old Woman Swamp. I wanted more than anything else someone to race to Horsehead Landing, someone to box with, and someone to perch with in the great pine behind the barn. I wanted a brother. But Mama, crying, told me that even if William Armstrong lived, he would never do these things with me. He might not, she sobbed, even be "all there." He might, as long as he lived, lie on the rubber sheet in the center of the bed in the front bedroom.

It was bad enough having an **invalid** brother, but having one who possibly was not all there was unbearable. I began to make plans to kill him by smothering him with a pillow. However, one afternoon as I watched him, my head poked between the iron posts of the foot of the bed, he looked straight at me and grinned. I skipped through the rooms, down the echoing halls, shouting, "Mama, he smiled. He's all there! He's all there!" and he was.

Word Power

invalid (in´ və lid) *n.* a person who is sick or disabled

Literary Element

Plot: Exposition Reread the sentence highlighted in blue and the rest of the paragraph. The exposition is the part of the story in which characters are introduced. You learn that Doodle is the narrator's brother who is six years younger than he is. List two other points you learn about Doodle in the exposition.

_____

_____

_____

_____

_____

_____

Reading Skill

Infer Reread the paragraph highlighted in green. Doodle is unable to do the same things his brother can do. What can you infer about Doodle from this detail?

_____

_____

_____

_____

Reading Skill

Sequence Reread the highlighted paragraph. The narrator is telling the story of Doodle's life. To help you keep track of time, you can pay attention to Doodle's age. At age two, Doodle is diagnosed with a weak heart. What takes place a year later?

_____

_____

_____

Connect to the Text

Reread the boxed text. How would you feel if someone you know tagged along with you everywhere you went?

_____

_____

_____

_____

When he was two, if you laid him on his stomach, he began to try to move himself, straining terribly. The doctor said that with his weak heart this strain would probably kill him, but it didn't. Trembling, he'd push himself up, turning first red, then a soft purple. He would then collapse back onto the bed like an old worn-out doll. But he learned to crawl (it was his third winter). For the first time he became one of us.

As long as he lay all the time in bed, we called him William Armstrong. But with his creeping around on the deerskin rug and beginning to talk, something had to be done about his name. It was I who renamed him. When he crawled, he crawled backwards, as if he were in reverse and couldn't change gears. If you called him, he'd turn around as if he were going in the other direction. Crawling backward made him look like a doodlebug, so I began to call him Doodle, and in time even Mama and Daddy thought it was a better name than William Armstrong. Renaming my brother was perhaps the kindest thing I ever did for him, because nobody expects much from someone called Doodle.

Although Doodle learned to crawl, he showed no signs of walking, but he wasn't idle. He talked so much that we all quit listening to what he said. It was about this time that Daddy built him a go-cart and I had to pull him around. At first I just paraded him up and down the porch. Then he started crying to be taken out into the yard and it ended up by my having to lug him wherever I went. If I so much as picked up my cap, he'd start crying to go with me and Mama would call from wherever she was, "Take Doodle with you."

He was a burden in many ways. The doctor had said that he mustn't get too excited, too hot, too cold, or too tired and that he must always be treated gently. A long list of don'ts went with him, all of which I ignored once we got out of the house.

To **discourage** his coming with me, I'd run with him across the ends of the cotton rows and **careen** him around corners on two wheels. Sometimes I accidentally turned him over, but he never told Mama. His skin was very sensitive, and he had to wear a big straw hat whenever he went out. When the going got rough and he had to cling to the sides of the go-cart, the hat slipped all the way down over his ears. He was a sight. Finally, I could see I was licked. Doodle was my brother and he was going to cling to me forever, no matter what I did. So, I dragged him across the burning cotton field to share with him the only beauty I knew, Old Woman Swamp. His eyes were round with wonder as he gazed about him, and his little hands began to stroke the rubber grass. Then he began to cry.

Comprehension Check

Reread the boxed text. The narrator shows both cruelty and kindness to his younger brother. How is the narrator cruel to Doodle? How is the narrator kind to Doodle?

_____

_____

_____

_____

_____

_____

A Wooded River Landscape, 1910. Peder Monsted. Oil on canvas, 43.25 x 43.25 cm. Private collection.

If the narrator brought Doodle to a place like the one pictured, how might Doodle react?

_____

Word Power

discourage (dis kur′ ij) *v.* to try to persuade someone not to do something
careen (kə rēn′) *v.* to tilt or sway while moving, as if out of control

"For heaven's sake, what's the matter?" I asked, annoyed.

"It's so pretty," he said. "So pretty, pretty, pretty."

After that day Doodle and I often went down into Old Woman Swamp. I would gather wildflowers, wild violets, snakeflowers, and water lilies, and with wire grass we'd weave them into necklaces and crowns. We'd wear our handiwork and **loll** about thus beautified. Then when the slanted rays of the sun burned orange in the tops of the pines, we'd drop our jewels into the stream and watch them float away toward the sea.

There is within me (and with sadness I have watched it in others) a knot of cruelty borne by the stream of love, and at times I was mean to Doodle. One day I took him up to the barn loft and showed him his casket, telling him how we all had believed he would die. Doodle studied the mahogany box for a long time, then said, "It's not mine."

"It is," I said. "And before I'll help you down from the loft, you're going to have to touch it."

"I won't touch it," he said **sullenly.**

"Then I'll leave you here by yourself," I threatened, and made as if I were going down.

Doodle was frightened of being left. "Don't go leave me, Brother," he cried, and he leaned toward the coffin. His hand, trembling, reached out, and when he touched the casket he screamed. An owl flapped out of the box into our faces, scaring us. Doodle was paralyzed, so I put him on my shoulder and carried him down the ladder. Even when we were outside in the bright sunshine, he clung to me, crying, "Don't leave me. Don't leave me."

Word Power

loll (lol) *v.* to act or move in a lazy and relaxed way
sullenly (sul′ ən lē) *adv.* in a bad-tempered, sulky, or gloomy way

When Doodle was five years old, I was embarrassed at having a brother of that age who couldn't walk, so I set out to teach him. We were down in Old Woman Swamp and it was spring. "I'm going to teach you to walk, Doodle," I said.

He was sitting comfortably on the soft grass, leaning back against the pine. "Why?" he asked.

I hadn't expected such an answer. "So I won't have to haul you around all the time."

"I can't walk, Brother," he said.

"Who says so?" I demanded.

"Mama, the doctor—everybody."

"Oh, you can walk," I said, and I took him by the arms and stood him up. He collapsed onto the grass like a half-empty flour sack. It was as if he had no bones in his little legs.

"Don't hurt me, Brother," he warned.

"Shut up. I'm not going to hurt you. I'm going to teach you to walk." I heaved him up again, and again he collapsed.

This time he did not lift his face up out of the rubber grass. "I just can't do it. Let's make honeysuckle wreaths."

"Oh yes you can, Doodle," I said. "All you got to do is try. Now come on," and I hauled him up once more.

It seemed so hopeless from the beginning that it's a miracle I didn't give up. But all of us must have something or someone to be proud of, and Doodle had become mine. I did not know then that pride is a wonderful, terrible thing, a seed that bears two vines, life and death. Every day that summer we went to the pine beside the stream of Old Woman Swamp, and I put him on his feet at least a hundred times each afternoon. Occasionally I too became discouraged because it didn't seem as if he was trying, and I would say, "Doodle, don't you *want* to learn to walk?"

Reading Skill

Infer Reread the highlighted text. What do you think the narrator means by this comment? Check the **best** response.

- [ ] It is wonderful to always have pride.
- [ ] Pride can lead to being disappointed in others.
- [ ] Good and bad things can happen because of pride.

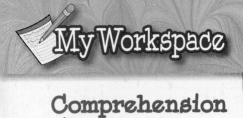

Comprehension Check

Reread the boxed text. What makes Doodle always want to try again?

_____

_____

_____

_____

_____

Reading Skill

Sequence Reread the highlighted text. What takes place at the party? Number the events in the order in which they occur.

_____ The narrator waltzes Aunt Nicey around.

_____ Doodle walks across the room.

_____ Mama cries and both parents hug Doodle.

_____ The narrator brings Doodle to the door in the go-cart.

He'd nod his head, and I'd say, "Well, if you don't keep trying, you'll never learn." Then I'd paint for him a picture of us as old men, white-haired, him with a long white beard and me still pulling him around in the go-cart. This never failed to make him try again.

Finally one day, after many weeks of practicing, he stood alone for a few seconds. When he fell, I grabbed him in my arms and hugged him. Now we knew it could be done. "Yes, yes," I cried, and he cried it too.

With success so close, we decided not to tell anyone until he could actually walk. Each day, except when it rained, we sneaked into Old Woman Swamp, and by cotton-picking time Doodle was ready to show what he could do. He still wasn't able to walk far, but we could wait no longer. We chose to reveal all on Doodle's sixth birthday, and for weeks ahead we promised everybody a most spectacular surprise.

On our chosen day, when Mama, Daddy, and Aunt Nicey were in the dining room, I brought Doodle to the door in the go-cart just as usual and had them turn their backs. I helped Doodle up, and when he was standing alone I let them look. There wasn't a sound as Doodle walked slowly across the room and sat down at his place at the table. Then Mama began to cry and ran over to him, hugging him and kissing him. Daddy hugged him too, so I went to Aunt Nicey, and began to waltz her around.

Doodle told them it was I who had taught him to walk, so everyone wanted to hug me, and I began to cry.

"What are you crying for?" asked Daddy, but I couldn't answer. They did not know that I did it for myself; that pride, whose slave I was, spoke to me louder than all their voices, and that Doodle walked only because I was ashamed of having a crippled brother.

Within a few months Doodle had learned to walk well and his go-cart was put up in the barn loft (it's still there) beside his little mahogany coffin. Now, when we roamed off together, resting often, we never turned back until our destination had been reached. To help pass the time, we took up lying. From the beginning Doodle was a terrible liar and he got me in the habit. Had anyone stopped to listen to us, we would have been sent off to Dix Hill.

My lies were scary and usually pointless, but Doodle's were twice as crazy. People in his stories all had wings and flew wherever they wanted to go. His favorite lie was about a boy named Peter who had a pet peacock with a ten-foot tail. Peter wore a golden robe that glittered so brightly that when he walked through the sunflowers they turned away from the sun to face him. When Peter was ready to go to sleep, the peacock spread his magnificent tail around the boy like a closing go-to-sleep flower. Yes, I must admit it. Doodle could beat me lying.

Doodle and I spent lots of time thinking about our future. We decided that when we were grown we'd live in Old Woman Swamp and pick dog-tongue for a living. Beside the stream, he planned, we'd build us a house. All day long (when we weren't gathering dog-tongue) we'd swing through the cypresses on the rope vines. If it rained we'd huddle beneath an umbrella tree and play stickfrog.

Once I had succeeded in teaching Doodle to walk, I prepared a terrific development program for him, unknown to Mama and Daddy, of course. I would teach him to run, to swim, to climb trees, and to fight. He, too, now believed in me, so we set the deadline for these accomplishments less than a year away, when Doodle could start to school.

Background Info

Dix Hill is the state mental hospital in Raleigh, North Carolina.

Comprehension Check

Reread the text boxed in green. Underline what the narrator plans to teach Doodle in his "development program."

That winter we didn't make much progress, for I was in school and Doodle suffered from one bad cold after another. But when spring came, rich and warm, we raised our sights again. Success lay at the end of summer like a pot of gold. On hot days, Doodle and I went down to Horsehead Landing and I gave him swimming lessons or showed him how to row a boat.

Connect to the Text

Do you like to swim or go boating in the summer? What other activities do you like to do?

_____

_____

_____

_____

_____

Young Fishermen in a Rowboat, 1909. Adam Emory Albright. Oil on canvas, 24 x 36 in. Private collection.

STOP Stop here for **Break Time** on the next page.

Break Time

When reading any story, it's important to keep track of the sequence of events. Knowing the order in which things happen can help you understand the plot. Read each event from "The Scarlet Ibis" in the boxes below. Write the numbers 2 through 8 in the spaces provided to show the order in which the events occur in the story. The first event has been marked for you.

The narrator takes Doodle to Old Woman Swamp for the first time.

_____

The narrator sees the grindstone outside and begins to remember Doodle.

1

The narrator names his brother Doodle because he crawls like a doodlebug.

_____

When Doodle is five years old, the narrator teaches him to walk.

_____

The narrator frightens Doodle by showing him the casket.

_____

Doodle and the narrator begin to plan their future.

_____

Doodle tells a story about a boy named Peter with a pet peacock.

_____

Doodle is born when the narrator is six years old.

_____

 GO Turn the page to continue reading.

Reading Skill

Infer Reread the text highlighted in green. Think about clues the narrator has given about his feelings toward his brother. Why do you think he tells Doodle that it's important not to be "different from everybody else"?

_____

_____

_____

_____

_____

_____

_____

English Coach

A simile is a comparison using *like* or *as*. The author says Doodle's eyes are: *round like two blue buttons*. The simile helps the reader visualize the surprised expression on Doodle's face. Write your own simile to describe Doodle's eyes, using the phrase "as round as."

_____

_____

_____

_____

That summer, the summer of 1918, was spoiled. In May and June there was no rain and the crops withered, then died under the thirsty sun. One morning in July a hurricane came out of the east, tipping over the oaks in the yard and splitting the limbs of the elm trees.

So we came to that change of seasons. School was only a few weeks away, and Doodle was far behind schedule. He could barely clear the ground when climbing up the rope vines and his swimming was certainly not passable.

We decided to double our efforts, to make that last drive and reach our pot of gold. I made him swim until he turned blue and row until he couldn't lift an oar. Wherever we went, I purposely walked fast, and although he kept up, his face turned red and his eyes became glazed. Once, he could go no further, so he collapsed on the ground and began to cry.

"Aw, come on, Doodle," I urged. "You can do it. Do you want to be different from everybody else when you start school?"

"Does it make any difference?"

"It certainly does," I said. "Now, come on," and I helped him up.

As we slipped through dog days, Doodle began to look feverish, and Mama felt his forehead, asking him if he felt ill. At night he didn't sleep well, and sometimes he had nightmares, crying out until I touched him and said, "Wake up, Doodle. Wake up."

It was Saturday noon, just a few days before school was to start. Daddy, Mama, Doodle, and I were seated at the dining-room table having lunch. It was a hot day, with all the windows and doors open in case a breeze should come.

Suddenly, from out in the yard, came a strange croaking noise. Doodle stopped eating, with a piece of bread poised ready for his mouth, his eyes popped round like two blue buttons. "What's that?" he whispered.

I jumped up, knocking over my chair, and had reached the door when Mama called, "Pick up the chair, sit down again, and say excuse me."

By the time I had done this, Doodle had excused himself and had slipped out into the yard. He was looking up into the bleeding tree. "It's a great big red bird!" he called.

The bird croaked loudly again, and Mama and Daddy came out into the yard. On the top branch a bird the size of a chicken, with scarlet feathers and long legs, was perched **precariously.**

"It's not even frightened of us," Mama said.

"It looks tired," Daddy added. "Or maybe sick."

Doodle's hands were clasped at his throat, and I had never seen him stand still so long. "What is it?" he asked.

Daddy shook his head. "I don't know, maybe it's—"

At that moment the bird began to flutter, but the wings were uncoordinated, and it tumbled down, bumping through the limbs of the bleeding tree and landing at our feet with a thud. Its long, graceful neck jerked twice into an S, then straightened out, and the bird was still. A white veil came over the eyes and the long white beak unhinged. Its legs were crossed and its clawlike feet were curved at rest. Even death did not spoil its grace, for it lay on the earth like a broken vase of red flowers. We stood around it, awed by its exotic beauty.

"It's dead," Mama said.

"What is it?" Doodle repeated.

"Go bring me the bird book," said Daddy.

I ran into the house and brought back the bird book. As we watched, Daddy thumbed through its pages. "It's a scarlet ibis," he said, pointing to a picture. "It lives in the tropics—South America to Florida. A storm must have brought it here."

Word Power

precariously (pri kār´ ē əs lē) *adv.* dangerously; insecurely

Connect to the Text

Reread the text boxed in purple. What kinds of animals have you seen in the area around your home? How do they react to humans?

_____

_____

_____

_____

_____

_____

Comprehension Check

Reread the text boxed in green. Where does Daddy say the scarlet ibis normally lives? How does the bird end up in the family's yard? Underline the answers in the text.

Sadly, we all looked back at the bird. A scarlet ibis! How many miles it had traveled to die like this, in our yard, beneath the bleeding tree.

"Let's finish lunch," Mama said, nudging us back toward the dining room.

"I'm not hungry," said Doodle, and he knelt down beside the ibis.

"We've got peach cobbler for dessert," Mama tempted from the doorway.

Doodle remained kneeling. "I'm going to bury him."

"Don't you dare touch him," Mama warned. "There's no telling what disease he might have had."

"All right," said Doodle. "I won't."

Daddy, Mama, and I went back to the dining-room table, but we watched Doodle through the open door. He took out a piece of string from his pocket and, without touching the ibis, looped one end around its neck.

Slowly, while singing softly "Shall We Gather at the River," he carried the bird around to the front yard and dug a hole in the flower garden. Now we were watching him through the front window, but he didn't know it. His awkwardness at digging the hole with a shovel whose handle was twice as long as he was made us laugh.

When Doodle came into the dining room, he found us seriously eating our cobbler. He was pale and lingered just inside the screen door. "Dead birds is bad luck," said Aunt Nicey, poking her head from the kitchen door. "Specially red dead birds!"

As soon as I had finished eating, Doodle and I hurried off to Horsehead Landing. Time was short, and Doodle still had a long way to go if he was going to keep up with the other boys when he started school.

Comprehension Check

Reread the boxed text. How does Doodle carry the ibis without touching it?

_____

_____

_____

_____

When we reached the landing, Doodle said he was too tired to swim, so we got into a small boat and floated down the creek with the tide. Doodle did not speak and kept his head turned away, letting one hand trail limply in the water.

After we had drifted a long way, I put the oars in place and made Doodle row back against the tide. Black clouds began to gather in the southwest, and he kept watching them, trying to pull the oars a little faster. When we reached Horsehead Landing, lightning was playing across half the sky and thunder roared. The sun disappeared and darkness descended, almost like night.

Doodle was both tired and frightened, and when he stepped from the small boat he collapsed onto the mud. I helped him up, and as he wiped the mud off his trousers, he smiled at me ashamedly. He had failed and we both knew it, so we started back home, racing the storm. We never spoke (What are the words that can fix cracked pride?), but I knew he was watching me, watching for a sign of **mercy.** The lightning was near now, and from fear he walked so close behind me he kept stepping on my heels. The faster I walked, the faster he walked, so I began to run. The rain was coming, roaring through the pines. Then, like a bursting Roman candle, a gum tree ahead of us was shattered by a bolt of lightning. When the deafening thunder had died, and in the moment before the rain arrived, I heard Doodle, who had fallen behind, cry out, "Brother, Brother, don't leave me! Don't leave me!"

The knowledge that Doodle's and my plans had failed was bitter, and that streak of cruelty within me awakened. I ran as fast as I could, leaving him far behind with a wall of rain dividing us. The drops stung my face. Soon I could hear his voice no more.

Word Power

mercy (mur´ sē) *n.* compassion or forgiveness

Reading Skill

Infer Reread the sentence highlighted in green. The narrator earlier says that Doodle begins to look feverish and isn't sleeping well. Now he is tired and falls. What inference can you make from this information? Check the **best** response.

☐ Doodle is stubborn.

☐ Doodle is ill.

☐ Doodle is angry.

Literary Element

Plot: Rising Action
Reread the text highlighted in blue. At this point, there is tension building in the story. What weather conditions are taking place that add to the rising action?

_____

_____

_____

_____

Literary Element

Plot: Climax The climax is the emotional high point of the story. Reread the text highlighted in blue. What is the climax of the story?

_____

_____

_____

_____

_____

Reading Skill

Infer Reread the text highlighted in green. What can you infer about how the narrator feels about his brother's death?

_____

_____

_____

_____

I hadn't run too far before I became tired, and the flood of childish **spite** faded as well. I stopped and waited for Doodle. The sound of rain was everywhere, but the wind had died and it fell straight down like ropes hanging from the sky. As I waited, I peered through the downpour, but no one came. Finally I went back and found him huddled beneath a red nightshade bush beside the road. He was sitting on the ground, his face buried in his arms, which were resting on his drawn-up knees. "Let's go, Doodle," I said.

He didn't answer, so I placed my hand on his forehead and lifted his head. Limply, he fell backwards onto the earth. He had been bleeding from the mouth, and his neck and the front of his shirt were stained a brilliant red.

"Doodle! Doodle!" I cried, shaking him, but there was no answer but the ropy rain. He lay very awkwardly, with his head thrown far back, making his scarlet neck appear unusually long and slim. His little legs, bent sharply at the knees, had never before seemed so fragile, so thin.

I began to weep, and the tear-blurred vision in red before me looked very familiar. "Doodle!" I screamed above the pounding storm and threw my body to the earth above his. For a long long time, it seemed forever, I lay there crying, sheltering my fallen scarlet ibis from the rain.

Word Power

spite (spīt) *n.* a mean feeling toward someone

98

Respond to Literature

The Scarlet Ibis

A Comprehension Check

Answer the following questions in the spaces provided.

1. Why does the narrator call his brother "Doodle"? _____

_____

_____

2. What does Doodle do with the scarlet ibis? _____

_____

_____

B Reading Skills

Complete the following activities in the spaces provided.

1. **Sequence** The narrator describes important events in Doodle's life. List four events in sequence. _____

_____

_____

_____

2. **Infer** What can you infer about Doodle's feelings about life and death when he buries the scarlet ibis? _____

_____

_____

_____

C Word Power

Complete each sentence below, using one of the words in the box.

invalid	discourage	careen	loll
sullenly	precariously	mercy	spite

1. The loose brick was hanging _____ off the building, so we moved out of the way.

2. After being hurt badly in a car accident, Yosef became an

   _____.

3. The bully finally showed _____ by not hurting Joaquin and letting him go.

4. After school, Wai Min likes to _____ on the couch and watch TV.

5. It's important to _____ young children from crossing the street by themselves.

6. The brakes on the go-cart failed, and we watched it _____ down the road.

7. After my mother told me I had to go to bed early, I _____ went upstairs.

8. Tyra was jealous of my new bike and tried to take it, out of _____
   .

D Literary Element: Plot

Read the following passages from the "The Scarlet Ibis." As you read, think about the elements of a plot. Then answer the questions that follow.

When the deafening thunder had died, and in the moment before the rain arrived, I heard Doodle, who had fallen behind, cry out, "Brother, Brother, don't leave me! Don't leave me!"[1]

I ran as fast as I could, leaving him far behind with a wall of rain dividing us.[2]

He was sitting on the ground, his face buried in his arms, which were resting on his drawn-up knees.[3] "Let's go, Doodle," I said.[4]

He didn't answer, so I placed my hand on his forehead and lifted his head.[5] Limply, he fell backwards onto the earth.[6]

1. In sentences 1–2, the *rising action* shows how the story intensifies. What details does the author use to describe the growing tension?

   _____

   _____

   _____

2. Reread sentences 3–6. Usually a *climax* follows the rising action. What is the climax here? How do you know?

   _____

   _____

   _____

E A Goodbye Letter to Doodle

Sometimes, people write letters to loved ones who have died as a way of saying things they did not say when the person was alive. Imagine that you are the narrator. Write a letter to Doodle about your memories and how you feel about him.

Dear Doodle,

When you were first born, I felt frustrated because

_____

Then, when you turned five, I decided to try to _____

_____

I know I was mean to you sometimes, like when I

_____

_____

But I remember having wonderful times with you too, like
when we _____

_____

On that last day, I'm sorry I left you behind. I feel _____

_____

because I couldn't save you.
I want you to know that I will always _____

_____

Love always,
Your Brother

Assessment

Fill in the circle next to each correct answer.

1. What does Doodle learn to do first?
   - ○ A. swim
   - ○ B. row a boat
   - ○ C. crawl
   - ○ D. walk

2. Which feeling motivates the narrator to teach Doodle to walk?
   - ○ A. fear
   - ○ B. pride
   - ○ C. envy
   - ○ D. anger

3. What can you infer from the fact that Doodle and the narrator start telling "lies" together and making plans for their future?
   - ○ A. The boys are growing closer, and the narrator grows to love Doodle.
   - ○ B. Doodle and the narrator never tell the truth about anything.
   - ○ C. The boys see no hope for their future and want to run away.
   - ○ D. Doodle hates his brother so much that he tells him terrible lies.

4. Which of the following sentences from the story is part of the plot's rising action?
   - ○ A. As long as he lay all the time in bed, we called him William Armstrong.
   - ○ B. Doodle was my brother and he was going to cling to me forever, no matter what I did.
   - ○ C. Doodle remained kneeling. "I'm going to bury him."
   - ○ D. I heard Doodle, who had fallen behind, cry out, "Brother, Brother, don't leave me!"

5. Which of the following words means "in a dangerous or insecure way"?
   - ○ A. sullenly
   - ○ B. precariously
   - ○ C. mercy
   - ○ D. discourage

Soul-Catcher

Meet Louis Owens

Louis Owens comes from both Native American and Irish ancestors. He worked as a wilderness ranger, which gave him knowledge of wild animals. He later worked as a teacher and as a writer. The author says that "Soul-Catcher" is based on an experience from his childhood: a panther had followed his father home, jumped on the roof, and paced across it all night! Louis Owens was born in 1948 and died in 2002.

What You Know

Do you know any stories or myths from your own culture, such as traditional stories told by a family member? Do you enjoy these stories? Do you think they are true?

Reason to Read

Read to learn about how a boy and his great-uncle each have a different understanding of a Native American myth.

Background Info

The selection's events take place in the Yazoo River basin in Mississippi, which is a habitat for panthers. Many Native American groups believe that large cats (such as panthers, mountain lions, and jaguars) have special, supernatural powers. According to a Choctaw myth, the spirit of *nalusachito,* which means "soul-catcher," "soul-eater," or "soul-snatcher," is said to sometimes appear in the form of a black panther.

Word Power

lanky (lang´ kē) *adj.* ungracefully thin and tall; p. 106
The *lanky* boys ran with long strides around the track.

cower (kou´ ər) *v.* to crouch down in fear; p. 108
I *cower* in the corner every time I see a spider in our house.

acrid (ak´ rid) *adj.* sharp, bitter, or irritating to smell or taste; p. 110
After the car raced by, the *acrid* smell of burnt rubber was in the air.

indestructible (in´ di struk´ tə bəl) *adj.* not able to be destroyed; p. 110
We keep our family's valuable things in an *indestructible* steel safe.

skeptically (skep´ ti kəl lē) *adv.* doubtfully; in an unconvinced manner; p. 112
I looked at my sister *skeptically* when she told me we had ghosts in the attic.

ventured (ven´ chərd) *v.* risked; dared to do something or go somewhere; p. 115
After a lot of hesitation, I finally *ventured* onto the rock-climbing wall.

consciousness (kon´ shəs nis) *n.* the state of being awake and aware of one's
surroundings; p. 118
The sound of my alarm clock startled me into *consciousness*.

**Answer the following questions that contain the new words above.
Write your answers in the spaces provided.**

1. If you are in a state of *consciousness,* are you asleep or awake? _____

2. If something is *indestructible,* can it be destroyed or is it unable to be destroyed?

   _____

3. If you *cower* from something, are you feeling afraid or courageous? _____

4. If you listen to a story *skeptically,* do you believe it is true or doubt it is true?

   _____

5. Is a *lanky* person tall and thin or short and heavy? _____

6. If you smell something *acrid,* does it smell bad or good? _____

7. If you *ventured* to do something, did you take a risk or not take a risk?

   _____

Adapted from

Soul-Catcher

Louis Owens

The old man held the rifle in one hand and walked bent over under the weight of the gunnysack on his back, as if studying the tangle of roots that was the trail. Behind him three **lanky** brown-and-black-and-white hounds crowded close to his thin legs and threw nervous glances at the wet forest all around. The only sound was that of the old man's boots and the occasional whine of one of the dogs. The sliver of moon had set, and the trail was very dark. The light on his hat cast a glow around the group, so that the old man, with his long silver hair, might have been one of the Choctaw shadows on the bright path home.

Out of the dark to the old man's right came a scream that cut through the swamp like jagged tin and sent the hounds trembling against his legs.

"Hah! Get back you!" he scolded, turning to shake his head at the cringing dogs. "That cat ain't going to eat you, not yet."

Word Power
lanky (lang ́ kē) *adj.* ungracefully thin and tall

The dogs whined and pushed closer so that the old man stumbled and caught himself and the light from the headlamp splashed upon the trail. He shook his head again and chuckled, making shadows dance around them. He knew what it was that stalked him. The black *koi* hadn't been seen in the swamps during the old man's lifetime, but as a child he'd heard the stories so often that he knew at once what the *koi* meant. It was an old and familiar story. He'd felt the black one out there in the swamps for a long time. The bird, *falachito,* had called from the trees to warn him, and he had listened and gone on because what else was there to do? All of his life he had been prepared to recognize the soul-catcher when it should come.

The old man also knew that the screamer was probably the panther that the fool white man, Reeves, had wounded near Satartia a couple of weeks before. He could feel the animal's anger there in the darkness, feel the hatred like grit between his teeth. And he felt great pity for the injured cat.

The boar coon in the sack was heavy, and the old man thought that he should have brought the boy along to help. Behind him, this time to his left, the panther screamed again. The cat had been circling like that for the past hour, never getting any closer or any farther away.

He paused at the edge of the clearing and spoke a few words in a low voice, trying to communicate his understanding and sympathy to the wounded animal and his knowledge of what was there to the soul-catcher. For a moment he leaned the rifle against his leg and reached up to touch a small pouch that hung inside his shirt. All of his life the old man had balanced two realities, two worlds, a feat that had never struck him as particularly noteworthy or difficult. But as the cat called out once more, he felt a shadow fall over him. The animal's cry rose from the dark waters of the swamp to the stars and then fell away like one of the deep, bottomless places in the river.

Comprehension Check

Reread the boxed text. The old man is returning home late at night after hunting. He believes a black panther, the *koi,* is the soul-catcher, and that it is stalking him. What is his reaction? Check the correct response.

☐ He is scared and wants to run away.

☐ He is ready to face the soul-catcher.

☐ He plans to capture the soul-catcher.

English Coach

The suffix *-less* often means "without." Here, *bottomless* means the river appears to be "without a bottom." Use the suffix *-less* to make the word that means "without hope." Then write one other word using the suffix *-less*.

_____

_____

_____

My Workspace

Reading Skill

Sequence Reread the highlighted text. Underline the sequence words that help you understand the sequence of events.

Background Info

Painter is the way the old man pronounces the word "panther."

English Coach

Mad is a word with more than one meaning. For example, it can mean either "angry" or "crazy." Below, write two sentences using the word *mad.* Use a different meaning for each sentence.

_____

_____

_____

_____

_____

_____

_____

When the old man opened the door, the hounds shot past and went to **cower** beneath the beds. He lowered the bag to the floor and pushed the door closed. After a moment's thought he dropped the bolt into place before reaching with one hand to hang the twenty-two on nails beneath a much larger rifle. Finally, he looked at the teenage boy sitting on the edge of one of the beds with a book in his lap. The lantern beside the boy left half of his upturned face in shadow, as if two faces met in one, but the old man could see one green eye and the fair skin, and he wondered once more how much Choctaw there was in the boy.

The boy looked up fully and stared at the old uncle. The distinct fold of each eye giving the boy's face an oddly Oriental quality.

"*Koi,*" the old man said. "A painter. He followed me home."

After a moment's silence, the boy said, "You going to keep him?" The old man grinned. The boy was getting better.

"Not this one," he replied. "He's no good. A fool shot him, and now he's mad." He studied the air to one side of the boy and seemed to make a decision. "Besides, this black one may be *nalusachito,* the soul-catcher. He's best left alone, I think."

The boy's grin died quickly, and the old man saw fear and curiosity in the pale eyes.

"Why do you think it's *nalusachito*?" The word was awkward on the boy's tongue.

"Sometimes you just know these things. He's been out there a while. The bird warned me, and now that fool white man has hurt him."

"*Nalusachito* is just a myth," the boy said.

The old man looked at the book in the boy's lap. "You reading that book again?"

The boy nodded.

"A teacher give that book to your dad one time, so's he could learn all about his people, the teacher said. He used to read that book, too, and tell me about us Choctaws." The old man grinned once more. "After he left, I read some of that book."

Word Power

cower (kou′ ər) *v.* to crouch down in fear

The old man reached a hand toward the boy. "Here, let me read you the part I like best about us people." He lifted a pair of wire-rimmed glasses from a shelf above the rifles and slipped them on.

The boy held the book out and the old man took it. Bending so that the lantern-light fell across the pages, he thumbed expertly through the volume.

"This is a good book, all right. Tells us all about ourselves. This writer was a smart man. Listen to this." He began to read, pronouncing each word with care, as though it were a foreign language.

The Choctaw warrior, as I knew him in his native Mississippi forest, was as fine a specimen of manly perfection as I have ever beheld.

He looked up with a wink.

He seemed to be as perfect as the human form could be. Tall, beautiful in symmetry of form and face, graceful, active, straight, fleet, with lofty and independent bearing, he seemed worthy in saying, "I am monarch of all I survey." His black piercing eye seemed to penetrate and read the very thoughts of the heart, while his firm step proclaimed a feeling sense of manly independence. Nor did their women fall behind in all that pertains to female beauty.

"I read this next part to Old Lady Blue Wood that lives 'cross the river. She says this is the smartest white man she ever heard of." He adjusted the glasses and read again.

They were of such unnatural beauty that they literally appeared to light up everything around them. Their shoulders were broad and their carriage true to Nature, which has never been excelled by the hand of art; their long, black tresses hung in flowing waves, extending nearly to the ground; but the beauty of the countenances of many of those Choctaw and Chickasaw girls was so extraordinary that if such faces were seen today in one of the parlors of the fashionable world, they would be considered as a type of beauty hitherto unknown.

Literary Element

Tone Reread the highlighted text and the rest of the page. The uncle is reading from a book about the Choctaw people. The author of the book describes Choctaw men and women. The tone of the book's author is supposed to be admiring. Underline two words or phrases that show the book's author is trying to be admiring.

Snapping Turtle, a Half Breed, or *Peter Pitchlynn.* 1834. Choctaw. George Catlin (1796–1872). Smithsonian American Art Museum, Washington, DC.

Think about the description of the Choctaw men you just read. Is this how you pictured a Choctaw man? How is it similar to or different from the picture you formed in your mind?

Reading Skill

Infer Reread the highlighted text. What inference can you make about the boy's mother? Was she a Choctaw?

_____

_____

_____

_____

He handed the book back to the boy and removed the glasses, grinning all the while. The boy looked down at the moldy book and then grinned weakly back at the old uncle. Beneath the floppy hat, surrounded by the **acrid** smell of the headlamp, the old man seemed like one of the swamp shadows come into the cabin. The boy thought about his father, the old man's nephew, who had been only half Choctaw but looked nearly as dark and **indestructible** as the uncle. Then he looked down at his own hand in the light from the kerosene lantern. The pale skin embarrassed him, gave him away. The old man, his great-uncle, was Indian, and his father had been Indian, but he wasn't.

There was a thud on the wood shingles of the cabin's roof. Dust fell from each of the four corners of the cabin and onto the pages of the damp book.

"*Nalasuchito* done climbed up on the roof," the old man said, gazing at the ceiling with amusement. "He moves pretty good for a cat that's hurt, don't he?"

The boy knew the uncle was watching for his reaction. He steeled himself and then the panther screamed and he flinched.

Word Power

acrid (ak´ rid) *adj.* sharp, bitter, or irritating to smell or taste
indestructible (in´ di struk´ tə bəl) *adj.* not able to be destroyed

The old man nodded. "Only a fool or a crazy man ain't scared when soul-catcher's walking around on his house," he said.

"You're not afraid," the boy replied, watching as the old man set the headlamp on a shelf and hung the wide hat on a nail beside the rifles.

The old man pulled a piece of canvas from beneath the table and spread it on the floor. As he dumped the coon out onto the canvas, he looked up with a chuckle. "That book says Choctaw boys always respected their elders. I'm scared alright, but I know about that cat, you see, and that's the difference. That cat ain't got no surprises for me because I'm old, and I done heard all the stories."

The boy glanced at the book.

"It don't work that way," the old man said. "You can't read them. A white man comes and he pokes around and pays somebody, or maybe somebody feels sorry for him and tells him stuff and he writes it down. But he don't understand, so he can't put it down right, you see."

How do you understand? the boy wanted to ask as he watched the uncle pull a knife from its sheath on his hip and begin to skin the coon, making cuts down each leg and up the belly so delicately that the boy could see no blood at all. The panther shrieked overhead, and the old man seemed not to notice.

"Why don't you shoot it?" the boy asked, looking at the big deer rifle on the wall.

The old man looked up in surprise.

"You could sell the skin to Mr. Wheeler for a lot of money, couldn't you?" Mr. Wheeler was the black man who came from across the river to buy the coonskins.

The old man squinted and studied the boy's face. "You can't hunt that cat," he said patiently. "*Nalusachito* something you got to accept, something that's just there."

Comprehension Check

Reread the boxed text. What is the uncle's response when the boy says he thinks his uncle isn't afraid?

_____

_____

_____

_____

_____

Reading Skill

Infer Reread the highlighted sentences. Based on what the uncle says here, what can you infer about how he feels about the white man's story he read aloud earlier?

_____

_____

_____

_____

_____

_____

My Workspace

Literary Element

Tone Reread the paragraph highlighted in blue. What is the tone of this passage? Check the **best** response.

☐ confusing and uncertain
☐ understanding and accepting
☐ happy and silly

Reading Skill

Sequence Reread the text highlighted in green. Then read the sentences below. Write 1, 2, or 3 on each line to show which event happens first, second, and third on a typical night and morning.

_____ The boy wakes up and sees the old man sleeping.

_____ The old man goes out to hunt.

_____ The old man comes back with his catch.

"You see," he continued, "what folks like that fool Reeves don't understand is that this painter has always been out there. We just ain't noticed him for a long time. He's always there, and that's what people forget. You can't kill him." He tapped his chest with the handle of the knife. "*Nalusachito* comes from in here."

The boy watched the old man in silence. He knew about the soul-catcher from the book in his lap. It was an old superstition, and the book didn't say anything about *nalasuchito* being a panther. That was something the old man invented. This panther was very real and dangerous. He looked **skeptically** at the old man and then up at the rifle.

"No," the old man said. "We'll just let this painter be."

He pulled the skin off over the head of the raccoon like a sweater, leaving the naked body shining like a baby in the yellow light. Under the beds the dogs sniffed and whined, and overhead the whispers moved across the roof.

The old man held the skin up and admired it, then laid it fur-side down on the bench beside him. "I sure ain't going outside to nail this up right now," he said, the corners of his mouth suggesting a grin. He lifted the bolt and pushed the door open and swung the body of the coon out into the dark. When he closed the door there was a snarl and an impact on the ground. The dogs began to growl and whimper, and the old man said, "You, Yvonne! Hoyo!" and the dogs shivered in silence.

The boy watched the old man wash his hands in the bucket and sit on the edge of the other bed to pull off his boots. Each night and morning since he'd come it had been the same. The old uncle would go out at night and come back before daylight with something in the bag. Usually the boy would waken to find the old man in the other bed, sleeping like a small child, so lightly that the boy could not see or hear him breathe.

Word Power

skeptically (skep´ ti kəl lē) *adv.* doubtfully; in an unconvinced manner

But this night the boy had awakened in the very early morning, torn from sleep by a sound he wasn't conscious of hearing, and he had sat up with the lantern and book to await the old man's return. He read the book because there was nothing else to read. The myths reminded him of fairy tales he'd read as a child, and he tried to imagine his father reading them.

The old man was a real Choctaw—Chahtaokia—a full-blood. Was the ability to believe the myths diluted with the blood, the boy wondered, so that his father could, when he had been alive, believe only half as strongly as the old man and he, his father's son, half as much yet? He thought of the soul-catcher, and he shivered, but he knew that he was just scaring himself the way kids always did. His mother had told him how they said that when his father was born the uncle had shown up at the cabin and announced that the boy would be his responsibility.

That was the Choctaw way, he said, the right way. A man must accept responsibility for and teach his sister's children. Nobody had thought of that custom for a long time, and nobody had seen the uncle for years, and nobody knew how he'd even learned of the boy's birth, but there he was come out of the swamps across the river with his straight black hair hanging to his shoulders under the floppy hat and his face dark as night so that the mother, his sister, screamed when she saw him. And from that day onward the uncle had come often from the swamps to take the boy's father with him, to teach him.

Connect to the Text

Reread the boxed text. Think about a cultural or family custom you have in your home. It can be anything from a traditional story to a special song or food. Describe the custom and how you feel about it. Would you like to pass it on to your children when you grow up?

_____

_____

_____

_____

_____

_____

STOP Stop here for **Break Time** on the next page.

Break Time

The young boy is one of the main characters in this story. We learn about the boy from his thoughts, his actions, and his words. For example, the boy reads a book about the Choctaw because he wants to understand his cultural heritage. Complete the word web with details from the story that help you understand what the boy is like. An example has been done for you.

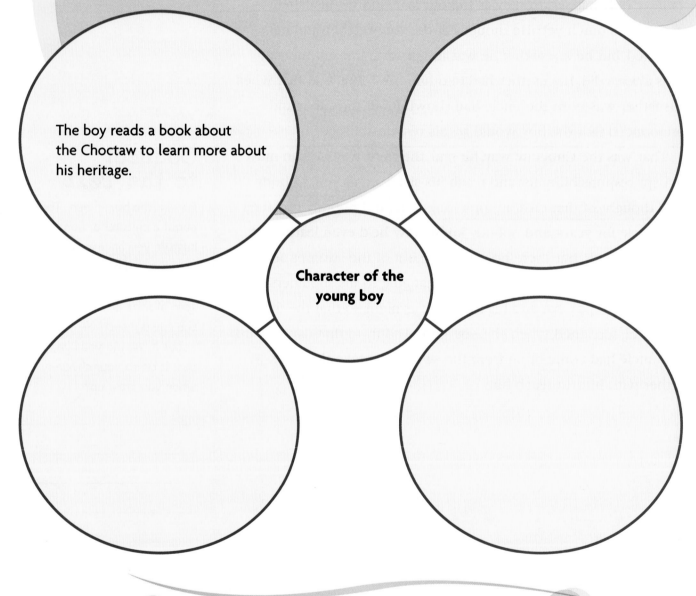

The boy reads a book about the Choctaw to learn more about his heritage.

Character of the young boy

GO Continue reading on the next page.

The old man rolled into the bed, pulled the wool blanket to his chin, turned to the wall, and was asleep. The boy watched him and then turned down the lamp until only a dim glow outlined the objects in the room. He thought of Los Angeles, the bone-dry hills and yellow air, the home where he'd lived with his parents before the accident that killed both. It was difficult to be Choctaw, to be Indian there, and he'd seen his father working hard at it, growing his black hair long, going to urban powwows where the fancy dancers spun like beautiful birds.

Did You Know?

Powwows are Native American ceremonies.

His father had taught him to hunt in the desert hills and to say a few phrases, like *Chahta isht ia* and *Chahta yakni,* in the old language. The words had remained only sounds, the powwow dancers only another Southern California spectacle for a green-eyed, fair-skinned boy. But the hunting had been real, a testing of desire and reflex he had felt all the way through.

Indians were hunters. Indians lived close to the land. His father had said those things often. He thought about the panther. The old man would not hunt the black cat, and had probably made up the story about *nalusachito* as an excuse. The panther was dangerous. For a month the boy had been at the cabin and had not **ventured** beyond the edges of the garden except to go out in the small rowboat onto the muddy Yazoo River. The swampy forest around the cabin was like the river, a place in which nothing was ever clear: shadows, swirls, dark forms rising and disappearing again, nothing ever clearly seen. And each night he'd lain in the bed and listened to the booming and cracking of the swamp like something monstrously evil and thought of the old man killing things in the dark, picturing the old man as a solitary light cutting the darkness.

Comprehension Check

Reread the boxed paragraph. Underline two things the boy's father did to connect the boy with his Choctaw heritage.

Reading Skill

Infer Reread the highlighted text. What can you infer about how the boy feels about the swamp?

_____

_____

_____

_____

Word Power

ventured (ven´ chərd) *v.* risked; dared to do something or go somewhere

A black panther is another name for a leopard, jaguar, or puma with a darker skin and hair color. Have you ever seen a large, wild cat, like a panther? How would you react if you saw one in the wild?

Reading Skill

Infer Reread the highlighted text. What advantage does the boy see "in not being really Choctaw"? Check the **best** response.

☐ He feels free to shoot the panther.

☐ He feels better about the color of his skin and eyes.

☐ He is glad that he is not very closely related to the old man.

Background Info

A mackinaw is a short coat made of woolen mackinaw cloth. The cloth is heavy and water-repellent. Mackinaw coats were first worn by loggers in the northern part of the Midwest in the mid-1900s.

The panther might remain, its soft feet whispering maddeningly on the cabin roof each night while the old man hunted in the swamp. Or it might attack the old man who would not shoot it. For the first time the boy realized the advantage in not being really Choctaw.

The old uncle could not hunt the panther, but he could, because he knew the cat for what it really was. It would not be any more difficult to kill than the wild pigs he'd hunted with his father in the coastal range of California, and it was no different than the cougars that haunted those same mountains. The black one was only a freak of nature.

Moving softly, he lifted the heavy rifle from its nails. In a crate on the floor he found the cartridges and, slipping on his red-plaid mackinaw, he dropped the bullets into his pocket. Then he walked carefully to the door, lifted the bolt, stepped through, and silently pulled the door closed. Outside, it was getting close to dawn and the air had the clean, raw smell mixed with a sharp odor of the river and swamp.

He pushed shells into the rifle and then stepped along the garden trail toward the trees, listening carefully for the sounds of the woods. Where even he knew there should have been the shouting of crickets, frogs, and a hundred other night creatures, there was only silence beating like the heartbeat drum at one of the powwows. At the edge of the clearing he paused.

In the cabin the old man sat up and looked toward the door. The boy had an hour before full daylight, and he would meet *nalusachito* in that transitional time. The old man fingered the medicine pouch on the cord around his neck and wondered about such a convergence. There was a meaning beyond his understanding, something that could not be avoided.

The boy brushed aside a vine and stepped into the woods, feeling his boots sink into the wet floor. It had all been a singular journey toward this, out of the light of California, across the burning earth of the Southwest, and into the darkness of this place. Beyond the garden, in the uncertain light, the trunks of trees, the brush and vines were like a curtain closing behind him. Then the panther cried in the damp woods somewhere in front of him. The boy began to walk on the faint trail toward the sound, his movements like those of a man walking on the floor of the sea. His eyes adjusted to the darkness and strained to isolate the watery forms surrounding him.

When he had gone a hundred yards the panther called again, a strange, dreamlike, muted cry different from the earlier screams, and he hesitated a moment and then left the trail to follow the cry. A form slid from the trail beside his boot, and he moved carefully away, deeper into the woods beyond the trail. Now the light was graying, and the leaves and bark of the trees became delicately etched as the day broke.

Reading Skill

Sequence Think about the sequence of events on this page. What happens after the boy decides to hunt the panther? Number the following events in the order in which they occur.

_____ The panther cries out somewhere in front of the boy.

_____ The boy loads the rifle and walks on the garden trail.

_____ The uncle wakes up and senses something mysterious is happening.

_____ The boy goes beyond the garden trail and enters the woods.

Literary Element

Tone Reread the highlighted text. Think about words and phrases that give clues to the author's tone, such as *strange* and *dreamlike*. Which of the following sentences **best** describes the tone? Check the correct response.

☐ It is mysterious and frightening.

☐ It is pleasant and enjoyable.

☐ It is boring and uneventful.

My Workspace

Comprehension Check

Reread the boxed paragraph. What does the boy do to the wounded panther?

_____

_____

_____

Reading Skill

Infer Reread the highlighted paragraph. What can you infer about the myth of *nalusachito*?

_____

_____

_____

_____

_____

The close scream of the panther jerked him into full **consciousness,** and he saw the cat. Twenty feet away, it crouched in a clutter of vines and brush, its yellow eyes burning at him. In front of the panther was the half-eaten carcass of the coon.

He raised the rifle slowly, bringing it to his shoulder and slipping the safety off in the same movement. With his action, the panther pushed itself upright until it sat on its haunches, facing him. It was then the boy saw that one of the front feet hung limp, a festering wound in the shoulder on that side. He lined the notched sight of the rifle against the cat's head, and he saw the burning go out of the eyes. The panther watched him calmly, waiting as he pulled the trigger. The animal toppled backward, kicked for an instant and was still.

He walked to the cat and nudged it with a boot. *Nalusachito* was dead. He leaned the rifle against a tree and lifted the cat by its four feet and swung it onto his back, surprised at how light it was and feeling the sharp edges of the ribs through the fur. He felt sorrow and pity for the hurt animal he could imagine hunting awkwardly in the swamps, and he knew that what he had done was right. He picked up the rifle and turned back toward the cabin.

When he opened the cabin door, with the cat on his shoulder, the old man was sitting in the chair facing him. The boy leaned the rifle against the bench and swung the panther carefully to the floor and looked up at the old man, but the old man's eyes were fixed on the open doorway. Beyond the doorway *nalusachito* crouched, ready to spring.

Word Power

consciousness (kon′ shəs nis) *n.* the state of being awake and aware of one's surroundings

Soul-Catcher

A Comprehension Check

Answer the following questions in the spaces provided.

1. What animal follows the old man home? What does the old man think the animal is? _____

   _____

2. Why is the boy living with his great-uncle? _____

   _____

B Reading Skills

Answer the following questions in the spaces provided.

1. **Sequence** What important event happens **after** the boy goes into the woods? _____

   _____

2. **Infer** Why does the boy go out and kill the panther after his uncle chose not to kill it? _____

   _____

   _____

3. **Infer** At the end of the story, the boy returns with the killed panther. However, the old man sees *nalusachito* in the doorway. What can you infer about the myth of *nalusachito*? _____

   _____

   _____

C Word Power

Complete each sentence below, using one of the words in the box.

lanky	cower	acrid	indestructible
skeptically	ventured	consciousness	

1. I was afraid of getting lost in the city, so I _____ only a short distance from the apartment building.

2. The _____ basketball player seemed to be all arms and legs.

3. The _____ smell of burnt toast drifted out of the kitchen.

4. Sergei had drifted off in class, but when the teacher called on him, he was brought back into _____ .

5. My little brother will _____ under his bed if he thinks there's a monster in the closet.

6. Yoshi listened _____ to his neighbor as she bragged about winning a free trip.

7. The bridge was so strong that it seemed _____ .

Respond to Literature

D Literary Element: Tone

Read the following passages from "Soul-Catcher." The first passage is from the book about the Choctaw people that the uncle reads aloud. The second passage shows the uncle's reaction to white people who write about the Choctaw people. As you read, think about the tone of the passages. Then answer the questions that follow.

He seemed to be as perfect as the human form could be.[1] Tall, beautiful in symmetry of form and face, graceful, active, straight, fleet, with lofty and independent bearing, he seemed worthy in saying, "I am monarch of all I survey."[2]

"A white man comes and he pokes around and pays somebody, or maybe somebody feels sorry for him and tells him stuff and he writes it down.[3] But he don't understand, so he can't put it down right, you see."[4]

1. Sentences 1–2 are from the book the uncle reads about the Choctaw people. How can you tell that the book's author tries to have an admiring tone? _____

_____

_____

2. Sentences 3–4 show what the uncle thinks of white writers who try to write about the Choctaw people. Here, the uncle reflects the tone of the author of "Soul-Catcher." How can you tell that the author's tone here is sad and frustrated? _____

_____

_____

E A Letter to an Author

Imagine that you are the boy. Think about your experience with the panther. Then write a letter to the man who wrote the book about the Choctaw. Tell him what you have learned about the myth of *nalusachito*.

Dear Sir,

I read your book about the Choctaw. I am not a full
Choctaw, because my parents were _____

_____

_____

I am just one-quarter Choctaw. Instead of dark skin, I have

_____

My great-uncle, however, is a full Choctaw. I spent some
time with him. He told me all about the myth of

_____

and that it lives in the body of _____

At first, I didn't believe the myth. But then I heard a
wounded panther. I went into the woods and I saw the
panther. Then I _____
I brought the panther back to my great-uncle. But even
though I killed the panther, I did not kill *nalusachito*.
It was standing in the doorway and then it _____

_____

I think it is important for you to learn something different
about the Choctaw people because _____

_____

Assessment

Fill in the circle next to each correct answer.

1. Why does the old man call Reeves a "fool white man"?
   - ○ A. because he is always coming over to borrow things
   - ○ B. because he wounded the panther and made it angry
   - ○ C. because he never went to school
   - ○ D. because he is rude to the boy

2. What is the **first** thing the old man does each night?
   - ○ A. He brings back his catch.
   - ○ B. He goes to sleep.
   - ○ C. He goes out to hunt.
   - ○ D. He wakes up the boy.

3. The boy's father tries to teach him Choctaw words and takes him to powwows. What can you infer about the father from this?
   - ○ A. He wants his son to feel connected to his heritage.
   - ○ B. He wants his son to see why they moved to the city.
   - ○ C. He doesn't want his son to learn in a white school.
   - ○ D. He doesn't want his son to be taken by the uncle.

4. Which of the following lines from the story has an eerie tone?
   - ○ A. Finally, he looked at the teenage boy sitting on the edge of one of the beds with a book in his lap.
   - ○ B. He handed the book back to the boy and removed the glasses, grinning all the while.
   - ○ C. The myths reminded him of fairy tales he'd read as a child, and he tried to imagine his father reading them.
   - ○ D. Out of the dark to the old man's right came a scream that cut through the swamp like jagged tin.

5. Which of the following words means "in a doubtful way"?
   - ○ A. lanky
   - ○ B. skeptically
   - ○ C. consciousness
   - ○ D. indestructible

Get Ready to Read!

Sweet Potato Pie

Meet Eugenia Collier

Eugenia Collier was born in 1928. She went to segregated schools before college. She became a college teacher and an award-winning writer. Of her career, Collier stated, "The fact of my blackness is the core and center of my creativity. . . .
I discovered the richness, the diversity, the beauty of my black heritage." "Sweet Potato Pie" was first published in 1972.

What You Know

Sometimes people make judgments about others based on visual clues, such as the style of their clothes or the kind of backpacks they carry. Do you think it's fair to make judgments based on visual clues? Discuss your opinions with other classmates.

Reason to Read

Read to see how two brothers view symbols of social standing or importance.

Background Info

Sharecropping was a farming system common in the South in the years between the Civil War and World War II. Sharecroppers, who were mostly African Americans, farmed land that belonged to someone else. The landowner allowed the sharecroppers to live on the land in exchange for a large portion of the crop. Sharecroppers worked very hard but almost never had enough money to meet their basic needs. In the 1940s, machines ended the need for sharecroppers. Hundreds of thousands of African Americans headed north to find work in cities.

Word Power

perspective (pər spek′tiv) *n.* point of view; p. 127
From the *perspective* of someone flying in an airplane, cars look like toys.

futilely (fū′til ē) *adv.* uselessly; without hope; p. 128
We searched *futilely* for the lost money and finally gave up.

inevitably (i nev′ə tə blē) *adv.* certainly; predictably; p. 128
Every winter, snow *inevitably* falls in the far north.

apex (ā′ peks) *n.* the highest point; p. 129
When the tennis player was at the *apex* of her career, nobody could beat her.

potential (pə ten′shəl) *n.* the ability to grow or develop; p. 130
Education helps people make the most of their *potential*.

saunter (sôn′ tər) *v.* to walk slowly and easily; to stroll; p. 132
On warm days, people *saunter* through the park to enjoy the sun.

panorama (pan′ə ram′ ə) *n.* a complete view of an area from every direction; p. 132
Climb to the top of the hill to see the grand *panorama* below.

reverently (rev′ ər ənt lē) *adv.* in a way that shows honor and love; p. 135
The man *reverently* held the faded photo of his beloved mother.

**Answer the following questions that contain the new words above.
Write your answers in the spaces provided.**

1. If you reach the *apex,* are you at a high or a low part? _____

2. If you speak *reverently* about someone, are you honoring or dishonoring that

    person? _____

3. When people *saunter,* do they move slowly or quickly? _____

4. If you saw a city *panorama,* would you see one or many parts of the city?

    _____

5. From the *perspective* of an ant, would a blade of grass look big or small?_____

6. Which happens *inevitably,* sunrise or a tornado? _____

7. If you work *futilely,* do you succeed or fail? _____

8. Would a singer with *potential* likely be a superstar or a failure?

    _____

Adapted from

Sweet Potato Pie

Eugenia Collier

From up here on the fourteenth floor, my brother Charley looks like an insect scurrying among other insects. A deep feeling of love surges through me. He seems to feel it, for he turns and scans the upper windows, but failing to find me, continues on his way.

I watch him moving quickly down Fifth Avenue and around the corner to his shabby taxicab. In a moment he will be heading back uptown.

I flop down on the bed, shoes and all. Perhaps because of what happened this afternoon or maybe just because I see Charley so seldom, my thoughts hover over him like hummingbirds. The cheerful tidiness of this room is a world away from Charley's flat in Harlem and a hundred worlds from the noisy shanty where he and the rest of us spent what there was of childhood. I close my eyes, and I see the Charley of my boyhood and the Charley of this afternoon, as clearly as if I were looking at a split TV screen.

As far as I know, Charley never had any childhood at all. The oldest children of sharecroppers never do. Mama and Pa were shadowy figures whose voices I heard vaguely in the morning as they left for the field or as they trudged wearily into the house at night.

They came into sharp focus only on special occasions. One such occasion was the day when the crops were in and the sharecroppers were paid. In our cabin there was so much excitement in the air that even I, the "baby," responded to it. On the evening of that day we waited anxiously for our parents' return. Then we would cluster around the rough wooden table, and all seven of us silent for once, waiting. Pa would place the money on the table—gently, for it was made from the sweat of their bodies and from their children's tears. Mama would count it out in little piles, her dark face stern and beautiful.

The other time when my parents were solid entities was at church. On Sundays we would wear our Sunday-go-to-meeting clothes and tramp to the Tabernacle Baptist Church.

My early memories of my parents are associated with special occasions. My everyday life was shaped by Lil and Charley, the oldest children, who rode herd on the rest of us while Pa and Mama toiled in fields. Not until years later did I realize that Lil and Charley were little more than children themselves.

Lil had the loudest, screechiest voice in the county. When she yelled, "Boy, you better git yourself in here!" you got yourself in there. It was Lil who caught and bathed us, Lil who fed us and sent us to school, Lil who punished us when we needed punishing and comforted us when we needed comforting.

Charley was taller than anybody in the world, including, I was certain, God. From his shoulders, the world had a different **perspective**: I looked down at tops of heads rather than at the undersides of chins.

As I grew older, Charley became more father than brother. Those days return in fragments of splintered memory: Charley's slender dark hands whittling a toy from a chunk of wood, his face thin and intense, brown as the loaves Lil baked when there was flour.

Word Power

perspective (pər spek´tiv) *n*. point of view

Literary Element

Tone Remember, tone is the attitude a writer takes toward a subject. It is expressed through the words and details the writer uses. Reread the text highlighted in blue. What is the tone? Check the correct response.

☐ serious and intense
☐ anxiety and despair
☐ sadness and loss

Reading Skill

Infer Reread the text highlighted in green. What clues suggest that Charley is a loving and caring brother?

_____

_____

_____

_____

_____

English Coach

The root word of *feverishly* is *fever*. A *fever* can mean "having a higher than normal temperature." It can also mean "intense excitement or anxiety." In the story, the children are eager to be educated—they "sought education feverishly." Write an original sentence using the word *feverishly*.

_____

_____

_____

Comprehension Check

Reread the boxed text. What does Pa tell Buddy?

_____

_____

_____

_____

_____

_____

_____

_____

Some memories are more than fragmentary. I can still feel the whap of the wet dish rag across my mouth. Somehow I developed a stutter, which Charley was determined to cure. Someone had told him that an effective cure was to slap the stutterer across the mouth with a sopping wet dish rag. Thereafter whenever I began, "Let's g-g-g—," whap! From nowhere would come the rag. Charley would always insist, "I don't want hurt you none, Buddy—" and whap again. I don't know when or why I stopped stuttering. But I stopped.

Already laid waste by poverty, we were easy prey for ignorance and superstition, which hunted us like hawks. We sought education feverishly—and, for most of us, **futilely. Inevitably** each child had to leave school and bear his share of the eternal burden.

Eventually the family's hopes for learning fastened on me, the youngest. I remember one frigid day Pa, huddled on a rickety stool before the coal stove, took me on his knee and studied me gravely. I was a skinny little thing, they tell me, with large, solemn eyes.

"Well, boy," Pa said at last, "if you got to depend on your looks for what you get out'n this world, you just as well lay down right now." His hand was rough from the plow, but gentle as it touched my cheek.

Did You Know?
Stoves fueled by coal were used for cooking and for heating the home.
· · · · · · · · · · · · · · · · · · · ·

"Lucky for you, you got a mind. And that's something ain't everybody got. You go to school, boy, get yourself some learning. Make something out'n yourself. Ain't nothing you can't do if you got learning."

Word Power
futilely (fū′ til ē) *adv.* uselessly; without hope
inevitably (i nev′ ə tə blē) *adv.* certainly; predictably

Charley was determined that I would break the chain of poverty, that I would "be somebody." As we worked our small vegetable garden in the sun, Charley would tell me, "You ain gon be no poor farmer, Buddy. You gon be a teacher or maybe a doctor or a lawyer. One thing, bad as you is you ain gon be no preacher."

I loved school with a passion, which became more intense when I began to realize what a struggle it was for my parents and brothers and sisters to keep me there. The cramped, dingy classroom became a battleground where I was victorious. I stayed on top of my class. With glee I out-read, out-figured, and out-spelled the country boys who mocked my poverty.

As the years passed, the economic strain was eased enough to make it possible for me to go on to high school. There were fewer mouths to feed, for one thing: Alberta went North to find work at sixteen; Jamie died at twelve.

I finished high school at the head of my class. For Mama and Pa and each of my brothers and sisters, my success was a personal triumph. One by one they came to me the week before commencement bringing crumpled dollar bills and coins, muttering, "Here, Buddy, put this on your graduation clothes." My graduation suit was the first suit that was all my own.

My graduation speech was the usual nonsense. I have forgotten what I said that night, but the sight of Mama and Pa and the rest is burned in my memory; Lil, her round face made beautiful by her proud smile; Pa, his head held high, eyes loving and fierce; Mama radiant. Years later when her shriveled hands were finally still, my mind kept coming back to her as she was now. I believe this moment was the **apex** of her entire life. All of them, even Alberta down from Baltimore—different now, but united with them in her pride. And Charley, on the end of the row, still somehow the protector of them all. Charley, looking as if he were in the presence of something sacred.

Word Power

apex (āʹ peks) n. the highest point

English Coach

The narrator uses the prefix *out-* to show how he did better than everyone else. *Out-* means "to go over and above," or "to do better." Write another word that uses the prefix *out-* to mean doing something better than someone else.

_____

_____

_____

Reading Skill

Sequence Find the following events on this page and underline them. Then, on the lines below, number the events from 1 to 4 to show the order in which they took place.

_____ Buddy gives the speech at his high school graduation.

_____ The family experiences less economic strain, which means Buddy can attend high school.

_____ Buddy thinks that his graduation was the apex of his mother's life.

_____ Buddy discovers that school is a battleground where he is victorious.

Literary Element

Tone Reread the highlighted words. Underline the other words in this paragraph that express a tone of deep affection and sympathy for the family.

Background Info

The GI Bill of Rights helped soldiers returning from World War II pay for college.

As I made my way through the carefully rehearsed speech it was as if part of me were standing outside watching the whole thing—their proud, work-weary faces, myself wearing the suit that was their combined strength and love and hope: Lil with her lovely, low-pitched voice, Charley with the hands of an artist, Pa and Mama with God knows what **potential** lost with their sweat in the fields. I realized in that moment that I wasn't necessarily the smartest—only the youngest.

And the luckiest. The war came along, and I exchanged three years of my life (including a fair amount of my blood and a great deal of pain) for the GI Bill and a college education. Strange how time can slip by like water flowing through your fingers. One by one the changes came—the old house empty at last, the rest of us scattered; for me, marriage, graduate school, kids, a professorship, and by now a thickening waistline and thinning hair. My mind spins off the years, and I am back to this afternoon and today's Charley—still long and lean, still gentle-eyed, still my greatest fan, and still determined to keep me on the ball.

Field Workers. Ellis Wilson (1899–1977). Oil on Masonite, 29 ¾ x 34 ⅞ in. National Museum of American Art, Washington, D.C.

How does the family in this painting resemble Buddy's family?

 Stop here for **Break Time** on the next page.

Word Power

potential (pə ten´ shəl) *n.* the ability to grow or develop

Break Time

Buddy's family is very important to him. He has warm memories of his family life while he was growing up. In the left column are scenes that he remembers. Fill in details of these scenes in the right column. The first one has been started for you.

Buddy's Family Life

Scene	Details
The crops are in, and Mama and Pa get paid.	Everyone gathers around the table.
Lil takes care of the younger children.	
Charley stops Buddy from stuttering.	
Buddy graduates from high school.	

 Turn the page to continue reading.

Rooftops (No. 1, This is Harlem), 1942–1943. Jacob Lawrence. Gouache on paper, 14 ⅜ x 21 ⅞ in. Hirshhorn Museum and Sculpture Garden, Washington, D.C.

How does this painting help you visualize Harlem?

Comprehension Check

Reread the boxed paragraph. Now it is the same afternoon that the narrator had mentioned at the start of the story. What does he plan to do this afternoon?

_____

_____

_____

Literary Element

Tone Reread the highlighted text. Buddy is expressing how he feels about being in Harlem. The tone is bittersweet—both pleasant and painful. Underline a sentence that expresses this bittersweet tone.

Background Info

Marcus Garvey (1887–1940) was an African American leader in the 1920s. Garvey Day is a day to honor his memory.

I didn't tell Charley I would be at a professional meeting in New York and would surely visit; he and Bea would have spent days in fixing up. No, I would drop in on them, take them by surprise. Yesterday and this morning were taken up with meetings in the posh Fifth Avenue hotel—a place we could not have dreamed in our boyhood. Late this afternoon I shook loose and headed for Harlem.

Whenever I come to Harlem I feel somehow as if I were coming home. The problems are real, the people are real—yet there is some mysterious quality about Harlem, as if all Black people began and ended there, as if each had left something of himself. As if in Harlem the very heart of Blackness pulsed its beautiful tortured rhythms. Joining the throngs of people that **saunter** Lenox Avenue late afternoons, I headed for Charley's apartment. Along the way I enjoyed the **panorama** of Harlem— women with shopping bags trudging wearily home; little kids flitting through the crowd; groups of adolescent boys striding boldly along; defeated men standing around on street corners or sitting on steps, heads down, hands idle; posters announcing Garvey Day; "Buy Black" stamped on pavements; store windows bright with things African; stores still boarded up, a livid scar from last year's rioting. There was a terrible tension in the air.

Word Power

saunter (sôn′ tər) v. to walk slowly and easily; to stroll

panorama (pan′ ə ram′ ə) n. a complete view of an area from every direction

I mounted the steps of Charley's building—old and in need of paint, like all the rest—and pushed the button to his apartment. Charley's buzzer rang. I pushed open the door and mounted the urine-scented stairs.

"Well, do Jesus—it's Buddy!" roared Charley. "Bea! Bea! Come here, girl, it's Buddy!" And somehow I was simultaneously shaking Charley's hand, getting clapped on the back, and being buried in the fervor of Bea's gigantic hug.

"Lord, Buddy, what you doing here? Whyn't you tell me you was coming to New York?" His face was so lit up with pleasure that in spite of the inroads of time, he still looked like the Charley of years gone by, excited over a new litter of kittens.

"The place look a mess! Whyn't you let us know?" put in Bea, suddenly distressed.

"Looks fine to me, girl. And so do you!"

And she did. Bea is a fine-looking woman, plump and firm still, with rich brown skin and thick black hair.

"Mary, Lucy, look, Uncle Buddy's here!" Two neat little girls came shyly from the TV. Uncle Buddy was something of a celebrity in this house.

We all sat in the warm kitchen, where Bea was preparing dinner. It felt good there. Charley sprawled in a chair near mine. No longer shy, the tinier girl sat on my lap, while her sister darted here and there like a merry little water bug. Bea bustled about, managing to keep up with both the conversation and the cooking.

I told them about the conference I was attending and, knowing it would give them pleasure, I mentioned that I had given a speech that morning. Charley's eyes glistened.

"You hear that, Bea?" he whispered. "Buddy done spoke in front of all them professors!"

Reading Skill

Sequence The information on this page is told in the order listed below. However, these events do not happen in this order. Find the following events on this page and underline them. Then, on the lines below, number the events from 1 to 3 in the order in which they actually happen.

_____ Buddy arrives at Charley's apartment.

_____ Everyone sits in the kitchen talking while Bea cooks dinner.

_____ Buddy gives a speech at the conference.

Background Info

Although traditional African American foods such as ham hocks, chitterlings, grits, black-eyed peas, corn bread, and collard greens have long been popular, the term "soul food" was coined around 1960. The expression may have come from the cultural spirit and soul-satisfying taste of the food.

Reading Skill

Infer Reread the highlighted text. What does Charley mean when he says, "You *somebody*." Check the correct response.

- ☐ You're somebody because you're a professor.
- ☐ You're somebody because you're a cab driver.
- ☐ You're somebody because you're a student.

"Sure I hear," Bea answered briskly, stirring something. "I bet he weren't even scared. I bet them professors learnt something, too."

We all chuckled. "Well anyway," I said, "I hope they did."

We talked about a hundred different things after that—Bea's job in the school cafeteria, my Jess and the kids, our scattered family.

They insisted that I stay for dinner. Persuading me was no hard job: fish fried golden, ham hocks and collard greens, corn bread— if I'd *tried* to leave, my feet wouldn't have taken me. It was good to sit there in Charley's kitchen surrounded by soul food and love.

"Say, Buddy, a couple months back I picked up a kid from your school."

"No stuff."

"I axed him did he know you. He say he was in your class last year."

"Did you get his name?"

"No, I didn't ax him that. Man, he told me you were the best teacher he had. He said you were one smart cat!"

"He told you that cause you're my brother."

"Your *brother*—I didn't tell him I was your brother. I said you was a old friend of mine."

I put my fork down and leaned over. "What you tell him that for?"

Charley explained patiently as he had explained things when I was a child and had missed an obvious truth. "I didn't want your students to know your brother wasn't nothing but a cab driver. You *somebody*."

"You're a nut," I said gently. "You should've told that kid the truth." I wanted to say, I'm proud of you, you've got more on the ball than most people I know, I wouldn't have been anything at all except for you. But he would have been embarrassed.

Bea brought in the dessert—homemade sweet potato pie! "Buddy, I must of knew you were coming! I just had a mind I wanted to make some sweet potato pie."

There's nothing in this world I like better than Bea's sweet potato pie! "Lord, girl, how you expect me to eat all that?"

The slice she put before me was outrageously big—and moist and covered with a light, golden crust—I ate it all.

"Bea, I'm gonna have to eat and run," I said at last.

Charley guffawed. "Much as you et, I don't see how you gonna *walk*, let alone *run*." He went out to get his cab from the garage several blocks away.

Bea was washing the tiny girl's face. "Wait a minute, Buddy, I'm gon give you the rest of that pie to take with you."

"Great!" I'd eaten all I could hold, but my *spirit* was still hungry for sweet potato pie.

Bea got out some waxed paper and wrapped up the rest of the pie. "That'll do you for a snack tonight." She slipped it into a brown paper bag.

I gave her a long good-bye hug. "Bea, I love you for a lot of things. Your cooking is one of them!" We had a last comfortable laugh together. I kissed the little girls and went outside to wait for Charley, holding the bag of pie **reverently.**

In a minute Charley's ancient cab limped to the curb. I plopped into the seat next to him, and we headed downtown. We chatted as Charley skillfully managed the heavy traffic. I looked at his long hands on the wheel and wondered what they could have done with artist's brushes.

We stopped a bit down the street from my hotel. I invited him in, but he said he had to get on with his evening run. But as I opened the door to get out, he commanded in the old familiar voice, "Buddy, you wait!"

English Coach

Guffawed means "laughed." So, if someone guffaws, is he or she more likely to be happy or sad?

Literary Element

Tone Reread the paragraph highlighted in blue. Underline words or phrases that communicate an affectionate and loving tone.

Word Power

reverently (rev´ ər ənt lē) *adv.* in a way that shows honor and love

Reading Skill

Infer Reread the highlighted paragraph. Why won't Charley let Buddy take the bag of pie into the hotel?

_____

_____

_____

_____

_____

For a moment I thought my fly was open or something. "What's wrong?"

"What's that you got there?"

I was bewildered. "That? You mean this bag? That's a piece of sweet potato pie Bea fixed for me."

"You ain't going through the lobby of no big hotel carrying no brown paper bag."

"Man, you *crazy!* Of course I'm going—Look, Bea fixed it for me—*That's my pie—*"

Charley's eyes were miserable. "Folks in that hotel don't go through the lobby carrying no brown paper bags. That's *country*. And you can't neither. You *somebody*, Buddy. You got to be *right*. Now, gimme that bag."

"I want that pie, Charley. I've got nothing to prove to anybody—"

I couldn't believe it. But there was no point in arguing. Foolish as it seemed to me, it was important to him.

"You got to look *right,* Buddy. Can't nobody look dignified carrying a brown paper bag."

So finally, thinking how tasty it would have been and how seldom I got a chance to eat anything that good, I handed over my bag of sweet potato pie. If it was that important to him—

I tried not to show my irritation. "Okay, man—take care now." I slammed the door harder than I had intended, walked rapidly to the hotel, and entered the brilliant, crowded lobby.

"That Charley!" I thought. Walking slower now, I crossed the carpeted lobby toward the elevator, still thinking of my lost snack. I had to admit that of all the herd of people who jostled each other in the lobby, not one was carrying a brown paper bag. Or anything but expensive attaché cases or slick packages from exclusive shops.

I suppose we all operate according to the symbols that are meaningful to us, and to Charley a brown paper bag symbolizes the humble life he thought I had left. I was *somebody*.

Did You Know?

An *attaché* (at´ ə shā´) case is a slim briefcase.

. . . .

I don't know what made me glance back, but I did. And suddenly the tears and laughter, toil and love of a lifetime burst around me like fireworks in a night sky.

For there, following a few steps behind, came Charley, proudly carrying a brown paper bag full of sweet potato pie.

Connect to the Text

Reread the boxed text. Charley sees Buddy as a successful person. For Charley, the paper bag symbolizes "a humble life." What is a symbol that suggests success to you?

_____

_____

Literary Element

Tone Reread the highlighted sentence. How would you describe the tone? Check the correct response.

☐ anxiety and despair
☐ respect and love
☐ sadness and loss

137

Respond to Literature

Sweet Potato Pie

A Comprehension Check

Answer the following questions in the spaces provided.

1. Why is Buddy in New York City? _____

   _____

2. What does Buddy accomplish that his parents and his older brothers and

   sisters do not? _____

   _____

B Reading Skills

Complete the following activities in the spaces provided.

1. **Sequence** At the beginning of the story, Buddy is at his hotel room in New York City. His brother has just dropped him off and is heading back home. Buddy then starts to recall his childhood. Explain where Buddy had been

   and what he was doing earlier that afternoon. _____

   _____

   _____

2. **Infer** At the end, Charley is "proudly carrying" a brown paper bag into the hotel lobby. Why might Charley be proud to carry the brown paper bag?

   _____

   _____

   _____

   _____

C Word Power

Complete each sentence below, using one of the words in the box.

perspective	futilely	inevitably	apex
potential	saunter	panorama	reverently

1. All the people bowed _____ when the king entered the hall.

2. Let's walk quickly because we don't have time to _____.

3. She looked down from the _____ of the mountain.

4. Hold the camera in a different way to show the scene from a new _____.

5. Children have the _____ to learn languages easily.

6. The movie began with a view of a beautiful _____ of mountains, rivers, and fields.

7. The workers tried _____ to stop the flood, and water filled the streets.

8. The children will _____ want to go to the amusement park.

D Literary Element: Tone

A writer's tone may be communicated through particular words and details that express emotions. Read the passage below from "Sweet Potato Pie." As you read, think about the tone. Then answer the questions that follow.

Whenever I come to Harlem I feel somehow as if I were coming home. The problems are real, the people are real—yet there is some mysterious quality about Harlem, as if all Black people began and ended there, as if each had left something of himself. As if in Harlem the very heart of Blackness pulsed its beautiful tortured rhythms.

I enjoyed the panorama of Harlem—women with shopping bags trudging wearily home; little kids flitting through the crowd; groups of adolescent boys striding boldly along; defeated men standing around on street corners or sitting on steps, heads down, hands idle; posters announcing Garvey Day, "Buy Black" stamped on pavements; store windows bright with things African; stores still boarded up, a livid scar from last year's rioting. There was a terrible tension in the air.

The narrator is telling about how he feels in Harlem. The tone is bittersweet—both pleasant and painful.

1. Which phrases from the passage express what the narrator finds pleasant about Harlem? _____

_____

_____

2. Which phrases from the passage express what the narrator finds painful about Harlem? _____

_____

_____

E Family Album

Buddy, the narrator of "Sweet Potato Pie," describes some members of his family in loving detail. He also tells about himself. Look back through the story to find descriptions of the people listed below. What are the most important things to know about each person? In each box, draw a picture of the person or a picture of something connected to that person. Then add a caption to tell about the person.

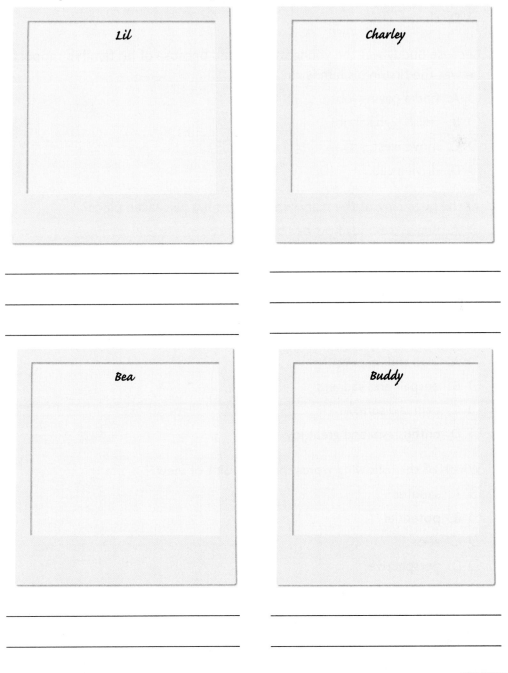

Lil

Charley

_____

_____

_____

Bea

Buddy

_____

_____

_____

Assessment

Fill in the circle next to each correct answer.

1. What is Buddy's main feeling toward Charley?
   - ○ A. love
   - ○ B. hope
   - ○ C. disappointment
   - ○ D. shame

2. Because Buddy was the youngest child and because of his family's support, he was the first in his family to
   - ○ A. find a paying job.
   - ○ B. finish high school.
   - ○ C. move west.
   - ○ D. drive a cab.

3. At the beginning of the story, which event has just taken place?
   - ○ A. Bea asks Buddy how he's been.
   - ○ B. Charlie drops Buddy off at his hotel.
   - ○ C. Buddy visits Harlem.
   - ○ D. Buddy speaks about his childhood.

4. What is the overall tone of "Sweet Potato Pie"?
   - ○ A. love and respect
   - ○ B. despair and sadness
   - ○ C. pain and sorrow
   - ○ D. enthusiasm and great joy

5. Which of the following words means "point of view"?
   - ○ A. saunter
   - ○ B. potential
   - ○ C. apex
   - ○ D. perspective

UNIT 2 **Wrap-up**

Compare and Contrast

Tone is the attitude a writer takes toward a subject. A writer can express tone through his or her choice of words and details. In both "Soul-Catcher" and "Sweet Potato Pie" there are moments where the tone conveys respect, and there are moments where the tone conveys tension.

Complete the chart below. In the left column, provide details that show how the tone of "Soul-Catcher" conveys respect and how it conveys tension. In the right column, provide details that show how the tone of "Sweet Potato Pie" conveys respect and how it conveys tension. Examples have been done for you.

"Soul-Catcher"	"Sweet Potato Pie"
Respect:	Respect: • When Buddy talks about family members, the tone is one of deep respect. He calls his mother's face "beautiful" and understands that she made sacrifices for the family.
Tension: • The boy has trouble respecting his heritage because he's only part Choctaw.	Tension:

UNIT 3 Drama

What's Drama?

Have you ever laughed, cried, or screamed during a movie or play? If so, you were being engaged by a drama.

A **drama**, which is written to be performed by actors in front of an audience, is a story told mainly through the speech and actions of characters. Any story performed by actors on the stage or screen is a drama.

The text, or script, for a drama includes elements similar to fiction, but it also has its own unique elements.

- The **cast of characters**, listed at the beginning of a drama, names the characters. Sometimes the cast list includes a brief description of one or more characters.

- Long dramas are broken up into shorter sections called **acts** and **scenes.** A new act or scene shows that the time or setting has changed.

- **Stage directions** describe how a scene should look and how the characters should speak or move.

- Much of the text of a drama consists of **dialogue,** or the conversation between characters. Most of the plot and characterization in a drama are revealed through dialogue.

What is your favorite movie, play, or TV series?

Why Read Drama?

Dramas can be great entertainment. They can also give you new insights about the way people live. By reading a drama, you can imagine how it should be presented on a stage or in a film.

How Do I Read Drama?

Focus on a key **literary element** and key **reading skills** to get the most out of reading the drama in this unit. Here are one key literary element and two key reading skills that you will practice in this unit.

Key Literary Element

• Conflict

A **conflict** is a struggle between two opposing forces. There are two basic kinds of conflicts:

- An *external conflict* is a struggle between a character and an outside force, such as another person, nature, or society.

- An *internal conflict* is a problem in a character's mind. A character might be torn between opposing feelings, such as greed versus generosity.

Key Reading Skills

• Main Idea

Determining an author's **main idea** means finding the most important thought in a passage or selection. When you look for the main idea, look for the idea that all the sentences in the passage are about. Some writers directly state main ideas in the passage, while others present a main idea through examples and other clues.

• Interpret

When you **interpret,** you are making meaning from what you have read. Interpreting is more than just understanding the facts or story you are reading. It's asking yourself, "What's the writer really saying here?" and then using what you know to help answer that question. Interpreting can give you a much better understanding of the work—as well as a personal connection to it.

Get Ready to Read!

Romeo and Juliet

Meet William Shakespeare

William Shakespeare (1564–1616) has often been called the greatest playwright ever to write in English. He wrote 37 plays that are still performed throughout the world. Shakespeare joined a theater company in London, England. He wrote his plays for the actors in the company. Few details about Shakespeare's personal life are known. But it is clear from his plays and poetry that he read widely and had a unique ear for the music of language. *Romeo and Juliet* is thought to have been written in 1595.

What You Know

When teenagers fall in love, their parents may have reasons to disapprove of the match. What are some reasons that parents would not allow teenagers to marry?

Reason to Read

Read to find out what happens when a young man meets a young woman from an enemy's family.

Background Info

Although the play *Romeo and Juliet* was written more than 400 years ago, it is still popular today. The setting of the play is northern Italy in the 1300s. Romeo and Juliet come from two upper-class families. Romeo is a member of the family of the House of Montague (mon′tə gū). Juliet is a member of the House of Capulet (kap′yə lət). The Montagues and the Capulets have been enemies for years. A long-term fight, called a feud, can involve every family member—brothers, sisters, uncles, cousins— and even household servants. In northern Italy during the Renaissance (1300s to 1600s), such feuds between families were common.

Word Power

mocks (moks) *v.* makes fun of; shows no respect for; p. 150
Even though Mercedes *mocks* Nigel's acting abilities, he still dreams of being a star.

kin (kin) *n.* relatives; family members; p. 150
None of our *kin* knew where our ancestors first came from.

shrine (shrīn) *n.* a place to offer prayers or to honor someone; p. 153
The woman lit a candle before the *shrine* to the dead soldiers.

despair (di spār´) *v.* to lose all hope; p. 153
The lost children began to *despair* as darkness came, and they sobbed with fear.

rile (rīl) *v.* to make upset; p. 157
It is a mistake to *rile* a person who has a bad temper.

grieve (grēv) *v.* to feel great sadness; p. 162
We let Leroy *grieve* in private when his grandfather died.

**Answer the following questions that contain the new words above.
Write your answers in the spaces provided.**

1. If you *rile* a dog, do you make it happy or angry? _____

2. When you *despair,* do you feel hopeful or hopeless? _____

3. When Tim *mocks* his sister, does he praise her or make fun of her?

   _____

4. When you *grieve,* are you more likely to cry or to laugh? _____

5. When people visit a *shrine,* are they more likely to act respectful or disrespectful?

   _____

6. If Tanya is *kin*, is she related to you or is she just a friend? _____

Romeo and Juliet

William Shakespeare

Comprehension Check

As you read *Romeo and Juliet,* look back at this page whenever you need to understand who's who. Read the character names below. Then write the letter that precedes each name next to his or her description.

A. Tybalt

B. Mercutio

C. Capulet

D. Benvolio

___ Romeo's friend

___ Romeo's cousin

___ Juliet's father

___ Juliet's cousin

CHARACTERS

The House of Montague	The House of Capulet
ROMEO the only son of Montague, the head of the House	**CAPULET** Juliet's father and head of the House
BENVOLIO cousin and friend of Romeo	**JULIET** Capulet's only daughter
Other	**TYBALT** Juliet's cousin
MERCUTIO relative of the Prince of Verona and friend of Romeo	**COUSIN CAPULET** an old man, cousin of Capulet
	NURSE Juliet's nurse and companion

The scenes you are about to read are the final scene in Act 1 and the first scene in Act 2. Earlier in the play, Capulet plans a party so that his thirteen-year-old daughter, Juliet, can meet a man she might marry. Romeo and his cousin Benvolio learn about the party. Because the two are members of the Montague family, they are not invited. Benvolio wants to take Romeo to the party anyway; he wants to help Romeo get over his lovesickness for Rosaline. Benvolio wants to show Romeo there are other beautiful women in the world. The two decide to crash the party, wearing masks so that they will not be recognized. They have arrived at Capulet's house when this scene begins.

Act 1, Scene 5. A hall in Capulet's house.

[MUSICIANS stand waiting. SERVANTS enter with napkins. CAPULET, JULIET, and others of his house enter, meeting the GUESTS and MASKERS.]

CAPULET. Welcome, gentlemen!

The ladies without corns on their feet will dance with you.

Ah ha, my ladies! Which of you refuses to dance?

If you play shy, I'll tell everyone that you have corns!

Welcome, gentlemen! I remember the days

When I used to wear a mask

And whisper in a lady's ear.

Oh, those days are gone, but you are welcome!

Come, musicians, play. Make room!

Dance, girls. [*Music plays, and they dance.*] Servants!

More light! Move these tables!

Put out the fire, the room is too hot.

Ah hello! Please sit, good cousin Capulet!

You and I are past our dancing days.

How long is it since you and I were in masks?

Comprehension Check

Reread the boxed text. Underline the reason why Benvolio wants to crash Capulet's party with Romeo.

Background Info

Corns are bumps or thickening of skin on the foot caused by pressure or friction.

149

Reading Skill

Interpret When you interpret what a character says, you explain the meaning behind the character's words.

Reread the lines highlighted in green. Romeo is describing Juliet as he sees her for the first time. What is the meaning of Romeo's speech? Check the correct response.

☐ He has fallen in love.

☐ He is afraid of Juliet's family.

☐ He misses Rosaline.

☐ He is impressed with Juliet's house.

Literary Element

Conflict Reread the lines highlighted in blue. What is the cause of the external conflict between Tybalt and Romeo? What does Tybalt say he will do about it?

_____

_____

_____

_____

_____

_____

COUSIN CAPULET. My word! Thirty years.

CAPULET. What! It hasn't been that long.

We wore masks at Lucentio's wedding, twenty-five years ago.

COUSIN CAPULET. More than that! His son is thirty.

CAPULET. He was only a child two years ago.

ROMEO. [_to a SERVANT_]: What lady is that

Who dances with that knight?

SERVANT. I know not, sir.

ROMEO. Oh, she teaches the torches to burn bright!

She hangs like a jewel upon the cheek of night.

Her beauty is too rich for earth—she glows!

She's like a snowy dove among crows.

The song is over. I'll see where she stands.

Simply touching her will bless my hands.

Did my heart love till now?

Not at this sight!

For I never saw true beauty till this night.

TYBALT. That voice! I know he is a Montague.

Fetch me my sword, boy.

How dare that slave come here, with such a happy face.

He **mocks** us at our own party.

By the honor of my **kin,**

I'll strike him dead, and not count it a sin.

CAPULET. Tybalt! Where are you storming off to?

TYBALT. Uncle, a villain Montague, our foe,

Has come here in spite

To mock us and spoil our party tonight.

Word Power

mocks (moks) _v._ makes fun of; shows no respect for

kin (kin) _n._ relatives; family members

CAPULET. Young Romeo is it?

TYBALT. It is he, that villain Romeo.

CAPULET. Calm down. Leave him alone.

He looks like a well-behaved gentleman.

From what I hear, all of Verona

Says he is decent and well-mannered.

Not for all the wealth of this town

Will I insult him in my own house.

Take no note of him.

Respect my wishes and stop frowning.

Your sour face is wrong for a party.

Reading Skill

Main Idea Reread the highlighted lines. What is the main idea of this passage?

_____

_____

_____

_____

_____

_____

In this scene, Tybalt dances with Juliet's mother, Lady Capulet. Why do you think he looks so serious?

TYBALT.   It fits, when such a villain is a guest.

I won't allow it.

CAPULET.   You will allow it! Am I the master here,

Or are you? Stop.

You're going to make a scene

In front of my guests!

TYBALT.   Uncle, it is a shame.

CAPULET.   Ignore it. My, you are an angry young boy.

Now be quiet.

[*to SERVANTS*] More light, more light!

Everyone, more cheer!

TYBALT.   My patience is wearing thin.

It makes my skin crawl. I must leave.

[*TYBALT exits.* ROMEO *goes to* JULIET *and takes her hand.*]

Comprehension Check

Reread the boxed text. What does Tybalt do in response to Capulet's allowing Romeo to stay at the party?

_____

_____

_____

_____

Look at the expressions on Juliet's and Romeo's faces in this scene. What are their attitudes?

_____

152

ROMEO. If my hand is unworthy of holding yours,

That holy **shrine,**

Charge me with this gentle fine:

My lips are like two blushing pilgrims,

Ready to smooth the hand's rough touch

With a tender kiss.

JULIET. Good sir, you do your hands a great wrong.

Is it not palm-to-palm that pilgrims pray?

ROMEO. But pilgrims pray with pilgrims' lips as well.

JULIET. Yes. We must use lips to pray.

ROMEO. Oh then, dear saint, answer my prayer,

And let our lips meet, or I **despair.**

[*They kiss.*]

JULIET. You kiss by the book.

NURSE. Madam, your mother craves a word with you.

[*JULIET exits.*]

ROMEO. Who is her mother?

NURSE. Her mother is the lady of the house.

I nursed the girl you just spoke with.

I tell you, whoever marries her will be rich.

[*NURSE walks away.*]

ROMEO. Is she a Capulet? Oh no!

My life is in the hands of my foe.

BENVOLIO. Let's leave. The party is over.

ROMEO. Ah, so I fear.

Word Power

shrine (shrīn) *n.* a place to offer prayers or to honor someone

despair (di spār´) *v.* to lose all hope

Reading Skill

Interpret Reread the highlighted lines at the top of the page. Romeo is comparing Juliet's hand to a shrine that is visited by pilgrims. What is the meaning of Romeo's comparison? Check the correct response.

☐ He wants to see whether he and Juliet share a religion.

☐ He is flirting with her by worshipping her hand.

☐ He wants Juliet to go to a shrine.

Reading Skill

Main Idea Reread the highlighted lines. The main idea of these lines is about Romeo's discovery. What does Romeo discover?

_____

_____

Reading Skill

Interpret Reread the lines highlighted in green. Juliet asks the nurse about three men at the party. What is Juliet really trying to find out?

_____

_____

_____

_____

_____

Literary Element

Conflict Reread the lines highlighted in blue. What is the internal conflict Juliet is struggling with at this point?

_____

_____

_____

_____

_____

_____

CAPULET. *[to everyone]:* Gentlemen, do not go.

We have refreshments.

You must go?

Why, then, I thank you, honest gentlemen. Good night.

[*ALL begin to file out except JULIET and NURSE.*]

JULIET. Come here, Nurse. Who is that gentleman?

NURSE. The son and heir of old Tiberio.

JULIET. Who is that, now going out the door?

NURSE. That, I think, is young Petruchio.

JULIET. And who is that there, who would not dance?

NURSE. I do not know.

JULIET. Go ask his name.

[*NURSE leaves.*]

If he is married,

A grave will be my wedding bed.

NURSE. [*returning*]: His name is Romeo,

And a Montague!

The only son of your great enemy.

JULIET. My only love comes from my only hate!

If I'd known earlier! But it is too late!

How awful love is to me,

That I must love my enemy.

NURSE. What are you saying?

JULIET. A rhyme I learned from someone tonight.

[*A voice from offstage calls for JULIET.*]

NURSE. Come, let's go up. The guests have all gone.

[*They exit.*]

STOP Stop here for **Break Time** on the next page.

Break Time

As you read *Romeo and Juliet,* keep track of the characters and what they say to help you understand the play. Read each of the lines of dialogue below. Think about what the lines reveal about the characters who speak them. Then write the name of the character who speaks the words on the line next to the dialogue. The first one has been done for you.

Names of Characters	Dialogue
Romeo **Juliet** **Nurse** **Tybalt** **Capulet**	_____Nurse_____ His name is Romeo, And a Montague! The only son of your great enemy. _____ Uncle, a villain Montague, our foe, Has come here in spite To mock us and spoil our party tonight. _____ Her beauty is too rich for earth—she glows! She's like a snowy dove among crows. _____ My only love comes from my only hate! If I'd known earlier! But it is too late! How awful love is to me, That I must love my enemy. _____ Not for all the wealth of this town Will I insult him in my own house. Take no note of him.

 Turn the page to continue reading.

Literary Element

Conflict Reread the lines highlighted in blue. Explain the conflict expressed in these lines. Is it an internal or external conflict?

_____

_____

_____

_____

_____

Reading Skill

Interpret Reread the lines highlighted in green. What is Mercutio trying to do in this speech? Check the correct response.

☐ Mercutio is teasing Romeo to make him respond.

☐ Mercutio is trying to make Romeo go back to the party.

☐ Mercutio is trying to warn Romeo about Rosaline.

Act 2, Scene 1. A lane by the wall of Capulet's orchard.

[*ROMEO enters.*]

ROMEO.   How can I leave when my heart is here?

I must turn around and find my center.

[*He climbs the wall, and leaps down behind it.*]

[*BENVOLIO enters with MERCUTIO.*]

BENVOLIO.   Romeo! My cousin, Romeo!

MERCUTIO.   If he is wise, he has gone home to bed.

BENVOLIO.   No, I think he ran this way

And leaped over this orchard wall.

Call him, Mercutio.

MERCUTIO.   I'll call him with magic words.

Oh Romeo! Madman! Passion! Lover!

Appear here in the form of a sigh.

Say just one rhyme, and I will be satisfied.

Cry out "Ah me!" or just "love" or "dove."

Speak now to the goddess of love.

Say just one fair word for her son Cupid.

He doesn't hear or stir. He won't move.

That ape is dead! I must bring him back to life.

I'll use the magic of his Rosaline.

By her bright eyes, high forehead, and red lips,

By her fine foot, straight leg, and all the rest,

Appear to us now!

Did You Know?

In Roman mythology, *Cupid* is the god of love and the son of the goddess Venus. Cupid is often shown in art as a boy with a bow and arrow. It is said that anyone struck with Cupid's arrow falls in love.
. . . .

BENVOLIO. If he hears you, you will make him angry.

MERCUTIO. No. My spell is fair and honest.

I'm only using Rosaline's name to **rile** him.

BENVOLIO. Forget it. He is hiding in the trees,

To be alone with the night.

His blind love is best in the dark.

MERCUTIO. If love is blind, how can it hit its target?

He is probably sitting under a tree,

Wishing that his love were the fruit.

Oh Romeo, that she were a pear!

Good night Romeo! I'm going to bed. Shall we go?

BENVOLIO. Let's go. It's useless to look for someone

Who does not want to be found.

[*They exit.*]

Scene 2.   Capulet's orchard.

[*ROMEO enters.*]

ROMEO. He laughs at love's scars,

But Mercutio has never felt such a wound.

[*JULIET appears above, at a window.*]

But, soft! What light through yonder window breaks?

It is the East, and Juliet is the sun.

Rise, fair sun, and kill the jealous moon,

Who is sick and pale with grief.

You are more fair than she, and the moon is jealous.

It is my lady. Oh, it is my love!

She speaks, yet she says nothing.

Her eyes speak, but not to me.

Two stars in heaven have business elsewhere,

And ask her eyes to twinkle in their place.

Comprehension Check

Reread the boxed lines. What do Mercutio and Benvolio do? Why?

_____

_____

_____

_____

_____

Word Power

rile (rīl) *v.* to make upset

English Coach

Here, *shame* is used as a verb meaning "to cause embarrassment by doing something better." Create a sentence using *shame* the same way it is used here.

_____

_____

_____

Background Info

Juliet's question, "Wherefore art thou Romeo?" is a famous one. But it is often misunderstood to mean *Where are you, Romeo?* It really means, *Why are you Romeo?* Juliet is asking why Romeo must have the name of a Montague.

ROMEO. What if her eyes were there, and the stars in her head?

The brightness of her cheek would shame those stars

As sunlight shames a lamp. Her eyes in heaven

Would burn so bright that the birds would sing,

Thinking it day, not night.

See how she places her cheek in her hand!

Oh, that I were a glove on that hand,

That I might touch that cheek!

JULIET. Oh my!

ROMEO. She speaks! Oh, speak again!

You are as glorious as a heavenly angel.

JULIET. Oh Romeo, Romeo! Wherefore art thou Romeo?

Deny your father Montague, refuse your name.

If you will not, swear and be my love,

And I'll no longer be a Capulet.

What do you think Juliet is thinking of in this scene?

_____

158

ROMEO. *(aside)*: Shall I hear more, or speak now?

JULIET. It is only your name that is my enemy.

You are yourself, not just a Montague.

What's a Montague? Not a hand, a foot,

An arm, face, or any other part of a man.

Oh be some other name!

What's in a name? That which we call a rose

By any other word would smell as sweet.

So Romeo would, were he not called Romeo,

Still have the perfection he owns. Oh, Romeo!

Drop thy name! Then take all of me.

ROMEO. I take you at your word.

From now on, I will never be Romeo.

JULIET. Who are you that lurks in the night?

ROMEO. I do not know how to tell you who I am.

I hate my name, because it is an enemy to you.

If my name were written, I would tear it up.

JULIET. My ears have heard less than a hundred words

From that mouth, yet I know the voice.

Aren't you Romeo, and a Montague?

ROMEO. Neither, fair lady, if you dislike either one.

JULIET. How did you come here, and why?

The orchard walls are high and hard to climb.

If any of my family find you here, you will die.

ROMEO. I scaled these walls with love's light wings.

Stone walls cannot keep love out.

Love dares to do what it can.

Your family is of no concern to me.

JULIET. If they see you, they will murder you.

ROMEO. There is more danger in your eye

Than twenty of their swords.

Look sweet, and I am ready for their anger.

Reading Skill

Main Idea Reread the highlighted lines. What is the main idea Juliet is expressing about the names of things and people?

_____

_____

_____

_____

_____

_____

_____

Reading Skill

Interpret Reread Juliet's speech, beginning with the line highlighted in green. What is she saying in this speech? Check the correct response.

☐ She is embarrassed that Romeo heard her but is truly in love with him.

☐ She is in love, so Romeo can't trust what she says.

☐ She likes Romeo, but is not really in love with him.

English Coach

Coy means "pretending to be shy or bashful." If Juliet is acting *coyly*, would she firmly state her love for Romeo or flirt with him and pretend that he must win her love?

_____

_____

_____

JULIET.   There is nothing in the world I want more

Than for them not to see you.

ROMEO.   I have night's cloak to hide me.

But if you don't love me, let them find me here.

It would be better to end my life by their hate,

Than to live without your love.

JULIET.   Who told you how to find this place?

ROMEO.   Love told me. I am not a ship's pilot,

But if you were a far shore on the farthest sea,

I would sail to find you.

JULIET.   The mask of night covers my face

Or you would see me blush.

You have heard me say too much tonight.

I wish I could pretend to deny it.

Do you love me? I know you will say yes.

But do not swear it, for sometimes lovers lie.

If you do love, say it faithfully.

If you think I am too quickly won over,

I'll frown so that you may charm me more.

But in truth, I am too fond of you to do so.

You may think I'm odd, but trust me.

I'll be more true than those who play hard to get.

I should be more coy, perhaps,

But you have already heard my true feelings.

So please forgive me,

My love is not as light as it might seem.

ROMEO.   Lady I swear by the moon that...

JULIET.   Don't swear by the moon,

For it changes month by month.

ROMEO.   What shall I swear by?

JULIET.   Do not swear at all. If you must,

Swear on yourself and I'll believe you.

ROMEO. By my heart's dear love...

JULIET. Do not swear. Although it makes me happy,

I have no joy about our love tonight.

It is too rash, too sudden.

It is like lightning, which is over

Before one can even say, "Look, lightning!"

Good night, my sweet.

The bud of our love will bloom when next we meet.

ROMEO. Oh, will you leave me so unsatisfied?

JULIET. What satisfaction can you have tonight?

ROMEO. Exchange your faithful vow of love for mine.

JULIET. I gave it to you before you asked for it.

But I will take it back.

ROMEO. Why? For what purpose, my love?

JULIET. To give it to you again.

My love is as deep as the deepest sea;

The more I give, the more I have.

[*NURSE calls offstage.*] I hear someone calling.

In a minute, good Nurse!

Wait here, I will come again. [*She exits.*]

ROMEO. I am afraid this is only a dream.

It is too sweet to be real.

JULIET. [*re-enters above*] Three words, dear Romeo,

And then good night. If your love is true,

And your purpose marriage, send me word tomorrow.

I will send someone to you

To ask where and what time we will marry.

Then I'll follow you throughout the world.

NURSE. [*offstage*]: Madam!

Reading Skill

Main Idea Reread the highlighted lines. Juliet is expressing how she feels about her new love. What is the main idea of these lines?

_____

_____

_____

_____

_____

_____

Comprehension Check

Reread the boxed text. What "word" does Juliet expect the next day, and what will she do if she gets it?

_____

_____

_____

_____

_____

_____

_____

Connect to the Text

Do you know people who have fallen in love this quickly? What happened to their relationships?

_____

_____

_____

_____

_____

_____

_____

Reading Skill

Interpret Reread the highlighted text. When Juliet speaks of "sweet sorrow," she is combining opposite ideas. What is she saying about parting with Romeo?

_____

_____

_____

_____

_____

JULIET.   I'm coming! [*to ROMEO*] But if you do not want to,

Leave me alone to **grieve.**

A thousand times good night! [*She exits.*]

ROMEO.   It is a thousand times worse

Now that she is gone.

JULIET.   [*re-enters, above*]: Romeo!

ROMEO.   My dear?

JULIET.   At what time tomorrow

Shall I send the messenger to you?

ROMEO.   At the hour of nine.

JULIET.   I will not fail. It seems like twenty years

Until then. Oh! I forgot why I called you back.

ROMEO.   Let me stand here until you remember.

JULIET.   I will forget, with you standing there.

I can only think about how I love your company.

ROMEO.   I'll stay, just to have you forget.

JULIET.   It is almost morning. I wish you would go,

But no farther than a bird's hop from here.

ROMEO.   I wish I were your bird.

JULIET.   Sweet, so do I.

But I might kill you with too much love.

Good night, good night! Parting is such sweet sorrow

That I shall say "good night" till it be tomorrow.

[*JULIET exits.*]

ROMEO.   Sleep well, and peace in your rest!

Now I must go to Friar Lawrence's cell,

To ask his help, and my happiness to tell.

[*ROMEO exits.*]

Word Power

grieve (grēv) *v.* to feel great sadness

162

Respond to Literature

Romeo and Juliet

A Comprehension Check

Answer the following questions in the spaces provided.

1. Where does Romeo first meet Juliet? _____

   _____

2. At the end of the selection, what are Romeo and Juliet planning to do?

   _____

B Reading Skills

Answer the following questions in the spaces provided.

1. **Main Idea** What main idea is Romeo expressing when he says "Her beauty is too rich for earth—she glows!/She's like a snowy dove among crows"?

   _____

   _____

2. **Interpret** What does Juliet mean when she says "My only love comes from my only hate!"?

   _____

   _____

3. **Interpret** What does Juliet mean when she says "What's in a name? That which we call a rose/By any other word would smell as sweet"?

   _____

   _____

C Word Power

Complete each sentence below, using one of the words in the box.

mocks	kin	shrine
despair	rile	grieve

1. The prisoners held on to hope and tried not to feel _____.

2. People stopped to pray at each _____ on the path to the temple.

3. We feel bad when someone _____ our ideas by calling them foolish.

4. It is hard to _____ Tony because he is always calm.

5. Fareed is not her _____; they just look alike.

6. You may _____ for what you have lost, but you can't get it back again.

D Literary Element: Conflict

Read the passages below from *Romeo and Juliet*. As you read them, think about the internal and external conflicts that the characters are facing. Then answer the questions that follow.

> **JULIET.** It is only your name that is my enemy.[1]
>
> You are yourself, not just a Montague.[2]
>
> What's a Montague?[3] Not a hand, a foot,
>
> An arm, face, or any other part of a man.[4]
>
> Oh be some other name![5]
>
> **JULIET.** If they see you, they will murder you.[6]
>
> **ROMEO.** There is more danger in your eye[7]
>
> Than twenty of their swords.[8]
>
> Look sweet, and I am ready for their anger.[9]

1. In lines 1–5, what internal conflict is Juliet struggling with? _____

   _____

   _____

   _____

2. What external conflict is described in lines 6–9? _____

   _____

   _____

   _____

E Advice Column

Imagine that you are Juliet writing a letter to an advice columnist. You want to know if you are doing the right thing. Complete the letter below. Then use your imagination to complete the columnist's reply.

Dear Professor Love,

At a party tonight, I met _____

_____

I feel in my heart that he and I _____

_____

But my parents will probably not allow us to marry because _____

_____

_____

What should I do?

—Giddy in Italy

Dear Giddy in Italy,

My advice to you is _____

_____

_____

Assessment

Fill in the circle next to each correct answer.

1. What does Romeo mean when he says "Her beauty is too rich for earth—she glows!"?
   - ○ A. Juliet is very rich.
   - ○ B. Juliet is very beautiful.
   - ○ C. Juliet is very smart.
   - ○ D. Juliet is very careless.

2. What is Tybalt's reaction when he learns that Romeo is at the party?
   - ○ A. He is angry and wants to fight.
   - ○ B. He is polite and wants the party to remain peaceful.
   - ○ C. He doesn't really care because he is having a good time.
   - ○ D. He is joyful since they are friends.

3. When Juliet says "It is only your name that is my enemy," what main idea is she expressing?
   - ○ A. She can learn to love her enemy, even though she feels hate now.
   - ○ B. She is supposed to hate anyone called Montague, but can't hate Romeo.
   - ○ C. She thinks a man should be able to choose any name he wishes.
   - ○ D. She wants to learn the name of the enemy who spoke to her at the party.

4. What is the main conflict that Romeo and Juliet confront?
   - ○ A. She doesn't know who he is.
   - ○ B. He falls in love too quickly.
   - ○ C. He has promised to marry someone else.
   - ○ D. Their families are feuding.

5. Which of the following words means "to lose hope completely"?
   - ○ A. mock
   - ○ B. rile
   - ○ C. despair
   - ○ D. shrine

UNIT 4 Epic

What's an Epic?

Have you ever seen a movie or read a book or comic book about superheroes fighting battles to save the world? Those are pretty close to the experience you get when you read an epic. Epics were told long before people invented writing. Storytellers repeated these tales from memory. Some of the most famous epics come from ancient Greece, dating from around 700 B.C.

All epics have certain elements in common.

- Epics are long stories that are divided into several **parts.** An epic's **setting** is often on a grand scale, spanning a continent or the whole world.

- A heroic central figure, or **epic hero,** undergoes tests and adventures. **Gods** and monsters often play a role in epics, and the action is frequently violent.

- The **quest,** or pursuit of a goal, is a common theme in epics.

On the lines below, write the name of a heroic character and describe his or her extraordinary abilities.

Hero: _____

Abilities: _____

Why Read Epics?

We read epics for some of the same reasons that ancient audiences listened to them. They are exciting stories that show us examples of strength, intelligence, and moral courage. We also get a glimpse of traits people found admirable long ago.

How Do I Read Epics?

Focus on the key **literary element** and **reading skills** to get the most out of reading the epic in this unit. Here is a key literary element and two key reading skills that you will practice in this unit.

Key Literary Element

Epic Hero

The central character in an epic is an **epic hero.** Epic heroes are larger-than-life figures with superhuman strength. They are stronger, smarter, and braver than the average person. They are often courageous and adventurous, traveling on long, dangerous journeys, or quests. They have many qualities that their culture finds admirable. In fact, their great deeds bring honor and fame both to themselves and to the nation they represent. However, epic heroes are human, and at times make human errors.

Key Reading Skills

• Visualize

When you **visualize** a person, place, object, or event, you see it in your mind. Try to imagine the person, thing, or scene being described. Build on any details the writer provides. Pay special attention to descriptions of the setting and characters. Trying to visualize what you are reading can give you a feeling of being part of the story. "See" in your mind the clothes that a character is wearing or the house that character lives in, based on the words used to describe it.

• Summarize

Summarizing is stating the main ideas or important events in a logical sequence. Summarizing teaches you to rethink what you've read and to separate main ideas from supporting information. It can also help you better understand and remember the information in a story.

Get Ready to Read!

The Odyssey

Meet Homer

Homer was one of the greatest poets of the ancient world, but little is known about him. It has been said that he was a blind man who lived in Greece or in what is now Turkey, probably before 700 B.C. His version of the story of Odysseus was a long poem that he spoke or sang. *The Odyssey* was not written down for a long time, perhaps as long as two hundred years after Homer's death.

What You Know

Think about the challenges you have faced in sports, school, or your personal life. What physical or mental qualities helped you handle each challenge? Were there any qualities you wished you had at the time?

Reason to Read

Read to learn the qualities Odysseus (ō dis′ ē əs) shows as he overcomes challenges during his journey home.

In the following three excerpts from an epic, you will read about the difficult challenges Odysseus faces on his journey home from the Trojan War. In Greek mythology, the Trojan War was a war fought by the Greeks against the city of Troy.

Background Info

The Odyssey describes the adventures of the general Odysseus. He is heading home to the Greek island of Ithaca following the end of the Trojan War. Odysseus helped lead the Greeks to victory. Odysseus is a hero known for his bravery. He is also known for being clever and sly. The events in the *The Odyssey* take place shortly before 1200 B.C.

Word Power

replenished (ri plen´ isht) *v.* made full or complete again; p. 174
The campers *replenished* their supply of juice and now have enough for a week.

companions (kəm pan´ yənz) *n.* people who accompany others; p. 174
Mona and her two *companions* took turns driving the car across the country.

savages (sav´ ij əz) *n.* people who are brutal and cruel; people who live in a basic, uncivilized way; p. 175
Without rules or laws, people can become *savages.*

abundance (ə bun´ dəns) *n.* a great amount; p. 175
There was an *abundance* of rain falling, and we feared there would be a flood.

strategy (strat´ ə jē) *n.* a plan of action; p. 181
The coach explained the *strategy* to make the best use of teamwork.

surged (surjd) *v.* grew higher and stronger like a wave; p. 184
The boat rocked as the sea *surged* around it.

**Complete the following sentences that contain the new words above.
Write your answers in the spaces provided.**

1. In the summer, if you have an *abundance* of fruit, do you have a lot of fruit or a little? _____

2. If the water *surged*, would the level get higher or lower? _____

3. If Joey has *companions*, is he alone or with other people? _____

4. If Connor has a *strategy*, does he have a plan or doesn't he have a plan?
_____

5. If the grocery store *replenished* the supply of cereal, was cereal put on the shelves or taken off the shelves? _____

6. Do you think that *savages* have good manners or no manners? _____

Adapted from
The Odyssey
Homer

Comprehension Check

Reread the boxed text. Underline the sentences that tell which god is Odysseus's most bitter enemy and which god is Odysseus's friend.

English Coach

The word *immortal* begins with the prefix *im-*, meaning "not." The word *mortal* means "sure to die." An immortal is a being, such as a god, that will not die. What is another word in which the prefix *im-* means "not"?

_____

_____

_____

FOREWORD

After the Trojan War, the Greek heroes left Troy for their homelands in Greece. Odysseus set out cheerfully for Ithaca, far across the sea. The sea! Odysseus's most bitter enemy among the gods was Poseidon, God of the Sea, ruler of the very oceans that Odysseus had to cross. How Poseidon became his enemy and how the god brought about many disasters Odysseus himself will tell. Fortunately, though, Odysseus had a good friend among the gods—Athena, goddess of wisdom, powerful daughter of the ruler of the gods, Zeus himself.

When Poseidon was off on a visit to the ends of the earth, Athena took the opportunity to plead with Zeus on behalf of Odysseus. For after many strange adventures and after the loss of all his men, he had become the prisoner of a goddess, Calypso, who loved him. Though wanting to return to his home he was powerless against the strength of an immortal. Zeus agreed to help. The god Hermes was sent to tell Calypso to release him, and Calypso had to bow before the will of the most powerful. The tale opens in the tenth year of his wanderings after the fall of Troy.

The One-Eyed Giant

"King Alcinous," replied Odysseus, "I really enjoyed listening to your wonderful singer. But you have asked about my troubles. How can I tell you all of them? Where can I begin? Well, first of all I'll tell you my name. I am Odysseus, son of Laertes, famed throughout the entire world. My home is Ithaca, one of the islands off the coast of Greece. It is rugged country, but a wonderful place just the same. Both Calypso and that other witch Circe kept me practically a prisoner, hoping that I would stay with them. But they never made me forget my home, for there is nothing sweeter than a man's own country. If you like, I'll tell you about my attempt to return home from Troy."

And this is the story Odysseus told.

We had a good start. A favorable wind took us from Troy to the land of the Ciconians in Ismarus. Needing provisions we destroyed the city and killed all the men. We divided the loot from the city, each one getting an equal share. I suggested that we leave at once, but the others were foolish and decided to stay on. They drank heavily and killed many sheep and cattle for a feast. In the meantime, though, word got through to a neighboring tribe of the Ciconians. These neighbors were much better fighters, skilled on horse as well as on foot.

They attacked us in the morning. Matters went badly for us. They formed ranks near the ships and attacked us from both sides. We fought them off as best we could, though we were far outnumbered. By evening we were trying to run away. We lost six men from each ship, but the rest of us fortunately escaped. We set sail at once, grieving at the loss of our comrades, but rejoicing at our own good luck.

Literary Element

Epic Hero Epic heroes face many challenges during their story.

Reread the text highlighted in blue. What is one challenge that Odysseus confronts while trying to return home?

_____

_____

_____

Reading Skill

Summarize Reread the last two paragraphs starting with the text highlighted in green. Summarize the most important events by completing each statement below.

Odysseus and his men sail away from Troy. In Ismarus, they _____

_____

Then a neighboring tribe of the Ciconians _____

_____

They are very skilled fighters, and Odysseus loses

_____

_____

Finally, Odysseus and his crew

_____

My Workspace

Comprehension Check

Reread the boxed text. Where did Odysseus and his crew end up after the wind blew them in the wrong direction for ten days?

_____

_____

Literary Element

Epic Hero Reread the highlighted text. Some of Odysseus's men have eaten the lotus flowers, which makes them forgetful. Odysseus forces the men to return to the ship. How is this action characteristic of an epic hero? Check the correct response.

☐ It shows he's a brute and a bully.

☐ It shows he seeks fame.

☐ It shows he's an extremely strong leader.

After we were at sea a short time, Zeus stirred up a frightening storm. The clouds covered the sky, and night set in too early. Our sails were torn in so many places we let them down so that we'd not be completely lost. For two days and two nights there was no let-up. On the morning of the third day the clouds scattered and we drew up the sails again. We set our course and hoped for the best. I probably would have reached my home if a powerful north wind had not swept us off our course. Just as we were rounding the dangerous straits of Malea, off the coast of southern Greece, the north wind blew us off to the southwest. The wicked wind took me in the wrong direction for nine days.

Did You Know?
Zeus, the ruler of all the Greek gods, controlled thunder and lightning.
. . . .

The tenth day brought us to the land of the Lotus-Eaters. These people eat flowers for food. We went ashore, **replenished** our water supply, and ate our supper.

After we had eaten, I sent three of my **companions** as messengers to find out what kind of people these were—these flower-eaters.

The messengers went among the natives. Innocently enough, the Lotus-Eaters offered lotus for my comrades to taste. When my men ate of the flowers, they forgot everything that had happened to them. They no longer wanted to return home, but wished to stay on there, eating the lotus in forgetfulness. I had to drag them off by force and bind them in the ships. I urged my other comrades to sail immediately, for I dreaded what would happen if more men tasted the lotus. We set out promptly, rowing steadily away from land.

Word Power

replenished (ri plen´ isht) *v.* made full or complete again
companions (kəm pan´ yənz) *n.* people who accompany others

174

We were in low spirits at our bad luck thus far. But we hadn't an idea of what was in store for us. We reached next the land of the Cyclopes. These monsters are **savages** without laws or culture. They live by themselves. Each family is a law unto itself. No man cares for his neighbor.

Across their harbor there lies a beautiful wooded island. Wild goats are plentiful there, for there are no hunters to kill them. The Cyclopes just don't have the ships to reach the island, and so it is neglected. It is a rich, fertile place, with drinking water in **abundance.** A wonderful island! We lay down on the shore, not knowing where we were.

In the morning we awoke and were amazed at our good fortune. We explored the island and found the goats in abundance. We killed a great number of them. As a matter of fact, each of my twelve ships had nine goats. We feasted all day long, adding to our meal the wine we had stolen from the Ciconians. I became curious at the sight of the mainland. We could see the smoke and hear the voices of the Cyclopes. The next day I addressed my men, having called them all together for a meeting.

"My beloved companions, please wait for me here. I am taking one ship over to the mainland. I'd like to find out what kind of people these Cyclopes are. I'd like to know whether they are rude, cruel, and unjust, or kindly and friendly."

I set out, with my men, for the mainland. When we neared land, we saw a lonely cave in which cattle, sheep and goats were housed.

Literary Element

Epic Hero Reread the highlighted text. How can you tell that Odysseus is the kind of character who seeks new adventures and experiences?

_____

_____

_____

_____

_____

_____

Word Power

savages (sav´ ij əz) *n.* people who are brutal and cruel; people who live in a basic, uncivilized way

abundance (ə bun´ dəns) *n.* a great amount

Reading Skill

Visualize Reread the highlighted text. Odysseus describes Polyphemus as a "monster." Sketch Polyphemus in the frame below.

Your sketch

English Coach

Kids has many different meanings. Here, *kids* are "young goats." *Kid* can also mean "to tease", and it can mean "a child." Write a sentence using two of the meanings of *kid.*

_____

_____

_____

_____

There lived a giant, evidently an outcast even from his own people. His name, as I learned later, was Polyphemus. He was really a monster, not like a man at all but like a mountain! He had but one round eye in the middle of his forehead. I ordered my men to stay there near the ship. I chose twelve of my best comrades and went to investigate. I took with me a goatskin of dark wine, which had been given me by a priest of Apollo. I brought some supplies, too, for I had a feeling that we were about to meet a man powerful and savage.

When we reached the cave, we found it empty. Food there was in abundance! There were baskets filled with cheeses. Pans were swimming with milk and cream. Lambs and kids were separated according to their size. My men urged me to take some of the cheeses, lead the animals into the ships, and be off. I didn't listen to them. If I only had! I wanted to meet the Cyclops and receive the stranger's gifts from him. As it happened, his gifts were far from pleasant to me or my companions.

We lit a fire and waited, eating of his cheeses. He came in with a great shout. We were terrified and hid in the back of the cave. He drove the animals into the cave for milking, and closed off the entrance with a huge rock. After he had milked the animals, he spied us.

"Who are you?" he cried out. "What place did you come from? Are you merchants, or sea-robbers ready to kill and be killed for gain?"

We trembled at his words, for we feared him. His monstrous size and heavy voice were no comfort to us. Yet I had to answer him; so I said, "We are Greeks on our way home from Troy. We have been driven far out of our course by wind and storm. We are proud to be followers of Agamemnon, leader of all the Greeks against Troy. His fame has spread to all corners of the earth. We are here to make a request of you. We ask for friendly treatment and gifts as are due to strangers. Honor the gods, O noble sir, and treat us well. For Zeus protects strangers and those who need help."

He answered cruelly, "You're a fool, my friend, to think that I would fear the gods. We Cyclopes have no respect for any of the 'blessed' gods. We are much above them. If I wish to lay hands upon you or your companions, Zeus won't stop me. But tell me where you keep your ship. Near here? Let me know."

He thought he could trick me into revealing the hiding place of the ship. But I gave him a dishonest answer.

"Poseidon the Earth-Shaker wrecked my ship against the rocks of your island. These men with me are all that escaped destruction."

He didn't bother to answer. Instead he rushed forward and grasped two of my companions. Snatching them like puppies he dashed them against the ground, crushing their skulls. Their brains oozed out on the earth. Cutting them up, limb by limb, he prepared his supper. He devoured them like a mountain lion, leaving no trace of the poor men.

> We wept aloud, raised our hands heavenward and prayed for Zeus' help. We were without hope. After the Cyclops had eaten, he lay stretched out in the cave and slept. I drew my sword and approached him, thinking to kill him or at least wound him seriously. I stopped. How would I get out? We could never have moved the stone from the cavern's opening. Miserably we waited for morning.

The Cyclops awoke after many hours. He went about his business, milking his cattle and performing other chores. After he finished, he snatched two more of my men and prepared his meal. He ate them and then proceeded to drive the cattle from the cage. When the last had gone through, he again rolled the stone in front of the cave's mouth.

 Stop here for **Break Time** on the next page.

Literary Element

Epic Hero Reread the text highlighted in blue. Odysseus is famous for using his brains to get out of trouble. How does he show his cleverness at this point in the story?

_____
_____
_____
_____
_____

Reading Skill

Visualize Reread the text highlighted in green. Underline the phrases that help you vividly picture this terrible action being described.

Comprehension Check

Reread the boxed text. Why doesn't Odysseus kill the monster when he falls asleep?

_____
_____
_____
_____
_____
_____

Break Time

So far, Odysseus and his crew have faced some amazing challenges on their journey home from the war. Practice your visualization skills by drawing some of the events that have taken place so far. Use details and descriptions from the story to help you draw the events in the frames below.

The land of the Ciconians	Zeus stirs up a storm

The land of the Lotus-Eaters	Polyphemus meets Odysseus and his men

 GO Continue reading on the next page.

I considered many plans for getting revenge if Athena would only grant my prayer. One plan seemed to be best. There was a huge club in the cave, which the Cyclops had been preparing as a walking stick. It was as big as the mast of a good-sized ship. I cut off a piece about six feet long and had my companions sharpen it. I burned the end and brought it to a good point. I asked the men to draw lots to see who would have the job, with me, of thrusting the stick into the eye of the sleeping Cyclops. Four good men were chosen.

In the evening he again herded his fine cattle and sheep into the cave. He put his barrier back into place and milked the animals. Again, after his chores were finished, he snatched two men and prepared his supper. I went close to the Cyclops and said, "Here, Cyclops, have a drink of wine after your meal of human flesh. I want you to know what kind of drink we had aboard my ship. I brought it originally as a gift offering, so that you would pity me and help me return home. Now I see you are mad beyond all cure. How can you expect men to visit you? You have behaved so cruelly."

He took the wine and gulped it down. Licking his lips he spoke again.

"Some more, please, and tell me your name. I'd like to give you a present that you'll approve. Our wine is good, but this is fit for the gods."

I gave him more, and he drank quickly. Again I offered, and again he drank the wine. At last, when he began to feel the effect of the wine, I said gently, "Cyclops, did you ask my name? Well then, I'll tell you, but don't forget that gift you promised me. No-man is my name. My mother, my father, and all my companions call me No-man."

Did You Know?

Athena was the goddess of wisdom and war. In Greek mythology, she helped her chosen heroes.
. . . .

Reading Skill

Summarize When you summarize, you tell the main idea in your own words.

Reread the highlighted paragraph. Summarize Odysseus's plan.

_____

_____

_____

_____

_____

_____

Comprehension Check

Reread the boxed text. What did Odysseus give the Cyclops? Check the correct response.
☐ some of his men
☐ a lot of wine
☐ some cattle and sheep
☐ a huge club

Reading Skill

Visualize Reread the paragraph starting with the highlighted text. Put yourself in the scene. Describe what you see, smell, feel, and hear.

_____

_____

_____

_____

_____

_____

_____

_____

Comprehension Check

Reread the boxed text. Odysseus calls himself "No-man" to trick the Cyclops. How does Odysseus's trick work when Polyphemus says "No-man is killing me..."?

_____

_____

_____

_____

_____

_____

_____

"No-man," he replied with a cruel grin, "this is my present to you. I'll eat all your companions first. I'll save you till last!"

As he said this, he staggered and fell upon his back. Sleep overcame him. He became ill in his drunken stupor and vomited wine and bits of human flesh. I put the wood stick in the ashes until it was warm. I kept encouraging my companions to keep their spirits high. The stick was green; when it was about to take fire, green though it was, I took it out and approached the one-eyed monster. My companions hesitated a moment, but some god inspired them with courage. They took hold of the stake and thrust the point into his eye. I leaned on it from above and turned it round and round, as a man drills a hole. Taking the white-hot stake we twisted it in his eye, and the hot blood flowed around it. We scorched his eyebrows and eye-lids as the eyeball burned with a hissing sound.

The Cyclops howled horribly and we drew away in terror. He drew the stake from his eye and threw it. He called aloud to the other Cyclopes who lived around him in caves. They heard him and came to find out what was the matter. They stood around the cave and cried out his name.

"What terrible injury, Polyphemus, has made you cry out so in the middle of the night? Is some man driving away your sheep against your will? Is someone killing you by force or by trickery?"

"O my friends," answered mighty Polyphemus, "No-man is killing me, by trickery and not by force."

"Well then," they said, "if no man is assaulting you, you must be sick, and sickness is heaven sent. You'd better pray to your father, the great god Poseidon."

They left. I laughed inwardly because my name and **strategy** had worked. But the Cyclops, groaning and weeping from pain, rolled away the stone from the opening. Taking no chances, he sat within the gate and stretched forth his hands. As his flocks went out to graze, he felt each sheep to make certain that none of us tried to escape this way. He must have taken me for a fool! I had been casting about for some plan to save my companions and me, for the future still looked very dark.

At last I hit upon this trick. The rams were sturdy and large, with rich dark coats. I tied them in threes, putting one of my companions under each middle ram. Thus three sheep carried one man. I chose a different method for myself. I picked out the biggest and heaviest ram. I laid hold of its back and slung myself under its shaggy belly. I hung upside down, holding on to the wonderful wool. Thus we awaited the morning.

At dawn the animals rushed to the pasture. The Cyclops, still suffering greatly, felt the backs of all the sheep as they went out. The fool did not realize that my men were tied underneath the sheep. My own sturdy ram went out last, weighed down by his heavy coat and by me. Putting his hand on the ram's back, Polyphemus said, "Dear ram, why are you the last out today? You are not usually the last. You're usually first out and first back. Now you're way behind. Do you feel sorry for the loss of my eye, which a foul villain has blinded after first making me drunk? Well No-man has not yet escaped. If you could only speak and tell me where he's hiding, I'd dash his brains out on the spot. Then and only then would I rest again."

Word Power

strategy (strat´ ə jē) *n.* a plan of action

English Coach

Casting has many different meanings. Which of the following phrases uses the same meaning of "casting" that is used in the story? Check the correct response.

☐ to throw, as in *casting a fishing line*

☐ to choose actors, as in *casting a movie*

☐ to think up a strategy, as in *casting about for a way to escape*

Reading Skill

Summarize Reread the highlighted text. Summarize Odysseus's plan for escaping from the cave.

_____

_____

_____

_____

_____

Connect to the Text

Imagine that you are the man hiding behind the ram on the left in the picture. What is going through your mind? What might the Cyclops be thinking in this scene?

_____

_____

_____

_____

_____

_____

_____

_____

_____

Odysseus. Jacob Jordaens (1593–1678). Oil on canvas, 61 x 97 cm. Pushkin Museum, Moscow.

At his last words he sent the ram away from him out of the cave. A little further on I dropped from the ram and freed my companions. We quickly drove his cattle on until we came to our ship. We were a welcome sight to the companions we had left aboard ship, but they began to weep for the men who had died. I gave them little time for weeping, for I ordered them to be off at once. When we were a good distance from the mainland, I couldn't resist a parting insult to Polyphemus.

"Hello there, Cyclops, you thought you had a weakling there in the cave when you murdered my companions. Your sins came home to roost, you monster. Since you didn't hesitate to eat your guests, the gods have had revenge upon you."

He was furious. He tore off the top of a large mountain and threw it in the direction of the voice. The missile landed in front of our boat and drove it back toward shore! I took a long pole and pushed powerfully, meanwhile urging my comrades to row with all their might. Soon we were twice as far away as before. I started to shout again.

My comrades tried to stop me. "Foolish man, why do you try to irritate a fierce monster? Just a moment ago he threw a huge rock into the sea and nearly brought us back to shore and our deaths. If he had heard any of us speaking, he'd have crushed us with a rock. He throws far enough."

I was too stubborn to listen. I spoke up again in my anger.

"O Cyclops, if anybody asks about that unsightly eye you have there, just say that Odysseus, destroyer of cities, son of Laertes, blinded you!"

He answered with a wail. "Alas, the old prophecies are coming true. They said I'd lose my sight through the trickery of Odysseus. I have always been expecting a strong, handsome man. Instead a puny weakling has blinded me after conquering me with wine. Come back, Odysseus, so that I can give you suitable presents. I shall urge my father, Poseidon, god of the sea, to get you back home safely. He will cure my loss of sight, if he chooses, without the help of any other gods."

"I wish I could kill you," I replied, "and send you to Hades where no one could ever cure you—not even Poseidon."

He stretched forth his hands and prayed aloud.

"Hear me, father Poseidon, see to it that Odysseus, destroyer of cities, never reaches his home. If you can't quite do that, if it is his fate to get there eventually, delay him and destroy all his companions. Arrange matters so that he finds great troubles at home."

Literary Element

Epic Hero Reread the highlighted text. Odysseus does not make a quick and quiet escape. Instead, his words and actions show him to be proud and stubborn—human faults. Underline the sentences showing these character traits.

Background Info

Prophecies are predictions of future events. Prophecies were important to the ancient Greeks.

Comprehension Check

Reread the boxed paragraph. The Cyclops is praying to the god Poseidon. Underline the things the Cyclops asks Poseidon to do.

My Workspace

Reading Skill

Summarize Reread the two paragraphs starting with the highlighted sentences. Summarize what happens to Odysseus and his men.

_____

_____

_____

_____

_____

_____

_____

So he prayed and his father heard him. But Polyphemus raised a much larger stone and sent it flying. This time it just missed the rudder, landing behind the ship. The sea **surged** up around us as the rock fell. The waves sent us forward to the little island. There we found the other ships and the rest of our comrades. They had almost given up hope, but were glad to see us. We divided the Cyclops' animals evenly. I sacrificed the ram to Zeus, but he did not listen. For as it turned out he had planned the destruction of all my ships and all my men.

We feasted throughout the whole day, and slept that night by the shore of the sea. In the morning we embarked on our ships, rejoicing at our narrow escapes and grieving at our losses.

Polyphemus Attacking Sailors in Their Boat, 1855. Alexandre Gabriel Decamps. Oil on canvas, 98 x 145 cm. Musée des Beaux-Arts, Rouen, France.

How does this painting help you visualize Odysseus's journeys and the creatures he meets?

_____

_____

Word Power

surged (surjd) *v.* grew higher and stronger like a wave

184

Respond to Literature

The Odyssey

A Comprehension Check

Answer the following questions in the spaces provided.

1. What do Odysseus and his men do at Ismarus, the land of the Ciconians?

   _____

   _____

2. What happens to the men who are sent to meet the Lotus-Eaters?

   _____

   _____

B Reading Skills

Use the reading skills to complete the activities.

1. **Summarize** Summarize the events that occur after Odysseus and his men become trapped inside the Cyclops's cave.

   _____

   _____

   _____

2. **Visualize** Describe what Odysseus looks like as he escapes from the Cyclops's cave.

   _____

   _____

   _____

C Word Power

Complete each sentence below, using one of the words in the box.

replenished	companions	savages
abundance	strategy	surged

1. Fruit grew in _____ on the warm, well-watered land.

2. With his dog and three _____, the young man set off in search of adventure.

3. _____ are uncivilized people.

4. Rushing water _____ over the banks of the river.

5. The clever leader suggested a _____ for tricking the enemy.

6. The hikers _____ their drinking water and moved on.

D Literary Element: Epic Hero

Reread the passages below from the epic *The Odyssey*. As you read, think about the personal qualities Odysseus exhibits.

I had to drag them off by force and bind them in the ships.[1] I urged my other comrades to sail immediately, for I dreaded what would happen if more men tasted the lotus.[2]

My comrades tried to stop me.[3] "Foolish man, why do you try to irritate a fierce monster?[4] Just a moment ago he threw a huge rock into the sea and nearly brought us back to shore and our deaths.[5]

I was too stubborn to listen.[6] I spoke up again in my anger.[7]

"O Cyclops, if anybody asks about that unsightly eye you have there, just say that Odysseus, destroyer of cities, son of Laertes, blinded you!"[8]

1. What characteristic traits of an epic hero does Odysseus display in sentences 1–2? _____

    _____

    _____

2. In sentences 3–8, Odysseus is acting against the advice of his men. What does this tell you about Odysseus? What character traits does Odysseus display in these lines? _____

    _____

    _____

E Comic Strip

Look at the four frames of the comic strip below. Add words to the speech balloons to show what Odysseus might be saying. Add words to the thought balloons to show what he might be thinking. If you wish, draw more details in the frames.

Assessment

Fill in the circle next to each correct answer.

1. Which god is Odysseus's enemy?
    ○ A. Zeus
    ○ B. Athena
    ○ C. Poseidon
    ○ D. Polythemus

2. Which sentences are an accurate summary of the events that take place in the land of the Lotus-Eaters?
    ○ A. Odysseus and his men eat lotus. They become very sick and want to return home.
    ○ B. Some of Odysseus's men eat lotus and become forgetful. Odysseus has to force them to return to the ship.
    ○ C. Some of Odysseus's men are eaten by the Cyclops. Odysseus helps others escape by hiding under rams.
    ○ D. Odysseus and his men destroy the city. They take many provisions such as cattle, sheep, and wine.

3. Why does Odysseus want to go to the island of the Cyclopes?
    ○ A. He is curious and wants to meet the Cyclopes.
    ○ B. He wants to steal more cattle.
    ○ C. He wants to show his strength by hurting the Cyclopes.
    ○ D. He wants to insult the Cyclopes.

4. Which of these descriptions **best** describes Odysseus?
    ○ A. gentle and caring
    ○ B. cowardly and honest
    ○ C. foolish and frightened
    ○ D. brave and stubborn

5. Which of the following words means "a kind of plan"?
    ○ A. abundance
    ○ B. strategy
    ○ C. surged
    ○ D. savages

Get Ready to Read!

The Odyssey
The Six-Headed Monster

Word Power

seize (sēz) *v.* to grab and hold suddenly; p. 193
The thief managed to *seize* the gold and run off.

fates (fāts) *n.* outcomes that have been determined to happen and over which human beings have no control; p. 194
Jessica and Manuel believed their *fates* involved always being together.

perils (per′ əlz) *n.* dangers; risks; p. 197
The travelers faced floods, earthquakes, and other *perils* before reaching safety.

weary (wēr′ ē) *adj.* very tired; p. 197
A child may grow *weary* in the afternoon and need a nap.

boldly (bōld′ lē) *adv.* in a way that shows no respect; arrogantly; p. 199
The boy *boldly* grabbed the fruit that was set out for everyone to share.

abruptly (ə brupt′ lē) *adv.* suddenly; without warning; p. 200
The rain stopped *abruptly*, and the sky was instantly clear.

**Answer the following questions that contain the new words above.
Write your answers in the spaces provided.**

1. If you felt *weary,* would you sit down or run? _____

2. If people were to hear their *fates,* would they be hearing about their pasts or their

   futures? _____

3. Which could you *seize,* a friend's hand or a friend's laugh? _____

4. If you were speaking too *boldly,* would you be speaking shyly or aggressively?

   _____

5. If a bus stopped *abruptly,* would the stop be quick or slow? _____

6. If you faced *perils,* would you feel you were safe or in danger? _____

Adapted from
The Odyssey
Homer

The Six-Headed Monster

*Odysseus continues the story of his adventures. At this point,
he and his men have just returned from Hades (hā′ dēz), the
land of the dead. They had been sent there by the goddess Circe
(sur′ sē). Odysseus and his men have been on Circe's island,
Aeaea (ē ē′ a), for a year. Now they are preparing to sail home.
But first they must bury a comrade, Elpenor (el pē′ nôr), who
had died accidentally on Circe's island and whose ghost they
met in Hades. Odysseus continues telling his hosts about his
adventures.*

Our ship left the ocean stream and went out into the open sea.
Soon we reached Aeaea, land of the dawn and the sunrise. We
drew up our ship upon the sands and went ashore. We slept on
the shore until morning. Soon after sunrise I sent my comrades
forward to the house of Circe to bring back the corpse of our
comrade Elpenor. We buried him sorrowfully, according to the
instructions his soul had given us. Having built his tomb we
placed the oar over it.

Background Info

Circe is the daughter of Helios,
the Sun God. She is known for
her knowledge and magic.

English Coach

Sunrise is a compound word
made from the words *sun*
and *rise*. Write two other
compound words that have
the word *sun* in them.

_____

_____

Background Info

The Sirens are three mythical sea nymphs—part bird and part woman. Their singing is said to have magical power. If sailors hear the songs of the Sirens, they either jump overboard and die on the rocky coasts, or they forget to eat and starve.

Reading Skill

Summarize Reread the highlighted text. Summarize the advice Circe gives Odysseus about sailing by the Sirens.

_____

_____

_____

_____

_____

_____

_____

_____

_____

Circe arrived soon after. Her attendants brought bread, meat, and wine. She stood among us and said, "What men you are! So you went down to Hades while still alive? You have the privilege of dying twice. Most other men have but one chance! Come now; eat, drink, and be merry. Tomorrow you will set sail. I'll give you full instructions to protect you from harm."

We agreed willingly. We feasted and drank till sunset. When night came on, the men slept near the ship. But Circe took me by the hand away from the others. She asked many questions about the trip, and I told it all as best I could. At last she said to me, "Good, that's over and done with. But now listen to what I have to say and don't forget it!

"On your way from here you'll sail by the Sirens first of all. They are charmers. Whoever sails near and hears the song of the Sirens immediately forgets wife and children. For the Sirens, sitting in a meadow, soothe him with a piercing song. Around them is a large heap of bones of men rotting away. Sail beyond them. Fill the ears of your companions with wax for fear they should hear the Sirens' song. But you can listen if you like. Have your men tie you, hands and feet, against the mast. Then you can listen to their song safely and enjoy it. If you beg your companions to free you, instruct them in advance to tie you still tighter."

"After you pass the Sirens, you have a choice of two courses. In one path you will find a pair of lofty rocks, surrounded by the waves of the sea. The gods call the rocks 'the Wanderers.' Not a bird can pass between them, not even the doves who are messengers of Zeus. The clashing rocks always crush them. Ships never get through these rocks. In all the years only one vessel has ever got through. That was the Argo, famous vessel of the Argonauts under Jason. Probably the Argo would have been destroyed, too, but Hera loved Jason and protected him."

"In the other direction lie two cliffs. One of them nearly touches the sky with its sharp peak. The summit is always in clouds. No man could ever climb this mountain, even if he had twenty hands and feet. The rock is smooth and polished. In the middle of this rock there is a shadowy cave toward the westward. Make for that cave, noble Odysseus. The cave is so high a strong archer could not reach it with his arrow. This is where Scylla lives, shrieking terribly. Her voice is like a newborn puppy's, it's true, but she herself is a huge monster. No one would like to meet her, I tell you, not even a god."

"She has twelve dangling feet and six long necks. On each neck there is a gruesome head, each head with three rows of teeth. She wallows in the middle of her hollow cave and pokes her heads out of the cavern. She fishes there, watching about the rock for dolphins and even whales, if they come by. No one has ever passed her unharmed. She always snatches a man from the ships with each of her heads."

"The other cliff is lower. Here there is a large wild fig-tree. Under this, Charybdis sucks in the black water. Three times a day she sucks it in, and three times a day she spouts it out. Don't be there when she sucks the water in, for then no one could save you, not even Poseidon himself. You'd better sail by Scylla. It's better to lose six of your companions than the whole ship."

"Tell me, O goddess," I said, "can I avoid Charybdis and attack Scylla when she rushes to **seize** my men?"

"Stubborn fool," she replied, "you're asking for trouble. Won't you yield even to the immortal gods? Scylla cannot be killed. She is a deathless evil, terrible and difficult and fierce. You cannot fight with her. There is no defense. Flight is the only course. If you delay for a fight, she'll come back for another round of six men. Make haste through that point and pray that Scylla takes no more men."

Word Power

seize (sēz) *v.* to grab and hold suddenly

Comprehension Check

Reread the boxed text. What does Circe warn Odysseus not to do on the island of Trinacria? Why?

_____

_____

_____

_____

Literary Element

Epic Hero Reread the highlighted text. Odysseus decides he wants to hear the Sirens' song. Which characteristic of an epic hero does this display? Check the correct response.

☐ He is stronger than the average person.

☐ He has human faults.

☐ He seeks adventure and new knowledge.

"Next you will come to the island of Trinacria. Here are kept the oxen and sheep of the Sun God, fifty of each. They never die, and they never have young. They have goddesses for shepherdesses. If you leave them unharmed, you may still get to your Ithaca with some minor misfortunes. But if you harm them, then I foretell the destruction of your ship and your companions. Even if you yourself should escape, you will return late, in misfortune, without your comrades."

As she finished, the first hints of morning announced the day. She left and I went to my companions and urged them to hurry. They went aboard and sat down on the benches. They rowed mightily, assisted by a wind that fair-haired Circe had sent on behind us. After the ship was well on its way, I addressed my companions.

"My comrades, it's not right that only one or two should know what's going to happen to us. I'll tell you about our **fates,** so that we may be forewarned and thus avoid destruction. First, Circe warned us against the song of the Sirens. She ordered me alone to hear their singing. Bind me to the mast. If I beg you and order you to loosen me, then tie me still tighter."

So I explained the prophecy to my men. Meanwhile the ship drew near to the isle of the Sirens. Suddenly the wind stopped. My companions rolled up the sail, storing it away. They began to row, whitening the water with long strokes. Then I took out the wax and warmed it in the sun. I put some into the ears of all my companions. They bound me to the mast, tying me securely. When we were within shouting distance of the Sirens, they began a beautiful song.

"Come here, admirable Odysseus, glory of all the Greeks! Stop your ship and listen to our singing. No one has ever passed by here without stopping to listen and enjoy our songs. We know all things—what the Greeks and Trojans suffered before Troy, and we know all that will happen on this earth."

Word Power

fates (fāts) *n.* outcomes that have been determined to happen and over which human beings have no control

The Sirens, c. 1875. Sir Edward Burne-Jones. South African National Gallery, Cape Town, South Africa.

Would you want to hear the song of the Sirens? Why or why not?

That was the message they gave. I wanted desperately to hear them. I ordered my companions to let me free, but they rowed all the faster. Two of them rose and bound me more tightly. After we had passed from earshot, my beloved comrades took away the wax and freed me.

After leaving the island behind, we saw smoke. A vast wave rolled toward us with a deafening roar. In their terror the men dropped their oars, which fell into the sea with a loud splash. The ship stopped when the oarsmen ceased rowing. I hurried through the vessel and urged on my comrades.

"Friends, we have seen misfortune face to face before. This evil is no greater than the one we experienced when the Cyclops imprisoned us in his cave. We escaped that time by my courage, wisdom, and good sense. You'll live to remember this occasion, too. Come; follow my instructions. Keep rowing strongly if you want to avoid death. And you, my pilot, keep the ship away from the smoke and the wave. Hug the cliff, or we'll surely be drowned."

Connect to the Text

Reread the boxed passage. Try to picture how Odysseus sounds and moves as he encourages his crew. What kinds of real-life leaders can you think of who talk that way?

_____

_____

_____

_____

_____

_____

_____

_____

Literary Element

Epic Hero Reread the text highlighted in blue. Odysseus does not follow Circe's warning against trying to fight Scylla. What does this tell you about Odysseus?

_____

_____

_____

_____

_____

_____

Reading Skill

Visualize Reread the sentence highlighted in green and the rest of the page. Form a picture in your mind of what is happening here. Underline the details that help you visualize the scene.

They hastened to obey. But I did not mention Scylla and the danger we could not avoid. For I feared my comrades would stop rowing from terror. In the excitement I forgot Circe's warning. I began to arm myself. Fully armed at last, I went to the prow of the ship. I thought Scylla, death-dealing monster that she is, would appear at that point. I looked carefully, but saw no sign of her.

We sailed through the strait, groaning in terror. On one side somewhere was Scylla. On the other was the dread whirlpool Charybdis, sucking in the waters of the sea. As she spouted the torrent out, it bubbled up as in a kettle. Foam covered the rocky shore. When she sucked the water in, it swirled furiously. The rocks echoed with the booming noise. We gazed at Charybdis horrified, fearing our destruction at any moment.

While we were so concerned, Scylla reached forth and snatched six of my best men. I looked toward the ship and my comrades at the same time. I saw them dangling pitifully above me. They called out and addressed me by name for the last time. That was a sight I'll never forget. They had been hooked like fish.

How does the artist's painting of this scene from *The Odyssey* compare with what you picture as you read? Does the image effectively convey how the men are powerless against the monsters?

Scylla and Charybdis, from the Ulysses Cycle, 1560. Alessandro Allori. Fresco. Banca Toscana, Florence, Italy.

After we had escaped the **perils**—both Scylla and Charybdis—we came at last to the island of the Sun God. Beautiful sheep and oxen roamed the island. When I saw them, I recalled the warnings of Tiresias and Circe, who had told me to avoid this island at any cost. I addressed my companions.

"My comrades, you have been having a hard time of it. Yet there is something else I must tell you. Both Tiresias and Circe urged me to avoid this island, no matter what other course we took. They insisted that a horrible fate lay in store for us here."

The men were sad at my words, but Eurylochus spoke up for the others.

"Odysseus, you're a powerful man. You are never **weary.** Surely you must be made of iron, for you don't wish your poor comrades to go ashore to sleep. We are weary. If we go ashore, we can prepare a good supper here. But you want us to go off wandering in the night again. Night is a bad time for ships. Winds come up suddenly. How can anyone escape when real hurricanes arise? Let us take a hint from the gathering dusk, and get supper ready near the ships. In the morning we can start again."

My other companions applauded his words. Then I knew we were in for it. I turned to the men and said, "You are a majority and I must yield. However, swear an oath to me that you will not, under any circumstances, kill any of the cattle or sheep we may find there. Eat only the food that Circe gave us."

They swore an oath as I commanded, and we went ashore. After supper they grieved, thinking of the comrades they had lost to Scylla. At last they fell asleep. Toward morning Zeus raised a terrible storm. Clouds covered the earth, and night returned in earnest. We drew our ship back into a safer harbor. I called my men together and again warned them.

Reading Skill

Summarize Reread the highlighted text. Summarize the argument between Odysseus and his men by completing the statements below.

The men are weary and decide they want to _____

_____

_____

Odysseus does not agree at first, but then gives his permission because _____

_____

_____

However, first he makes them swear that _____

_____

Word Power

perils (per ′ əlz) *n.* dangers; risks
weary (wēr ′ ē) *adj.* very tired

197

Comprehension Check

Reread the boxed paragraph. How does Eurylochus try to persuade the men to break their promise never to kill the Sun God's cattle?

_____

_____

_____

_____

_____

_____

_____

_____

English Coach

The word *stricken* means "to be overwhelmed by or full of." When someone is *grief-stricken*, he or she is overwhelmed by grief. What does it mean when someone is horror-stricken?

_____

_____

"My comrades, there is plenty of food and drink on shipboard. Don't touch the oxen, or we'll all suffer for it. These cattle belong to the God of the Sun. Nothing is hidden from him."

Once again they agreed to my words. But the unfavorable wind did not let up for a solid month. As long as they had plenty of food and drink, the men did not touch the oxen. At last, though, our provisions ran out. The men went fishing and hunting, hoping to find something to eat. Gradually hunger wore them down. I went off to pray to the gods for help to return from this island. I avoided my companions and at last fell asleep.

Once again it was Eurylochus who gave bad advice to the men.

> "Listen a moment, friends; you have had a hard time. No one wants to die, but death from starvation is most horrible. Let us drive off the best of the cattle and sacrifice them to the gods. If we ever reach our native Ithaca, we will build a lofty temple to the Sun God. If the Sun God is still angry and destroys our ship, I prefer drowning to wasting away here on a desert island."

The other men seconded his suggestion. They rounded up the heaviest oxen and made a prayer to the gods. Then they slaughtered the beasts and made fitting sacrifices. When they were preparing the animals for eating, I awoke. I rushed to the ships and smelled the odor of burning fat. Grief-stricken, I cried out to the gods.

"O Zeus and all other gods immortal, you plotted my ruin when you made me fall asleep. My companions have committed a horrible crime."

A messenger took the news at once to the Sun God. When he heard of the slaughter of his oxen, he addressed Zeus in rage.

"O father Zeus and all other blessed gods, punish the companions of Odysseus. They have **boldly** slain my oxen that I loved so much. If I do not get revenge, I'll be off to Hades, and shine among the dead—not among the living."

"O God of the Sun," replied Zeus the cloudgatherer, "continue to shine for the benefit of gods and men. I shall take care of Odysseus, striking his ship with a thunderbolt in the middle of the sea."

I heard all this later from Calypso, who declared she had heard it from Hermes.

When I came to the ship, I scolded the men, but there was nothing for me to do. The cattle were all dead. Then amazing things began to happen. The meat began to make noises, like the sounds of cattle. The skins crawled. But my companions ate. For six days they continued to feast. On the seventh day the tempest stopped, and we sailed off once more. After we had left the island, we saw no more land. Zeus brought a black cloud over our ship. The very sea became dark underneath it. The winds began to rise. The storm broke. The mast was split. As it fell, it crushed the pilot's head. Zeus thundered and sent a bolt which struck the ship. It was whirled round and round. All my companions were thrown off the ship. They bobbed up and down on the waves like seagulls. I tried to keep going until the storm tore the sides from the keel. I tied together keel and mast and rode upon them, drifting before the terrible winds.

Word Power

boldly (bōld´ lē) *adv.* in a way that shows no respect; arrogantly

My Workspace

Comprehension Check

Reread the boxed paragraphs. Underline the sentence that tells how Zeus plans to punish Odysseus for the deaths of the Sun God's animals.

Reading Skill

Summarize Reread the highlighted text. Summarize what happens to Odysseus and his men after they leave the island by completing the statements below.

Zeus creates a storm and

_____

_____

_____

Odysseus's crew _____

_____

_____

Odysseus survives by _____

_____

_____

Literary Element

Epic Hero Reread the highlighted text. Which characteristic of an epic hero is Odysseus displaying here? Check the correct response.

- ☐ human faults
- ☐ superhuman strength
- ☐ fame and honor

The west wind stopped **abruptly,** and the south wind sprang up. This was no comfort to me, for I realized it would bring me directly back to Scylla and Charybdis. All night long I drifted. At sunrise I came again to Charybdis. She gulped down the salty sea water, but I held on to a tall fig-tree, which hung over the whirlpool.

I couldn't climb up into the tree, and I couldn't climb down; there was no place for me to go. So I had to hold on until Charybdis spouted up the mast and keel again. How I longed for the reappearance of my raft as I hung on, but it took a long time! At last it came. I put down my feet and hands and fell back onto it. I began to paddle with my hands.

Fortunately Scylla did not appear, or I'd certainly have been lost. I drifted along for nine days. On the tenth I drifted to the island of Ogygia, where the goddess Calypso lives. She nursed me back to health. There I stayed for eight long years. The rest you know. Why should I tell you what you know already?

And so Odysseus concluded his tale before the Phaeacians.

Word Power
abruptly (ə brupt′ lē) *adv.* suddenly; without warning

Respond to Literature

The Odyssey

A Comprehension Check

Answer the following questions in the spaces provided.

1. How does Odysseus protect his men from the Sirens' song? How do his men protect him? _____

   _____

2. What does Zeus promise the Sun God? Why? _____

   _____

   _____

B Reading Skills

Use the reading skills to complete the activities.

1. **Summarize** Summarize what happens to Odysseus and his men as they sail through the passage between Scylla and Charybdis. _____

   _____

   _____

2. **Visualize** How does Odysseus manage to avoid Charybdis after the storm wrecks his ship? Make a sketch or describe what he does.

   > *Your Sketch*

C Word Power

Complete each sentence below, using one of the words in the box.

seize	fates	perils
weary	boldly	abruptly

1. Before the big game, the coach told her players that their

   _____ were all connected.

2. After the long hike, everyone was too _____ to stand.

3. When her parents told her to eat her vegetables, Renee

   _____ refused.

4. The little boy tried to _____ all the candy in
   the jar.

5. Hector spilled his coffee when the car stopped _____.

6. In adventure stories, the hero faces many _____
   but usually survives.

D Literary Element: Epic Hero

The passage below comes from the part of _The Odyssey_ you have just read. As you reread it, look for qualities that are characteristic of an epic hero. (To review qualities of an epic hero, see page 169.)

"Friends, we have seen misfortune face to face before.[1] This evil is no greater than the one we experienced when the Cyclops imprisoned us in his cave.[2] We escaped that time by my courage, wisdom, and good sense.[3] You'll live to remember this occasion, too.[4] Come; follow my instructions.[5] Keep rowing strongly if you want to avoid death.[6] And you, my pilot, keep the ship away from the smoke and the wave.[7] Hug the cliff, or we'll surely be drowned."[8]

They hastened to obey.[9] But I did not mention Scylla and the danger we could not avoid.[10] For I feared my comrades would stop rowing from terror.[11]

---

1. In sentences 1–8, how does Odysseus display qualities of an epic hero in his speech to his crew? _____

   _____

   _____

2. In sentences 9–11, Odysseus decides not to tell his crew Circe's prophecy— that six of his men will be killed. Do you think this shows that Odysseus is being very wise and strategic, or that he is weak? Explain. _____

   _____

   _____

   _____

E Warning Signs

Odysseus receives many warnings in this part of *The Odyssey*. Imagine that the warnings are posted as signs near the dangers that Odysseus and his men will face. Write the words that belong on each sign below. Draw Scylla's cave in the box.

DANGER!

SIRENS SING HERE!

Be sure to _____

_____

If you don't, _____

_____

_____

WARNING!

WATCH OUT FOR CHARYBDIS!

All ships should _____

_____

Obey these rules, or

_____

_____

BEWARE!

SCYLLA'S CAVE ABOVE!

Your Sketch

DANGER!

THE WANDERERS!

These rocks _____

_____

_____

_____

WARNING!

THIS IS THE ISLAND OF THE SUN GOD!

Do not _____

_____

Consider yourself warned!

Assessment

Fill in the circle next to each correct answer.

1. What does Charybdis look like?
   - ○ A. a six-headed monster
   - ○ B. a creature that is part bird, part woman
   - ○ C. a high cliff
   - ○ D. a whirlpool

2. Who gives Odysseus advice in this part of *The Odyssey*?
   - ○ A. Zeus
   - ○ B. Circe
   - ○ C. Athena
   - ○ D. the Sun God

3. How does Odysseus use his wits to survive the storm that kills his men?
   - ○ A. He quickly builds a raft.
   - ○ B. He talks Zeus into helping him.
   - ○ C. He tricks Scylla into letting him pass.
   - ○ D. He remembers the route to safety.

4. Which of these settings should be included in a summary of this part of *The Odyssey*?
   - ○ A. Hades
   - ○ B. Mount Olympus, home of Zeus
   - ○ C. the cave of the Cyclops
   - ○ D. the sea near the isle of the Sirens

5. Which of the following words means "to grab"?
   - ○ A. fates
   - ○ B. seize
   - ○ C. weary
   - ○ D. perils

Get Ready to Read!

The Odyssey
The Slaughter of the Suitors

Word Power

slaughter (slô´ tər) *n.* the killing of many people or animals; p. 207
The battle resulted in the *slaughter* of thousands of soldiers.

retrieving (ri trēv´ ing) *v.* taking or getting something back; p. 209
The dog is *retrieving* the stick I threw into the pond.

reinforcements (rē´ in fôrs´ mənts) *n.* fighters and weapons added for a battle; p. 210
The commander called for *reinforcements* when he saw the enemy troops.

deserted (di zurt´ id) *v.* left someone alone in time of need or danger; p. 212
When Allen's friends *deserted* him, he realized they were not true friends.

intervened (in´ tər vēnd´) *v.* played a role in changing an event; interfered; p. 213
In Greek myths, the gods often *intervened* in human events.

ruthless (rōōth´ lis) *adj.* without pity or mercy; cruel; p. 214
The *ruthless* boss fired anyone who dared to question him.

Answer the following questions, using one of the new words above. Write your answers in the spaces provided.

1. Which word goes with "abandoned someone"? _____

2. Which word goes with "getting something back"? _____

3. Which word goes with "affected an outcome"? _____

4. Which word goes with "merciless"? _____

5. Which word goes with "more soldiers"? _____

6. Which word goes with "murder of many"? _____

Adapted from
The Odyssey
Homer

The Slaughter of the Suitors

As this part begins, Odysseus has completed his 20-year-long journey home to Ithaca. Helped by the goddess Athena, he is reunited with his son, Telemachus (tə lem´ ə kəs). Father and son plan to kill the men who have taken over the palace of Odysseus. These men are suitors, seeking to marry Odysseus's faithful wife, Penelope (pə nel´ ə pē). Odysseus returns disguised as a beggar. He wins a contest that Penelope has set up for the suitors. Only he is able to shoot an arrow from the bow of Odysseus. But Penelope does not yet know that the beggar who shot the arrow is really her beloved husband. She leaves the great hall to return upstairs to her room.

Odysseus stripped aside the old rags he wore and leaped with his bow and arrow. He spread the arrows in front of him and cried out, "That contest has at last been won. Now I'll turn my attention to other targets."

Background Info

A suitor is one who tries to win the love and affection of another, with hopes of marrying that person.

Word Power

slaughter (slô´ tər) *n.* the killing of many people or animals

Reading Skill

Visualize Reread the text highlighted in green. This is a vivid description of the murder of Antinous (an tin´ ō əs), the leader of the suitors. Underline words in the paragraph that help you picture his death clearly.

Literary Element

Epic Hero Reread the text highlighted in blue. Odysseus is threatening to kill all of the suitors. What qualities must he have to fight these men successfully?

_____

_____

_____

Comprehension Check

Reread the boxed text. What does Eurymachus (yoo rim´ ə kəs) say is the reason Antinous wanted to marry Odysseus's wife? Check the correct response.

☐ He wanted to rule Ithaca.

☐ He was in love with her.

☐ He wanted Telemachus for a son.

With that he sent an arrow at Antinous. This suitor was just about to lift a beautiful cup filled with wine. Death was far from his mind. After all, who among them would expect that a single person would dare to attack! The shaft caught him in the throat, and the point pierced his neck. He sank back, and the cup fell from his lifeless hands. Blood spouted over the table, and he pushed aside the table with a jerk of his feet. All the food was spilled on the ground.

The suitors were angry when they saw Antinous fall. They leaped from their seats and rushed off, looking for the armor that used to be on the walls. No shield or spear was anywhere to be seen. They cried out to Odysseus in their fury, "Madman, this is the last time you'll ever draw a bow. You have just slain the noblest man in Ithaca. The vultures will be dining off you very shortly."

Poor fools! They didn't realize that he had intended to kill Antinous. They thought it was an accident. It didn't dawn on them how close to death they all were.

Odysseus cried out, "Dogs! You thought I'd never get back again from Troy. You thought you could continue to eat my food and insult my household. You thought you could flatter my wife while I still lived. Your doom is sealed."

The suitors were terrified. They looked back and forth for a means of escape. Eurymachus alone had courage to speak.

"If you are indeed Odysseus, then you have spoken the truth about the evil doings in your house. But the man who was the cause of all this now lies dead—Antinous. It wasn't that he wanted a wife. He wanted to rule Ithaca after slaying your son Telemachus. Now he is slain instead. Please spare the rest of us. We will make it up to you."

Odysseus looked sternly at Eurymachus and said, "Even if you gave me everything you own, Eurymachus, you couldn't stop me from revenge. You have the choice of fighting or trying to escape—though I don't think many of you will escape."

The suitors were shaking with fright, but Eurymachus spoke up again.

"Friends, it's easy to see this man will not stop plans for slaughter. Since he has the bow and arrows, he'll continue to shoot until he has killed us all. Be men. Draw your swords and use the tables for shields. Let us all rush together against him, and try to thrust him from the threshold. Once we get outside we can raise an alarm. Then this man will shoot an arrow for the last time."

As he spoke he drew his sword and leaped at Odysseus with a piercing cry, but Odysseus sent an arrow at the same time that struck Eurymachus in his chest. Eurymachus threw his sword down and staggered around the table. He thrust all the cups and food on the ground as he lurched forth. He fell upon the ground and his forehead struck the dust. A shadow of darkness fell before his eyes, and he lay still.

Amphinomus rushed Odysseus next, his sharp sword waving in the air. But Telemachus took care of him, striking him from behind with his spear. It came out his chest and he fell with a thud. Telemachus rushed away, not even **retrieving** the spear, for he feared being struck if he tried to regain it. He ran to Odysseus and cried, "My father, now I'll bring you a shield, two spears, and a bronze helmet. I'll equip myself and the two faithful herdsmen. We must be armed."

Reading Skill

Summarize Reread the highlighted text. Summarize Eurymachus's advice to the suitors.

_____

_____

_____

_____

_____

_____

_____

Word Power

retrieving (ri trēv´ ing) *v.* taking or getting something back

Reading Skill

Visualize Reread the text highlighted in green. Sketch a picture of how Odysseus looks at this point of the story. Be sure to include what he's wearing and holding.

Your Sketch

English Coach

A *goatherd* is someone who herds goats. A *shepherd* is someone who herds sheep. Underline the word on this page that names someone who herds swine, or pigs.

Odysseus replied, "Run and get the arms while I still have arrows to defend myself with, or they may drive me out while I am alone."

Telemachus rushed out for **reinforcements.** He armed himself and the two servants, all three men taking their stand beside Odysseus. Meanwhile Odysseus sent forth the death-dealing arrows until the suitors piled up before him. When the arrows gave out, he stood the bow against a pillar and put on a shield and his famous helmet. He took also the two strong bronze-tipped spears which Telemachus had brought.

Now there was a certain door high up in the wall. This led to an alley outside. Odysseus warned the swineherd to guard this door, since there was only one approach. Agelaus had already thought of this and said to the others, "Friends, can't someone get through that door up there and raise the alarm? Then we can stop this slaughter."

But the goatherd Melanthius shook his head and said, "Not possible, Agelaus! One man can hold the fort there, for the doors are so narrow. Wait a minute. I'll bring you arms from the storeroom. I think I know where Odysseus and his son have stored the arms."

Then Melanthius went up through a secret way into the storeroom. He took out twelve shields and spears, and twelve helmets. He quickly carried them down and gave them to the suitors.

When Odysseus saw this, he was troubled, for the suitors were putting on the armor Melanthius had brought them. He turned to his son and said, "Telemachus, one of the women must be acting against us, or else it's Melanthius who's doing the job."

Word Power

reinforcements (rē´ in fôrs´ mənts) *n.* fighters and weapons added for a battle

Telemachus replied, "Father, it's all my fault. I left the storeroom open, and their spy has found it. Eumaeus, close the storeroom door. Find out whether one of the women is the traitor, or Melanthius."

As they spoke Melanthius went in for another batch of arms. This time Eumaeus spied him and said to Odysseus, "The man we suspected is going for another batch of arms. Shall I kill him myself, or bring him here so that you can avenge yourself?"

Odysseus replied, "Telemachus and I will keep off the attackers. You two go back and seize the traitor. Bind him hand and feet and throw him into the storeroom. Raise him up a bit on the rafters. Let him live a while longer."

They went into the storeroom and surprised Melanthius, seizing him as he was leaving with arms. They bound him and raised him off the ground. It was Eumaeus's turn to laugh.

"Well now, Melanthius, you can be watchman tonight. You'll see dawn at about the time you usually bring in all the best goats for the suitors' feasts."

They left him there, struggling in his bonds. Putting on arms themselves, they went to the assistance of Odysseus. Thus there were four of them ready to face the survivors, among them many courageous men.

At this moment Athena appeared in the likeness of Mentor, an old friend of Odysseus. Odysseus was glad to see her.

"Mentor," he cried, "help me in this fight. Remember me, an old friend who has often helped you."

Reading Skill

Summarize Reread the highlighted text. Summarize the action by completing each statement below.

Melanthius is helping the suitors by sneaking into a storeroom to _____

_____
Eumaeus discovers the traitor is _____

Odysseus tells Eumaeus to

_____

_____

_____

Background Info

Mentor is the trusted friend of Odysseus. Mentor served as the teacher of Telemachus, giving the boy good advice. Today a helpful adviser is often called a mentor.

Literary Element

Epic Hero Reread the highlighted text. Athena is troubled that Odysseus is not the man of action he was when he fought the Trojans. Odysseus is talking instead of doing what?

_____

_____

Comprehension Check

Reread the boxed text. Underline the reason why Athena doesn't help Odysseus and Telemachus at first.

As he said this, he guessed that this was really Athena in human form. The suitors meanwhile spoke threateningly. Agelaus said, "Mentor, don't let Odysseus persuade you to fight with him against us. If you do, we'll kill you along with the others. And we'll take revenge on your wife and children, too."

Athena was furious at the words. She turned to Odysseus scornfully and said, "Odysseus, you're no longer the man you once were when you fought the Trojans. Then you killed many heroes. Troy was taken at last through your wisdom. What has happened? Now you have returned here and you talk at the suitors instead of acting. Come, my old friends; stand here and watch me to see how Mentor can repay old favors."

She ended, but did not bring about victory at once. She wished further to test the courage of Odysseus and Telemachus. In the shape of a swallow she fluttered off to the rafters and perched there.

Agelaus urged the suitors on to the battle. The most courageous of those still living moved among the others, trying to boost their courage. Agelaus at last spoke to the group. "Friends, this man will weaken at last. See! Even Mentor has **deserted** him, and the four of them are left alone. Come. Don't all throw the spears at once. Six of us will throw first to try to wound Odysseus. The other men will be no concern if Odysseus is struck."

Six eagerly hurled their spears, but Athena turned them aside in their courses. They all struck elsewhere.

"Now, my friends," ordered Odysseus, "when I give the signal, throw your spears into the mass of suitors. They would now add our deaths to the list of their abuses."

Word Power

deserted (di zurt´ id) _v._ left someone alone in time of need or danger

212

All four threw their spears together. Each one found a mark. Four of the suitors toppled over. The rest of the suitors rushed into the back of the hall. Odysseus and his men dashed to retrieve the four spears they had just sent forth. Once again the suitors sent their spears, and once again Athena **intervened.** One spear grazed Telemachus' wrist and another slightly wounded Eumaeus. This was the only damage.

Odysseus Slaying the Suitors.

Literary Element

Epic Hero What do you see in the picture that shows you Odysseus is brave and courageous—an epic hero?

_____

_____

_____

_____

_____

_____

Word Power

intervened (in´ tər vēnd´) *v.* played a role in changing an event; interfered

Once more the four threw their deadly spears, and again four more suitors fell. The herdsman Philoetius took on Ctesippus. Standing over him, he boasted, "You foul braggart, this is your gift for the one you gave Odysseus when he came begging through the house."

Odysseus wounded another suitor in hand-to-hand combat, and Telemachus wounded a second. Then Athena caused the suitors to become panic-stricken. They rushed about aimlessly, like stampeding cattle.

The four attackers pounced upon the suitors as vultures swoop down upon flocks of birds. The suitors fell on all sides, and the ground was soaked with blood. Leiodes rushed to Odysseus and fell on his knees before him, praying, "Pity me, Odysseus. I haven't done anything wrong. I tried to keep the other suitors from acting shamelessly, but they did not obey me. I have done nothing; yet I am to die, too. There is no gratitude for good deeds."

But Odysseus was **ruthless.** "You'll not escape death."

He took a sword and struck Leiodes on the neck and cut off his head.

But the harpist, who had entertained the suitors through no choice of his own, did escape death. He decided to beg his life of Odysseus. Placing the harp on the ground, he fell on his knees before Odysseus.

"I pray that you'll honor me and pity me, Odysseus. If you kill me, a singer, your name will not be famous. God has inspired me with all kinds of songs, and I am able to sing to you as to a god. Do not kill me. Telemachus will swear that I came here against my will."

Telemachus heard him and said, "Don't kill this innocent man. We will save the messenger Medon, too, for he always cared for me as a child—that is, if he's still alive."

Comprehension Check

Which two men do Odysseus and Telemachus decide to save? Check the correct responses.

- ☐ Leiodes
- ☐ the harpist
- ☐ Medon

Word Power

ruthless (rōōth′ lis) *adj.* without pity or mercy; cruel

Medon heard him. He lay crouching under a seat. He rose at once and fell on his knees before Telemachus.

"O friend," he cried, "here I am. Don't let your father kill me in his rage at the suitors who have wasted his wealth."

Odysseus smiled and said, "Don't worry. My son has saved your life, so that you can be living proof that it's better to act honorably than evilly. Go on, now. Leave the hall and take the harpist with you. I still have some work to do."

The two rushed out, looking to right and left as they went, as if yet in fear of death. Odysseus combed the house to see if any of the men were still alive.

At last Odysseus addressed Telemachus.

"Son, call the nurse Eurycleia to me. I must tell her something."

Telemachus went to the door and called out, "Come here, old nurse. My father wants to speak to you."

Eurycleia hurried in, following Telemachus. She found Odysseus standing among the dead, spattered with blood. He looked like a lion that has devoured an ox. His chest and cheeks were covered with gore. When she saw the dead and all the blood, she began to raise a shout of praise, but Odysseus stopped her on the spot.

"Old woman," he said, "rejoice quietly. It is not holy to boast over the slain. The gods have brought these men low because they had no respect for anyone. Come now. Tell me the names of the disloyal women in the palace."

Eurycleia replied, "I'll tell you the truth. You have fifty women-servants in the palace. We have taught them all kinds of skills and handicrafts. Of these fifty, twelve have been disloyal, respecting neither me nor Penelope. Well, come now to the upstairs room. I'll tell your wife. Some god has helped her to sleep through all this."

Reading Skill

Visualize Reread the highlighted paragraph. Underline the simile in the paragraph that helps you picture Odysseus. (Remember, a simile is a comparison using the word *like*.)

English Coach

The prefix *dis-* can mean "the opposite of." The word *disloyal* means "not loyal." Write another word that begins with the prefix *dis-*.

_____

Comprehension Check

Reread the boxed text. Why are the twelve women considered disloyal?

_____

_____

_____

_____

_____

English Coach

To *fumigate* means "to make pure and clean by spreading smoke or fumes." *Fumigate* and *purify* are synonyms, words with similar meanings. What are some other words that mean the same thing as *fumigate* and *purify*?

_____

_____

_____

"Wait a moment," answered Odysseus. "Don't awaken her yet. Send the traitorous women servants to me first. Then clean up the banquet hall thoroughly with rags and sponges. When you have arranged everything neatly again, take the shameless women out into the courtyard and put them to death."

> After he had finished, the twelve disloyal women came in, mourning aloud and weeping. They helped with the gruesome job of taking out the bodies, though they had to be forced by Odysseus. After the work had been completed, the women were led into the courtyard and shut up in a narrow space.
>
> Telemachus addressed them.
>
> "I will not give a decent death to those women who have insulted my mother and associated with the suitors."

He hanged the women like birds in a net. They struggled a while and then were still. Then the herdsmen brought out Melanthius. They cut off his nostrils and ears and threw them to the dogs. They lopped off his hands and feet in their fury and left him there to die. Then they went back to Odysseus. He was giving directions to Eurycleia.

"Bring sulphur and fumigate the palace. Then tell Penelope to come here with all the servants."

"I'll do that," replied Eurycleia. "First, though, let me get you a new change of clothes. You shouldn't be seen now in rags."

Odysseus answered, "First start the fires in the palace."

Eurycleia obeyed. After the halls were cleansed, the faithful women-servants came in and greeted Odysseus happily. He wept with joy to see them all.

The next day, Odysseus is reunited with his father, Laertes, as news of the death of the suitors passes through town. Families go to Odysseus's manor to gather the bodies for burial. There, Antinous's father rallies the families to avenge the deaths of their sons and brothers. As battle begins, however, Athena appears and calls the island to peace.

Respond to Literature

The Odyssey

A Comprehension Check

Answer the following questions in the spaces provided.

1. Who helps Odysseus in his fight against the suitors?

   _____

   _____

2. Why are twelve women killed? _____

   _____

   _____

B Reading Skills

Complete the activities in the spaces provided.

1. **Summarize** Summarize how the goddess Athena helps Odysseus in his

   fight against the suitors. _____

   _____

   _____

   _____

2. **Visualize** Describe Odysseus at the end of the battle when Eurycleia, the
   old woman, comes to rejoice that he has won.

   _____

   _____

   _____

C Word Power

Complete each sentence below, using one of the words in the box.

slaughter	retrieving	reinforcements
deserted	intervened	ruthless

1. The police needed more help controlling the mob, so they called for _____.

2. When his helpers _____ him, Lester finished the job by himself.

3. The players began to threaten each other, but the coach quickly _____ to make sure no one would fight.

4. News reporters described the terrible _____ of men, women, and children during the war.

5. Everyone felt safer when the _____ killer was finally caught.

6. We were _____ dropped coins from the bottom of the pool.

D Literary Element: Epic Hero

The passage below comes from the part of *The Odyssey* you have just read. As you reread it, think about what the sentences reveal about Odysseus's qualities as an epic hero.

Eurycleia hurried in, following Telemachus.[1] She found Odysseus standing among the dead, spattered with blood.[2] He looked like a lion that has devoured an ox.[3] His chest and cheeks were covered with gore.[4] When she saw the dead and all the blood, she began to raise a shout of praise, but Odysseus stopped her on the spot.[5]

"Old woman," he said, "rejoice quietly.[6] It is not holy to boast over the slain.[7] The gods have brought these men low because they had no respect for anyone."[8]

1. What details in sentences 1–5 help you understand that Odysseus is the kind of hero who takes action when faced with a conflict? _____

_____

_____

_____

2. In sentences 6–8, what does Odysseus tell Eurycleia to stop doing? What does that show about his character? _____

_____

_____

_____

_____

E Play Dialogue

This part of *The Odyssey* ends with the victory of Odysseus over the suitors. Imagine that the news is spreading throughout Ithaca. What might people say to one another as they learn of their king's return? Complete the dialogue below with your ideas.

Ithacan 1: (excitedly) Have you heard the news? Our great king, Odysseus, has at last returned from Troy!

Ithacan 2: (amazed) It's been 20 years! How did he deal with all the suitors in his home?

Ithacan 1: He _____

_____

Ithacan 2: What about young Telemachus?

Ithacan 1: He helped his father _____

_____

Ithacan 3: (breathlessly) I just heard that the lives of

_____ and _____

were spared.

Ithacan 2: What do you think will happen to Odysseus now?

Ithacan 1: _____

Ithacan 3: _____

Assessment

Fill in the circle next to each correct answer.

1. Where is Odysseus's palace?
   - ○ A. Ithaca
   - ○ B. Troy
   - ○ C. Hades
   - ○ D. Italy

2. Who are the suitors?
   - ○ A. Telemachus, Eumaeus, Eurycleia, and others
   - ○ B. men who have taken over the palace of Odysseus
   - ○ C. men who fought in Troy but returned to Ithaca before Odysseus
   - ○ D. Athena and Penelope

3. Which of these sentences belongs in the **beginning** of a summary of this part of *The Odyssey*?
   - ○ A. Telemachus forgets to close the door of the storeroom that holds weapons.
   - ○ B. Odysseus lets the harpist go free.
   - ○ C. The suitors do not recognize Odysseus because he is dressed as a beggar.
   - ○ D. Melanthius, the goatherd, is a traitor.

4. Which of these descriptions best fits Odysseus in this part of his story?
   - ○ A. a man who changes his mind easily
   - ○ B. a man who is deeply troubled
   - ○ C. a man who talks his way out of trouble
   - ○ D. a man of action

5. Which of the following words means "cruel"?
   - ○ A. ruthless
   - ○ B. reinforcements
   - ○ C. slaughter
   - ○ D. retrieving

UNIT 5 Nonfiction

What's Nonfiction?

You've heard people say, "This is true. I'm not making it up." That comment reminds us just how remarkable real life is. The world we live in provides lots of great stories—stories that are moving, exciting, sometimes unbelievable. No wonder authors use their writing skills to tell life's true stories. We call such writing nonfiction.

Nonfiction is writing that is "not fiction." It is about real events or situations. There are many kinds of nonfiction. Biographies, autobiographies, memoirs, and essays are popular forms of this kind of writing.

A **biography** is an account of a person's life written by someone other than the subject. An **autobiography** is the story of a person's life written by that person. A **memoir** is a story of the narrator's personal experience. An **essay** is a short piece of writing that communicates an idea or an opinion.

Some nonfiction tells about the lives of well-known people. **Put a check beside each kind of person you enjoy reading or hearing true stories about.**

_____ athletes	_____ artists
_____ rulers	_____ explorers
_____ military leaders	_____ scientists

Why Read Nonfiction?

Are you interested in space flight? What about a history of pro basketball, ancient Rome, or a journey across the arctic tundra? If it's a part of life, chances are you can read nonfiction about it.

How Do I Read Nonfiction?

Focus on key **literary elements** and **reading skills** to get the most out of reading the nonfiction in this unit. Here are two key literary elements and two key reading skills that you will practice in this unit.

Key Literary Elements

• Author's Purpose

The **author's purpose** is his or her reason for writing. An author's purpose can be to inform, to persuade, or to entertain—or a combination of these things. An author may want to capture the emotion and significance of a personal event. An author who wants to tell about a world event might want to educate the public, build support for a cause, honor a group of people, or simply tell a story.

• Autobiography

In an **autobiography,** a writer tells his or her life story from the first-person point of view, using the pronoun *I.* Writers create autobiographies to share memories of events, people, and feelings that are important to them. The incident may have happened in the past, when the author was a child, or it may be a recent event. Some autobiographies can also give readers an idea of what society was like during the author's lifetime.

Key Reading Skills

• Draw Conclusions

When you **draw conclusions,** you use clues in a story to gather evidence and make a general statement about characters and events. You can draw conclusions about characters by noting how they are described, what they say and do, and how other characters respond to them.

• Evaluate

To **evaluate** is to form opinions and make judgments about the story while you are reading. A writer may not always be right. Evaluate what you read by asking yourself questions: Are the events believable or unrealistic? How would I judge this character's thoughts and actions? You can also evaluate the writing. Is it interesting? Does the story hold your attention? Evaluate whether the message of a literary work makes sense.

Get Ready to Read!

Field Trip

Meet
Naomi Shihab Nye

Naomi Shihab Nye (shiˊhäb
nīˊ) is Palestinian American. She
was born in 1952 and spent most
of her childhood in St. Louis,
Missouri. Then she and her
family moved to Jerusalem. She
later attended high school in
Jordan before her family moved
back to the United States. She is
a poet, a teacher, and an essayist.
She says her inspiration has
always been "local life"—the
voices of friends, neighbors, and
people she meets on the street.

What You Know

When have you experienced an event that turned out differently
than you expected? Write a journal entry about an experience
that stands out in your mind. Explain why it was so different from
what you expected.

Reason to Read

Read to learn about the author's memories of a field trip that
turned out differently than she expected.

Background Info

"Field Trip" is a personal essay. The author recalls a field trip to
a commercial print shop where business cards, stationery, books,
and other printed products are made. One of the machines in a
print shop is an electric paper cutter that can cut through more
than 500 sheets of paper at one time with its razor-sharp blade.

Word Power

severance (sev′ ər əns) *n.* the act of cutting off or apart; p. 226
John had to cut the wires very carefully, because the *severance* could cause an electrical shock.

tediously (tē′ dē əs lē) *adv.* in a bored way; in a boring and tiresome way; p. 226
The kitchen workers yawned as the cook *tediously* explained how to wash dishes properly.

excruciating (iks kroo′ shē ā′ting) *adj.* extremely painful; p. 228
The woman had an *excruciating* toothache and hurried to the dentist.

mortality (môr tal′ ə tē) *n.* the condition of being sure to die; p. 229
Danger forces people to think about their own *mortality* and wonder whether they will survive.

parched (pärcht) *adj.* extremely dry; p. 229
Farmers hoped that the rain would save their *parched* crops.

consoling (kən sō′ ling) *v.* comforting or cheering someone who is sad or hurt; p. 230
The coach was *consoling* the players after the loss, telling them that they would surely win the next game.

**Answer the following questions, using one of the new words above.
Write your answers in the spaces provided.**

1. Which word goes with "great pain"? _____

2. Which word goes with "certainty of eventual death"? _____

3. Which word goes with "uninterestingly"? _____

4. Which word goes with "making someone feel better"? _____

5. Which word goes with "very thirsty"? _____

6. Which word goes with "the act of cutting apart"? _____

Field Trip

Adapted from

Naomi Shihab Nye

Only once did I ever take a large group of children on a field trip. I took a creative writing workshop to a printing office to see how pages were bound together to make books, and our cheerfully patient guide chopped her finger off with a giant paper cutter.

I had not prepared the children for experiences beyond typeface, camera-ready copy, collation. Standing toward the back like a shepherd, I felt their happy little backs stiffen at the moment of **severance.** A collective gasp rose from their throats as a blot of blood grew outward in a rapid pool, staining all the pages. Cupping her wounded hand against her chest, the woman pressed through the crowd, not screaming, but mouthing silently, "Hospital. Now. Let's go."

The children stood motionless, suspended. The motion of the workers was like the flurry of feathers and wings when anyone steps too quickly into a chicken coop. People dialed, then asked one another why they were dialing. Couldn't they drive her to the hospital themselves? Someone at the emergency room said to place the severed finger on ice, and a man who, moments before, had been **tediously** pasting up layouts ran for ice.

One boy tugged my shirt and croaked, "The last thing she said was—you have to be very careful with this machine."

Word Power

severance (sev´ ər əns) *n.* the act of cutting off or apart
tediously (tē´ dē əs lē) *adv.* in a bored way; in a boring and tiresome way

226

Someone dropped a ring of keys, and I immediately crawled around on the floor, reaching under a desk for them. It felt good to fall to my knees. For a second the stricken woman loomed above me, and I stuttered, apologizing for having distracted her from business, but she was distracted by something else.

"Honey, look at that thing!" she said, staring into the cup of ice where the index finger now rested like a rare specimen. "It's turning white! If that finger stays white, I don't want it on my body!"

We laughed long and hard and straight, and the children stared, amazed. Had we lost our senses? That she could joke at such a moment, as the big fans whirred and the collating machines paused over vast mountains of stacked paper . . . I wanted to sing her blackness, the sweet twist of her joy, to call out to those boys and girls, "This, my friends, is what words can do for you—make you laugh when your finger rests in a plastic cup!"

But she went quickly off into the day, and I shuffled an extremely silent group of budding writers back onto our bus. I wanted to say something promising recovery, or praising our guide's remarkable presence of mind, but my voice seemed lost among the seats. No one would look at me.

Later I heard how they went home and went straight to their rooms. Some had nightmares. A mother called my assistant to say, "What in the world happened on that field trip? Sarah came over today, and she and Molly climbed up on the bed and just sobbed."

At our next meeting we forgot poetry and made get-well cards. Or come-together-again cards. May the seam hold. May the two become one. They thought up all kinds of things. I had been calling the printing office to monitor her progress, and the reports sounded good. The students had been gathering stories: someone's farmer-uncle whose leg was severed in a cornfield but who lived to see it joined; someone's brother's toe.

Reading Skill

Evaluate As you read, evaluate—or form an opinion about—people and events.

Reread the text highlighted in green. What is your opinion about the woman's reaction to losing her finger?

_____

_____

_____

_____

_____

Literary Element

Author's Purpose Reread the text highlighted in blue. Think about the way the author tells this story and the details she includes. What do you think the author's purpose might be in writing this personal essay? Check the responses that apply.

☐ to entertain
☐ to persuade
☐ to express sympathy

Paler means "to become more pale." The suffix *-er* means "more than." Which word would you use to describe a movie that was "more scary" than another movie? Check the correct response.

☐ scared
☐ scarier
☐ scaring

I went to her home with a bundle of hopeful wishes tied in loops of pink ribbon. She was wearing a terry-cloth bathrobe and sitting in a comfortable chair, her hand hugely bandaged.

She shook her head. "I guess none of those cute kids will ever become printers now, will they? Gee, I hope they don't stop reading and writing! And to think of it happening in front of such an interested audience! Oh, I feel just terrible about it."

Reading their messages made her chuckle. I asked what the doctors had said about the finger turning black again. She said they thought it would, but it might be slightly paler than the rest of her hand. And it would be stiff, for a long time, maybe forever.

She missed being at work; vacations weren't much fun when they came this unexpectedly. The pain had been **excruciating** at first but was easing now, and wasn't modern medicine incredible, and would I please thank those kids for their flowers and hearts!

Describe the most exciting field trip you've taken.

Word Power
excruciating (iks krōō′ shē ā′ ting) *adj.* extremely painful

Once I'd dreamed of visiting every factory in town, the mattress factory, the hot sauce factory, the assembly line for cowboy boots, but I changed my mind. Now I took my workshops out onto the schoolyard, but no farther. I made them look for buttons and feathers, I made them describe the ways men and women stood as they waited for a bus.

By the time our workshops ended that summer, we felt more deeply bonded than other groups I'd known. Maybe our sense of **mortality** linked us, our shared vision of the fragility of body parts. One girl went on to become one of the best young writers in the city. I'd like to think her hands were blessed by our unexpected obsession with hands.

I continued to think about field trips in general. In San Antonio, school children are taken to the Hall of Horns, where exotic stuffed birds and beasts and fish stare back at them from glass habitats. They visit missions, where the Indians' mounded bread ovens still rise from **parched** grass. And they wander the Alamo, where David Crockett's fork and fringed vest continue to reside. Here, we say, for your information, soak it up. See what you can learn.

Did You Know?
David (Davy) Crockett was an American frontiersman who became a folk hero.
. . . .

It was not always predictable. At the state mental hospital, my high school health teacher unknowingly herded us into a room of elderly women who'd recently had lobotomies, just after telling us doctors didn't do that to people anymore.

Word Power
mortality (môr tal´ ə tē) *n.* the condition of being sure to die
parched (pärcht) *adj.* extremely dry

Reading Skill

Draw Conclusions
Reread the text highlighted in green. What conclusion can you draw about why the author goes camping even though she is afraid of spiders?

_____

_____

_____

_____

Literary Element

Author's Purpose Reread the text highlighted in blue and think about the message. What is the author's main purpose for writing this essay? Check the correct response.

☐ to inform readers that sometimes life takes unexpected turns

☐ to persuade readers to take field trips

☐ to give information about field trips

On the day Robert Kennedy was shot we found ourselves, numbed, staring at vats of creamy chocolate brew at the Judson Candy Factory. The air hung thick around us. It didn't make much sense to consider all that work for something that wasn't even good for you. A worker joked that a few of his friends had ended up in those vats, and no one smiled.

As a child I finally grew brave enough to plot a camping trip years after my friends had first done it—to Camp Fiddlecreek for Girl Scouts. I'd postponed such an adventure because of a profound and unreasonable fear of spiders. I felt certain a giant spider would crawl into my bedroll and entangle itself in my hair the moment I got there. The zipper on the sleeping bag would stick, and I would die, die, die. Luckily I finally decided a life without courage might be worse than death, so I packed my greenest duds and headed to the hills.

The first night I confided my secret fear to the girl who slept next to me. She said she'd always been more scared of snakes than spiders. I said, "Snakes, phooey!"

The next day while we were hiking, a group of donkeys broke out of a nearby field, ran at us, knocked me down, and trampled me. My leg swelled with three large, hard lumps. I could not walk. I would have to be driven back to the city for X rays. My friend leaned over my bruised face, smoothing back my bangs and **consoling** me. "Donkeys! Can you believe it? Who could ever dream a donkey would be so mean?"

So began a lifetime of small discoveries linked by a common theme: the things we worry about are never the things that happen. And the things that happen are the things we never could have dreamed.

Word Power

consoling (kən sō′ ling) *v.* comforting or cheering someone who is sad or hurt

Field Trip

A Comprehension Check

Answer the following questions in the spaces provided.

1. What happens to the students' guide at the print shop?

   _____

   _____

2. What unexpected event does the author recall from her first camping trip?

   _____

   _____

B Reading Skills

Answer the following questions in the spaces provided.

1. **Draw Conclusions** What can you tell about the injured woman from the

   way she reacts to her accident? _____

   _____

   _____

   _____

2. **Evaluate** The author mentions other field trips. Do you think that field trips are an important or necessary part of education? Explain.

   _____

   _____

   _____

C Word Power

Complete each sentence below, using one of the words in the box.

severance	tediously	excruciating
mortality	parched	consoling

1. No rain fell for weeks, and the ground was _____ as a result.

2. I have been _____ my friend, whose grandmother just died.

3. Janine spent the morning _____ washing the stairs.

4. No one lives forever, so we must all face our _____.

5. At first the pain was mild, but an hour later it was _____.

6. We had to leave our dog with the vet, and the sudden _____ from our family made him howl all night.

D Literary Element: Author's Purpose

Read the passage below from "Field Trip." As you read, think about the author's purposes for writing the essay. Then answer the questions that follow.

As a child I finally grew brave enough to plot a camping trip years after my friends had first done it—to Camp Fiddlecreek for Girl Scouts.[1] I'd postponed such an adventure because of a profound and unreasonable fear of spiders.[2] I felt certain a giant spider would crawl into my bedroll and entangle itself in my hair the moment I got there.[3] The zipper on the sleeping bag would stick, and I would die, die, die.[4] Luckily I finally decided a life without courage might be worse than death, so I packed my greenest duds and headed to the hills.[5]

1. How do sentences 1–4 show that the author wants to entertain her readers? _____

_____

_____

_____

2. What important lesson about life is the author trying to teach in sentence 5? _____

_____

_____

_____

E Thank-You Note

The woman from the printing office receives many get-well cards from the author's students. She asks the author to "please thank those kids for their flowers and hearts!" Imagine that you are the woman writing a thank-you note to the kids. Fill in the missing parts of her note below with your ideas.

Dear Students,

    I am recovering nicely here at home. I enjoyed reading your good wishes. Many of you wanted to know how I felt when _____

_____

But I feel much better now! And you'll be pleased to know that _____

_____

The lesson I have learned is _____

_____

    I am sorry you had to see my accident! I know it must have been upsetting. But I hope you _____

_____

    Thank you again for your kind thoughts!

Sincerely yours,

_____

Assessment

Fill in the circle next to each correct answer.

1. The woman at the printing office says, "If that finger stays white, I don't want it on my body!" Why does she say that?
   - ○ A. She is holding her wounded hand to her body.
   - ○ B. She is confused.
   - ○ C. She is making a joke.
   - ○ D. She knows that her finger has been chopped off.

2. What happens to the woman at the hospital?
   - ○ A. Her index finger is put in a cup of ice.
   - ○ B. She waits four hours in the emergency waiting room.
   - ○ C. Her finger swells and turns black.
   - ○ D. Doctors reattach her finger to her hand.

3. What conclusion can you draw about why the author decides to go camping even though she is afraid of spiders?
   - ○ A. She wants to wear her greenest duds.
   - ○ B. She wants to hike and ride the donkeys.
   - ○ C. She decides that a life full of fear is worse than death.
   - ○ D. She wants to be with others in the Girl Scout troop.

4. At the end of the essay, the author states a lesson that she wants people to learn. What lesson does the author want us to learn?
   - ○ A. Always have a plan.
   - ○ B. Life is not predictable.
   - ○ C. Accidents can be avoided.
   - ○ D. Everyone has fears.

5. Which of the following words means "giving comfort"?
   - ○ A. consoling
   - ○ B. excruciating
   - ○ C. parched
   - ○ D. tediously

Get Ready to Read!

ONLY DAUGHTER

Meet Sandra Cisneros

Sandra Cisneros (sis nā´rōs) was born in Chicago, Illinois in 1954. She grew up in a Mexican American family. She says that her background has given her "two ways of looking at the world" and "twice as many words to pick from." Although Cisneros uses Spanish words in her fiction and poetry, she writes mainly in English. She tells stories about people like those she grew up with—"poor families, brown families," she has said.

What You Know

Does being the only daughter or son in a big family affect who a person is? Do you think that being the oldest, middle, or youngest child affects who a person is? Why?

Reason to Read

Read this essay to find out how being an only daughter has affected the author.

Background Info

"Only Daughter" is a personal essay in which the author recalls growing up in Chicago, Illinois. She also describes a visit to her parents the year before she wrote this essay.

Spanish words and expressions are in the essay, and the author explains the meanings of most of them. In Spanish, the word *hijo* (ē´hō) means "son," and *hija* (ē´hä) means "daughter." The plural noun *hijos* means "sons," but it also means "sons and daughters" or "children." When the father in the story talks directly to his daughter, he uses a shortened phrase meaning "my daughter": *mi´ja* (mē´hä).

Word Power

anthology (an thol´ə jē) *n.* a collection of poems, stories, or other writing, in a single book; p. 238
Every night, Carlos reads a story from an *anthology* of horror stories.

retrospect (ret´rə spekt´) *n.* the act of looking back or thinking about the past; p. 239
Jackson faced hardships growing up, but in *retrospect*, he says his childhood was happy.

philandering (fi lan´dər ing) *adj.* carrying on a love affair with someone who is not one's spouse; p. 239
No woman is pleased with a *philandering* husband.

nostalgia (nos tal´jə) *n.* a sentimental longing for the past; p. 240
Looking through the old family photo album, Aunt Miranda sighed with *nostalgia*.

investment (in vest´mənt) *n.* spending in the present for a gain in the future; p. 241
Learning requires an *investment* of time and effort.

leisure (lē´zhər) *n.* free time that is not spent doing a job or other work; p. 242
Connie's job gave her no time for *leisure*, but she hoped someday to take piano lessons.

horizontally (hôr´ə zon´tə lē) *adv.* in a position that is parallel to the horizon; p. 242
When you lie down, you place yourself *horizontally*.

**Answer the following questions, using one of the new words above.
Write your answers in the spaces provided.**

1. Which word goes with "lying and cheating"? _____

2. Which word goes with "memories"? _____

3. Which word goes with "a collection of literature"? _____

4. Which word goes with "free time"? _____

5. Which word goes with "buying now for a profit later"? _____

6. Which word goes with "a view of the past"? _____

7. Which word goes with "along the line of the horizon"? _____

ONLY DAUGHTER

Sandra Cisneros

Once, several years ago, when I was just starting out my writing career, I was asked to write my own contributor's note for an **anthology** I was part of. I wrote: "I am the only daughter in a family of six sons. *That* explains everything."

Well, I've thought about that ever since, and yes, it explains a lot to me, but for the reader's sake I should have written: "I am the only daughter in a Mexican family of six sons." Or even: "I am the only daughter of a Mexican father and a Mexican-American mother." Or: "I am the only daughter of a working-class family of nine." All of these had everything to do with who I am today.

I was/am the only daughter and *only* a daughter. Being an only daughter in a family of six sons forced me by circumstance to spend a lot of time by myself because my brothers felt it beneath them to play with a girl in public. But that aloneness, that loneliness, was good for a would-be writer—it allowed me time to think and think, to imagine, to read and prepare myself.

Word Power

anthology (an thol′ə jē) *n.* a collection of poems, stories, or other writing, in a single book

Being only a daughter for my father meant my destiny would lead me to become someone's wife. That's what he believed. But when I was in the fifth grade and shared my plans for college with him, I was sure he understood. I remember my father saying, "*Qué bueno, mi'ja*, that's good." That meant a lot to me, especially since my brothers thought the idea hilarious. What I didn't realize was that my father thought college was good for girls—good for finding a husband. After four years in college and two more in graduate school, and still no husband, my father shakes his head even now and says I wasted all that education.

In **retrospect,** I'm lucky my father believed daughters were meant for husbands. It meant it didn't matter if I majored in something silly like English. After all, I'd find a nice professional eventually, right? This allowed me the liberty to putter about embroidering my little poems and stories without my father interrupting with so much as a "What's that you're writing?"

But the truth is, I wanted him to interrupt. I wanted my father to understand what it was I was scribbling, to introduce me as "My only daughter, the writer." Not as "This is only my daughter. She teaches." *Es maestra*—teacher. Not even *profesora*.

In a sense, everything I have ever written has been for him, to win his approval even though I know my father can't read English words, even though my father's only reading includes the brown-ink *Esto* sports magazines from Mexico City and the bloody *¡Alarma!* magazines that feature yet another sighting of *La Virgen de Guadalupe* on a tortilla or a wife's revenge on her **philandering** husband by bashing his skull in with a *molcajete* (a kitchen mortar made of volcanic rock). Or the *fotonovelas*, the little picture paperbacks with tragedy and trauma erupting from the characters' mouths in bubbles.

Word Power

retrospect (ret´rə spekt´) *n.* the act of looking back or thinking about the past

philandering (fi lan´dər ing) *adj.* carrying on a love affair with someone who is not one's spouse

Reading Skill

Evaluate Reread the sentence highlighted in green. Do you think that studying English in college is silly? Explain.

_____

_____

_____

_____

Literary Element

Author's Purpose Reread the text highlighted in blue. What is one purpose that the author has for writing stories?

_____

_____

_____

My father represents, then, the public majority. A public who is disinterested in reading, and yet one whom I am writing about and for, and privately trying to woo.

When we were growing up in Chicago, we moved a lot because of my father. He suffered bouts of **nostalgia.** Then we'd have to let go our flat, store the furniture with mother's relatives, load the station wagon with baggage and bologna sandwiches and head south. To Mexico City.

We came back, of course. To yet another Chicago flat, another Chicago neighborhood, another Catholic school. Each time, my father would seek out the parish priest in order to get a tuition break, and complain or boast: "I have seven sons."

He meant *siete hijos,* seven children, but he translated it as "sons." "I have seven sons." To anyone who would listen. The Sears Roebuck employee who sold us the washing machine. The short-order cook where my father ate his ham-and-eggs breakfasts. "I have seven sons." As if he deserved a medal from the state.

Woman in Cordilleran Night, 1996. Maria Eugenia Terrazas. Watercolor, 70 x 70 cm. Kactus Foto, Santiago, Chile.

How does the woman in this painting represent the author?

_____

Reading Skill
Draw Conclusions
Reread the highlighted paragraph. What conclusion can you draw about why the father tell everyone that he has seven sons?

_____

_____

_____

_____

_____

Word Power
nostalgia (nos tal´jə) *n.* a sentimental longing for the past

My papa. He didn't mean anything by that mistranslation, I'm sure. But somehow I could feel myself being erased. I'd tug my father's sleeve and whisper: "Not seven sons. Six! and *one daughter*."

When my oldest brother graduated from medical school, he fulfilled my father's dream that we study hard and use this—our heads, instead of this—our hands. Even now my father's hands are thick and yellow, stubbed by a history of hammer and nails and twine and coils and springs. "Use this," my father said, tapping his head, "and not this," showing us those hands. He always looked tired when he said it.

Wasn't college an **investment**? And hadn't I spent all those years in college? And if I didn't marry, what was it all for? Why would anyone go to college and then choose to be poor? Especially someone who had always been poor.

Last year, after ten years of writing professionally, the financial rewards started to trickle in. My second National Endowment for the Arts Fellowship. A guest professorship at the University of California, Berkeley. My book, which sold to a major New York publishing house.

At Christmas, I flew home to Chicago. The house was throbbing, same as always: hot *tamales* and sweet *tamales* hissing in my mother's pressure cooker, and everybody—my mother, six brothers, wives, babies, aunts, cousins—talking too loud and at the same time, like in a Fellini film, because that's just how we are.

Did You Know?

Tamales (tä mä´lēs) are a Mexican dish made of highly seasoned ground meat that is rolled in cornmeal dough, wrapped in corn husks, and steamed.

Reading Skill
Draw Conclusions
Reread the highlighted sentence. What conclusion can you draw about how much money the author is earning as a writer?

_____

_____

_____

Word Power

investment (in vest´mənt) *n.* spending in the present for a gain in the future

Background Info

Movies with Pedro Infante (in fän´tā), a Mexican movie star, were shown on a Spanish-language cable-TV channel called Galavision.

Literary Element

Author's Purpose Reread the highlighted sentences. What is the author's purpose in writing about this wonderful event? Check the **best** response.

☐ to persuade readers of the importance of family

☐ to give information about being a writer

☐ to describe how great it feels to have a father's approval

I went upstairs to my father's room. One of my stories had just been translated into Spanish and published in an anthology of Chicano writing, and I wanted to show it to him. Ever since he recovered from a stroke two years ago, my father likes to spend his **leisure** hours **horizontally.** And that's how I found him, watching a Pedro Infante movie on Galavision and eating rice pudding.

There was a glass filmed with milk on the bedside table. There were several vials of pills and balled Kleenex. And on the floor, one black sock and a plastic urinal that I didn't want to look at but looked at anyway. Pedro Infante was about to burst into song, and my father was laughing.

I'm not sure if it was because my story was translated into Spanish, or because it was published in Mexico, or perhaps because the story dealt with Tepeyac, the *colonia* my father was raised in and the house he grew up in, but at any rate, my father punched the mute button on his remote control and read my story.

I sat on the bed next to my father and waited. He read it very slowly. As if he were reading each line over and over. He laughed at all the right places and read lines he liked out loud. He pointed and asked questions: "Is this So-and-so?" "Yes," I said. He kept reading.

When he was finally finished, after what seemed like hours, my father looked up and asked: "Where can we get more copies of this for the relatives?"

Of all the wonderful things that happened to me last year, that was the most wonderful.

Word Power

leisure (lē´zhər) *n.* free time that is not spent doing a job or other work
horizontally (hôr´ə zon´tə lē) *adv.* in a position that is parallel to the horizon

Respond to Literature

ONLY DAUGHTER

A Comprehension Check

Complete the following activities in the spaces provided.

1. Describe Sandra Cisneros's family. _____

_____

_____

2. When the author visits her father at Christmas, what does she give him to
   read? How does he react? _____

_____

_____

B Reading Skills

Answer the following questions in the spaces provided.

1. **Draw Conclusions** The author comes from a large family, but this essay is
   mostly about her father. Why does she focus on her father?

_____

_____

_____

2. **Evaluate** Do you think going to college to study English was a good
   "investment" for Sandra Cisneros, even though she didn't find a husband?

_____

_____

_____

C Word Power

Complete each sentence below, using one of the words in the box.

anthology	retrospect	philandering	nostalgia
investment	leisure	horizontally	

1. Thelma enjoys golf, tennis, bowling, and other _____ activities.

2. Mr. Liu often has a feeling of _____ for his childhood in China.

3. The Woodsons want to buy a house because they think it is the best _____ a family can make.

4. The _____ is titled *All Year Long,* and the poems in it are about the seasons.

5. The movie shows how a husband gets even with his _____ wife.

6. Place each shelf _____ in the bookcase.

7. Thomas hated moving away from the city, but now, in _____, he is glad he left.

D Literary Element: Author's Purpose

Reread the passage below from "Only Daughter." As you read, think about the author's purpose for writing and answer the questions that follow.

> But when I was in the fifth grade and shared my plans for college with him, I was sure he understood.[1] I remember my father saying, "*Qué bueno, mi'ja,* that's good."[2] That meant a lot to me, especially since my brothers thought the idea hilarious.[3] What I didn't realize was that my father thought college was good for girls—good for finding a husband.[4] After four years in college and two more in graduate school, and still no husband, my father shakes his head even now and says I wasted all that education.[5]

1. In sentences 1–3, how does Sandra Cisneros show that it is important for her to go to college? _____

   _____

   _____

   _____

2. How do sentences 4–5 show that her father's views are different from her own? _____

   _____

   _____

E A Letter to Sandra Cisneros

Write a letter to Sandra Cisneros. Tell her what you liked about her essay "Only Daughter." Then tell her something about your own experiences in your family and share some of your dreams for the future. If you do not feel comfortable writing about your own family, write about a pretend family.

Dear Ms. Cisneros,

   I read your essay "Only Daughter," and I thought it
was _____ I especially liked the part
about _____

_____

   You said that you gained a lot by being the only
daughter. For example, you said that you _____

_____

In my family, I am _____ I think that my
experience as the _____ child in my family
will help me too. My family has helped me _____

_____

   When I grow up, I want to be a _____
I hope that when I _____

_____ my family
will be as proud of me as your father was of you.

Sincerely,

_____

Assessment

Fill in the circle next to each correct answer.

1. How many brothers does the author have?
   - ○ A. four
   - ○ B. five
   - ○ C. six
   - ○ D. seven

2. Based on details from the essay, which statement could you make about the author?
   - ○ A. She thinks her family is too noisy.
   - ○ B. She loves her visits to Mexico City.
   - ○ C. College was not what she hoped it would be.
   - ○ D. Her father's approval makes her happy.

3. At the start of the essay, the author sets out to
   - ○ A. describe her family members in detail so that readers get to know them all.
   - ○ B. persuade readers that a college education is valuable.
   - ○ C. explain why being an only daughter has made her who she is.
   - ○ D. inform readers about a culture they may not know well.

4. In this essay, the author is
   - ○ A. a writer and a college professor.
   - ○ B. a mother and wife.
   - ○ C. a student in high school.
   - ○ D. a publisher of Spanish books.

5. Which of the following words means a collection of writings?
   - ○ A. retrospect
   - ○ B. anthology
   - ○ C. investment
   - ○ D. horizontally

Get Ready to Read!

Of Dry Goods and Black Bow Ties

What You Know

In your opinion, what does it mean to be successful? What accomplishments, personal traits, or possessions might make one a successful person?

Reason to Read

Read to learn how a Japanese man met with success—and failure—after immigrating to the United States.

Background Info

The events in this essay take place in the late 1800s and the first half of the 1900s. In the United States, the Great Depression began in 1929. It was a period of severe economic hardship. Banks failed and businesses closed. Many people lost their jobs and struggled to feed their families. The Great Depression ended after the United States entered World War II in 1941. During the war, thousands of new jobs became available in factories that made war materials.

Meet Yoshiko Uchida

Yoshiko Uchida (yō shē´ kō ōō chē´ dä) was born and raised in California. Uchida became an award-winning author of twenty-eight books. She said she hoped her books would inspire readers not only to appreciate Asian American life and history, but above all, to "celebrate our common humanity." Uchida was born in 1921 and died in 1992. This essay, based on her own life, was first published in 1979.

Word Power

elated (i lā´ tid) *adj.* filled with joy; p. 251
I was *elated* when I got the lead part in the school play.

imposing (im pō´ zing) *adj.* impressive in appearance or manner; p. 254
King Kong was *imposing,* standing over three stories tall.

exhilarated (ig zil´ ə rāt´ id) *adj.* cheerful, lively, or excited; refreshed; p. 255
I was *exhilarated* when I found out our family was taking a camping trip.

collateral (kə lat´ər əl) *n.* money or property that is given to a lender as a pledge
that a loan will be repaid; p. 255
When I lent my friend money, he gave me his video game as *collateral.*

eloquence (el´ ə kwəns) *n.* an expressive or strong way of speaking; p. 257
If you want to make the debate team, you must learn to speak with *eloquence.*

**Answer the following questions that contain the new words above.
Write your answers in the spaces provided.**

1. If you are feeling *exhilarated,* are you excited or bored? _____

2. If something is *imposing,* is it remarkable or dull? _____

3. If you give someone *collateral,* are you likely or unlikely to repay the loan?

   _____

4. If you are *elated,* are you miserable or extremely happy? _____

5. If someone speaks with *eloquence,* does he or she speak well or poorly?

   _____

Adapted from

Of Dry Goods and Black Bow Ties

Yoshiko Uchida

Background Info

A four-in-hand tie is a man's necktie that is tied in a slip knot with the ends hanging down vertically.

Long after reaching the age of sixty, when my father was persuaded at last to wear a conservative four-in-hand tie, it was not because of his family's urging, but because Mr. Shimada (I shall call him that) had died. Until then, for some forty years, my father had always worn a plain black bow tie, a formality which was required on his first job in America and which he had continued to observe as faithfully as his father before him had worn his samurai sword.

Did You Know?

For centuries, the *Samurai* (sam′ oo rī′) were a class of fearsome warriors in Japan.

My father came to America in 1906 when he was not yet twenty-one. Sailing from Japan on a small six-thousand-ton ship which was buffeted all the way by rough seas, he landed in Seattle on a bleak January day. He revived himself with the first solid meal he had enjoyed in many days, and then allowed himself one day of rest to restore his sagging spirits. Early on the second morning, wearing a stiff new bowler, he went to see Mr. Shozo Shimada to whom he carried a letter of introduction.

Did You Know?
Bowler hats were worn in the nineteenth century by British gentlemen.
· · · · · · · · · · · · · · · · · · · ·

At that time, Shozo Shimada was Seattle's most successful Japanese business man. He owned a chain of dry goods stores which extended not only from Vancouver to Portland, but to cities in Japan as well. He had come to America in 1880, penniless but enterprising, and sought work as a laborer. It wasn't long, however, before he saw the futility of trying to compete with American laborers whose bodies were twice his in muscle and bulk. He knew he would never go far as a laborer, but he did possess another skill that could give him a start toward better things. He knew how to sew. It was a matter of expediency over masculine pride. He set aside his shovel, bought a second-hand sewing machine, and hung a dressmaker's sign in his window. He was in business.

In those days, there were some Japanese women in Seattle who had neither homes nor families nor sewing machines, and were delighted to find a friendly Japanese person to do some sewing for them. They flocked to Mr. Shimada with bolts of cloth, **elated** to discover a dressmaker who could speak their native tongue and, although a male, sew western-styled dresses for them.

Word Power
elated (i lā′ tid) *adj.* filled with joy

Literary Element

Author's Purpose Reread the highlighted paragraph. Why do you think the author gives such a detailed account of her father's journey to America? What is her purpose? Check the **best** response.

☐ to inform readers about what it is like to be an immigrant coming to America to start a new life

☐ to persuade readers not to move to a foreign country

☐ to entertain readers with funny details about the journey, such as the weather and her father's clothes

Comprehension Check

Reread the boxed text. Why does Mr. Shimada decide to leave his laboring job and become a dressmaker?

_____
_____
_____
_____
_____
_____
_____

English Coach

According to Japanese custom, the suffix *-san* is added after a person's name to express respect. In English, there are different titles (words used to address people) to express respect. Write at least two English titles of respect you know.

_____

_____

_____

_____

Background Info

Before supermarkets became widespread in the late 1940s and early 1950s, people bought fabric, clothing, and canned or packaged foods in dry goods stores.

Mr. Shimada acquainted himself with the fine points of turning a seam, fitting sleeves, and coping with the slippery folds of satin, and soon the women ordered enough dresses to keep him thriving and able to establish a healthy bank account. He became a trusted friend and confidant to many of them and soon they began to bring him what money they earned for safekeeping.

"Keep our money for us, Shimada-san," they urged, refusing to go to American banks whose tellers spoke in a language they could not understand.

At first the money accumulated slowly and Mr. Shimada used a pair of old socks as a repository, stuffing them into a far comer of his drawer beneath his union suits. But after a time, Mr. Shimada's private bank began to overflow and he soon found it necessary to replenish his supply of socks.

He went to a small dry goods store downtown, and as he glanced about at the buttons, threads, needles and laces, it occurred to him that he owed it to the women to invest their savings in a business venture with more future than the dark recesses of his bureau drawer. That night he called a group of them together.

"Think, ladies," he began. "What are the two basic needs of the Japanese living in Seattle? Clothes to wear and food to eat," he answered himself. "Is that not right? Every man must buy a shirt to put on his back and pickles and rice for his stomach."

The women marveled at Mr. Shimada's cleverness as he spread before them his fine plans for a Japanese dry goods store that would not only carry everything available in an American dry goods store, but Japanese foodstuff as well. That was the beginning of the first Shimada Dry Goods Store on State Street.

How might this 1903 dry goods store in Sacramento, California, compare with Mr. Shimada's store?

By the time my father appeared, Mr. Shimada had long since abandoned his sewing machine and was well on his way to becoming a business tycoon. Although he had opened cautiously with such stock items as ginghams, flannel, handkerchiefs, socks, shirts, overalls, umbrellas, and ladies' silk and cotton stockings, he now carried tins of salt, rice crackers, bottles of soy sauce, vinegar, ginger root, fish-paste cakes, bean paste, Japanese pickles, dried mushrooms, salt fish, red beans, and just about every item of canned food that could be shipped from Japan.

In addition, his was the first Japanese store to install a U.S. Post Office Station, and he therefore flew an American flag in front of the large sign that bore the name of his shop.

When my father first saw the big American flag fluttering in front of Mr. Shimada's shop, he was overcome with admiration and awe. He expected that Mr. Shozo Shimada would be the finest of Americanized Japanese gentlemen, and when he met him, he was not disappointed.

Reading Skill

Evaluate When you evaluate something, you make judgments or develop your own opinions about it. Reread the highlighted paragraph. Mr. Shimada set up a post office in his store. Do you think this was a good idea? Why?

_____

_____

_____

_____

_____

_____

Although Mr. Shimada was not very tall, he gave the illusion of height because of his erect carriage. He wore a spotless black alpaca suit, an immaculate white shirt, and a white collar so stiff it might have overcome a lesser man.

He also wore a black bow tie, black shoes that buttoned up the side and a gold watch whose thick chain looped grandly on his vest. He was probably in his fifties then, a ruddy-faced man whose hair, already turning white, was parted carefully in the center.

He was an **imposing** figure to confront a young man fresh from Japan with scarcely a future to look forward to. My father bowed, summoned as much dignity as he could muster, and presented the letter of introduction he carried to him.

Mr. Shimada was quick to sense his need. "Do you know anything about bookkeeping?" he inquired.

"I intend to go to night school to learn this very skill," my father answered.

Mr. Shimada could assess a man's qualities in a very few minutes. He looked my father straight in the eye and said, "Consider yourself hired." Then he added, "I have a few basic rules. My employees must at all times wear a clean white shirt and a black bow tie. They must answer the telephone promptly with the words, 'Good morning or good afternoon, Shimada's Dry Goods,' and they must always treat each customer with respect. It never hurts to be polite," he said thoughtfully. "One never knows when one might be indebted to even the lowliest of beggars."

My father was impressed with these modest words from a man of such success. He accepted them with a sense of mission and from that day was committed to white shirts and black bow ties, and treated every customer, no matter how humble, with respect and courtesy. When, in later years, he had his own home, he never failed to answer the phone before it could ring twice if at all possible.

Connect to the Text

Reread the boxed text. Think about a time when you met someone who impressed you. How did you feel? How did you act toward the person?

_____

_____

_____

_____

Reading Skill

Draw Conclusions

Reread the highlighted text. Think about Mr. Shimada's rules. What conclusions can you draw about Mr. Shimada's character?

_____

_____

_____

_____

_____

Word Power

imposing (im pō´ zing) *adj.* impressive in appearance or manner

My father worked with Mr. Shimada for ten years, becoming first the buyer for his Seattle store and later, manager of the Portland branch. During this time Mr. Shimada continued on a course of **exhilarated** expansion. He established two Japanese banks in Seattle, bought a fifteen-room house outside the dreary confines of the Japanese community and dressed his wife and daughter in velvets and ostrich feathers. When his daughter became eighteen, he sent her to study in Paris, and the party he gave on the eve of her departure, with musicians, as well as caterers to serve roast turkey, venison, baked ham and champagne, seemed to verify rumors that he had become one of the first Japanese millionaires of America.

In spite of his phenomenal success, however, Mr. Shimada never forgot his early friends nor lost any of his generosity, and this, ironically enough, was his undoing. Many of the women for whom he had once sewn dresses were now well established, and they came to him requesting loans with which they and their husbands might open grocery stores and laundries and shoe repair shops. Mr. Shimada helped them all and never demanded any **collateral.** He operated his banks on faith and trust and gave no thought to such common prudence as maintaining a reserve.

When my father was called to a new position with a large Japanese firm in San Francisco, Mr. Shimada came down to Portland to extend personally his good wishes. He took Father to a Chinese dinner and told him over the peanut duck and chow mein that he would like always to be considered a friend.

"If I can ever be of assistance to you," he said, "don't ever hesitate to call." And with a firm shake of the hand, he wished my father well.

English Coach
You may never have heard the word *expansion* before, but its base word is *expand*, which means "to grow in size." So, if there is an *expansion* of something, does it increase or decrease?

_____

Reading Skill
Evaluate Reread the highlighted paragraph. What is your opinion of Mr. Shimada's character? What is your opinion of the choices he makes in business?

_____
_____
_____
_____
_____
_____
_____

Word Power

exhilarated (ig zil´ ə rāt´ id) *adj.* cheerful, lively, or excited; refreshed
collateral (kə lat´ ər əl) *n.* money or property that is given to a lender as a pledge that a loan will be repaid

Literary Element

Author's Purpose Reread the highlighted paragraph. Why do you think the author includes so many details about what happens to Mr. Shimada in 1929, the year the Great Depression begins? Check the **best** response.

☐ She wants to inform readers about her father's success in San Francisco despite the Great Depression.

☐ She wants to show that Mr. Shimada was rude for not answering her father's letters.

☐ She wants to capture the emotion of the Great Depression by telling the story of a good man who fell on hard times.

That was in 1916. My father wrote regularly to Mr. Shimada telling him of his new job, of his bride, and later, of his two children. Mr. Shimada did not write often, but each Christmas he sent a box of Oregon apples and pears, and at New Year's a slab of heavy white rice paste from his Seattle shop.

In 1929 the letters and gifts stopped coming and Father learned from friends in Seattle that both of Mr. Shimada's banks had failed. He immediately dispatched a letter to Mr. Shimada, but it was returned unopened. The next news he had was that Mr. Shimada had had to sell all of his shops. My father was now manager of the San Francisco branch of his firm. He wrote once more asking Mr. Shimada if there was anything he could do to help. The letter did not come back, but there was no reply, and my father did not write again. After all, how do you offer help to the head of a fallen empire?

It seemed almost irreverent.

Did You Know?

A *morning coat* is a man's jacket for formal daytime wear, traditionally worn with striped trousers and a top hat.

It was many years later that Mr. Shimada appeared one night at our home in Berkeley. In the dim light of the front porch my mother was startled to see an elderly gentleman wearing striped pants, a morning coat and a shabby black hat. In his hand he carried a small black satchel. When she invited him inside, she saw that the morning coat was faded, and his shoes badly in need of a shine.

"I am Shimada," he announced with a courtly bow, and it was my mother who felt inadequate to the occasion. She hurriedly pulled off her apron and went to call my father. When he heard who was in the living room, he put on his coat and tie before going out to greet his old friend.

Mr. Shimada spoke to them about Father's friends in Seattle and about his daughter who was now married and living in Denver. He spoke of a typhoon that had recently swept over Japan, and he drank the tea my mother served and ate a piece of her chocolate cake. Only then did he open his black satchel.

"I thought your girls might enjoy these books," he said, as he drew out a brochure describing The Book of Knowledge.

"Fourteen volumes that will tell them of the wonders of this world." He spread his arms in a magnificent gesture that recalled his **eloquence** of the past. "I wish I could give them to your children as a personal gift," he added softly.

Without asking the price of the set, my father wrote a check for one hundred dollars and gave it to Mr. Shimada.

Mr. Shimada glanced at the check and said, "You have given me fifty dollars too much." He seemed troubled for only a moment, however, and quickly added, "Ah, the balance is for a deposit, is it? Very well, yours will be the first deposit in my next bank."

"Is your home still in Seattle then?" Father asked cautiously.

"I am living there, yes," Mr. Shimada answered.

And then, suddenly overcome with memories of the past, he spoke in a voice so low he could scarcely be heard.

"I paid back every cent," he murmured. "It took ten years, but I paid it back. All of it. I owe nothing."

"You are a true gentleman, Shimada-san," Father said.

"You always will be." Then he pointed to the black tie he wore, saying, "You see, I am still one of the Shimada men."

That was the last time my father saw Shozo Shimada. Some time later he heard that he had returned to Japan as penniless as the day he set out for America.

Word Power

eloquence (el ′ ə kwəns) *n.* an expressive or strong way of speaking

Background Info

A typhoon is a type of tropical storm, like a hurricane, that occurs in the areas of the Indian and western Pacific Oceans.

Reading Skill
Draw Conclusions
Reread the highlighted text. What is the best conclusion you can draw about why Mr. Shimada has come to the father's house and how he feels about it? Check the **best** response.

☐ He now works as a door-to-door salesman; he is embarrassed and wants to maintain his dignity.

☐ He thinks the father's girls are not very smart, and in need of his books.

☐ He is sorry for the father because he does not own a set of encyclopedias, but does not want to give him a gift.

Reading Skill

Evaluate Reread the highlighted text. Then evaluate the way the author chooses to end her story. Did you feel this was a good ending? Why or why not?

_____

_____

_____

_____

_____

It wasn't until the Christmas after we heard of Mr. Shimada's death that I ventured to give my father a silk four-in-hand tie. It was charcoal gray and flecked with threads of silver. My father looked at it for a long time before he tried it on, and then fingering it gently, he said, "Well, perhaps it is time now that I put away my black bow ties."

Buildings in Landscape, in black, gold, silver and red lacquer inlaid with gold and pearl-shell. Japanese, for the export market, c. 1640. Victoria and Albert Museum, London, Great Britain.

Respond to Literature

Of Dry Goods and Black Bow Ties

A Comprehension Check

Answer the following questions in the spaces provided.

1. What skill does Mr. Shimada first use to start his own business? What is his business? _____

   _____

2. When does the author's father decide it is time to put away his black bow ties? _____

   _____

B Reading Skills

Answer the following questions in the spaces provided.

1. **Draw Conclusions** Think about the business relationship that Mr. Shimada has with the author's father. What conclusion can you draw about why the father continues to wear black bow ties even after he no longer works for

   Mr. Shimada? _____

   _____

   _____

2. **Evaluate** Think about the descriptions of Mr. Shimada throughout the selection. Do you think he is a good boss to work for? Why or why not?

   _____

   _____

   _____

C Word Power

Complete each sentence below, using one of the words in the box.

elated   imposing   exhilarated
collateral   eloquence

1. The court house is a grand, _____ building, with wide steps and huge columns in the front.

2. Taylor felt _____ after her refreshing swim in the cold lake.

3. My little sister was _____ when she got the dollhouse she wanted for her birthday.

4. People may not lend you money unless you give them

   _____.

5. The speaker spoke with _____ at our graduation ceremony.

Circle the word that best completes each sentence.

6. Jamal's **(eloquence, imposing)** brought tears to the eyes of the audience.

7. Sadao was **(elated, collateral)** at the happy news.

8. Sarah was **(imposing, exhilarated)** by the climb up the mountain and greatly enjoyed the view.

9. Nate was reluctant to use his house as **(eloquence, collateral)** for the loan.

10. The tall woman wearing the long robe was very **(elated, imposing)**.

D Literary Element: Author's Purpose

Read the passage below from "Of Dry Goods and Black Bow Ties." As you read, think about the author's purpose. Then answer the questions that follow.

That was the last time my father saw Shozo Shimada.[1] Some time later he heard that he had returned to Japan as penniless as the day he set out for America.[2]

It wasn't until the Christmas after we heard of Mr. Shimada's death that I ventured to give my father a silk four-in-hand tie.[3] It was charcoal gray and flecked with threads of silver.[4] My father looked at it for a long time before he tried it on, and then fingering it gently, he said, "Well, perhaps it is time now that I put away my black bow ties."[5]

1. An author's purpose for writing can be to entertain, persuade, or give information. Which of these three purposes best applies to sentences 1–2?

   Explain your answer. _____

   _____

   _____

2. Sometimes an author's purpose is to capture the emotion and significance of a personal event. How do sentences 3–5 support this purpose?

   _____

   _____

   _____

   _____

   _____

E A Letter to Mr. Shimada

Imagine that you are the author's father, and you have just learned that Mr. Shimada has gone back to Japan as a poor man. Write a letter to Mr. Shimada to tell him what he has done for you and how you feel about him.

Dear Mr. Shimada,

I heard that you have moved back to Japan. I am writing to tell you how much you have meant to me over the years. When I first came to America and saw your shop, I felt

_____

_____

Even after I stopped working for you, I continued to

_____

When you came to my house in California, I was happy to see you. Even though you were no longer wealthy, I was proud of you because _____

_____

I just want you to know one thing: whether you are rich or poor, I will always think of you as _____

_____

Thank you for everything,
Mr. Uchida

Assessment

Fill in the circle next to each correct answer.

1. How did Mr. Shimada pay for his first dry goods store?
   - ○ A. with a loan from a bank
   - ○ B. with a loan from Mr. Uchida
   - ○ C. with deposits from his two Seattle banks
   - ○ D. with money from his dressmaking customers

2. Based on evidence in the selection, what is the **best** conclusion you can draw about how the author's father feels about Mr. Shimada?
   - ○ A. He feels he is greedy for opening so many businesses.
   - ○ B. He thinks he is stuck-up and thinks too much of himself.
   - ○ C. He feels he is a kind, generous, and honorable man.
   - ○ D. He thinks his manners are intimidating and overly formal.

3. According to the author, what was the reason for Mr. Shimida's business failures?
   - ○ A. He was too generous and lent money too freely.
   - ○ B. He knew nothing about running a business.
   - ○ C. He was too proud to ask for help.
   - ○ D. He was unable to adjust to life in the United States.

4. Which of the following statements **best** describes the author's purpose in telling the story?
   - ○ A. to persuade readers not to lend money to others
   - ○ B. to entertain readers with a humorous story about a Japanese businessman
   - ○ C. to inform readers about Japanese foods sold in dry goods stores
   - ○ D. to inform readers about an immigrant's experience

5. Which of the following words means "happy and joyful"?
   - ○ A. imposing
   - ○ B. elated
   - ○ C. collateral
   - ○ D. eloquence

Get Ready to Read!

Black Boy

Meet Richard Wright

Richard Wright's autobiography, *Black Boy*, tells of his childhood in the South, where he coped with poverty and discrimination. At fifteen, Wright began writing stories, poems, and essays. In 1940 he published the novel *Native Son*. In 1941 he received the Springam Medal, given by the NAACP for "the highest achievement by a black American." Wright was born in 1908 and died in 1960. *Black Boy* was first published in 1945.

What You Know

Have you ever done something that might have put other people in danger without thinking about the consequences? What happened?

Reason to Read

Read part of an autobiography to learn about a scary incident in a young boy's life.

Background Info

Many house fires are caused by cooking accidents, electrical shorts, or gas leaks. House fires can also be caused by children playing with lighters, matches, or other flammable materials. The fire described in this excerpt is a *Class A* fire, which means it involves ordinary dry materials such as wood or cloth.

Word Power

yearningly (yur´ ning lē) *adv.* with strong and deep desire; longingly; p. 266
I looked *yearningly* at the lake, wishing it was warm enough to jump in.

placidly (plas´ id lē) *adv.* in a serene, peaceful way; calmly; p. 266
My pet lizard lies *placidly* on his rock and suns himself all day long.

deny (di nī´) *v.* to refuse to admit something; to say something is untrue; p. 269
I tried to *deny* that I'd eaten the last cookie, but no one believed me.

taut (tôt) *adj.* stretched tight; tense or showing strain; p. 270
To play tug-of-war, both teams pull on the rope until it is *taut.*

elude (i lo͞od´) *v.* to avoid; escape the grasp of; p. 271
The dog managed to *elude* the dog catcher by racing into the woods.

perished (per´ ishd) *v.* ceased to exist; died; p. 271
I was sure my cat had *perished* in the car accident, but we got her to the vet just in time.

Answer the following questions that contain the new words above.
Write your answers in the spaces provided.

1. If you *elude* capture, do you escape or are you caught? _____

2. If a rope is *taut,* is it stretched tightly or hanging loosely? _____

3. If Arman is sitting *placidly,* is he still or fidgety? _____

4. If something has *perished,* is it alive or dead? _____

5. If your sister is looking at something *yearningly,* does she want it or not want it?

   _____

6. If Kendra and Alyssa *deny* that they have done something, are they saying they did

   or did not do it? _____

Black Boy

Richard Wright

Literary Element

Autobiography An autobiography is a person's life story written by that person. Reread the highlighted text. Look for clues in the opening sentences that tell you the selection is an autobiography. Below, list at least two clues you find.

_____
_____
_____
_____
_____
_____

One winter morning in the long-ago, four-year-old days of my life I found myself standing before a fireplace, warming my hands over a mound of glowing coals, listening to the wind whistle past the house outside. All morning my mother had been scolding me, telling me to keep still, warning me that I must make no noise. And I was angry, fretful, and impatient. In the next room Granny lay ill and under the day and night care of a doctor and I knew that I would be punished if I did not obey. I crossed restlessly to the window and pushed back the long fluffy white curtains— which I had been forbidden to touch—and looked **yearningly** out into the empty street. I was dreaming of running and playing and shouting, but the vivid image of Granny's old, white, wrinkled, grim face, framed by a halo of tumbling black hair, lying upon a huge feather pillow, made me afraid.

The house was quiet. Behind me my brother—a year younger than I—was playing **placidly** upon the floor with a toy. A bird wheeled past the window and I greeted it with a glad shout.

Word Power

yearningly (yur´ ning lē) *adv.* with strong and deep desire; longingly
placidly (plas´ id lē) *adv.* in a serene, peaceful way; calmly

"You better hush," my brother said.

"You shut up," I said.

My mother stepped briskly into the room and closed the door behind her. She came to me and shook her finger in my face.

"You stop that yelling, you hear?" she whispered. "You know Granny's sick and you better keep quiet!"

I hung my head and sulked. She left and I ached with boredom.

"I told you so," my brother gloated.

"You shut up," I told him again.

I wandered listlessly about the room, trying to think of something to do, dreading the return of my mother, resentful of being neglected. The room held nothing of interest except the fire and finally I stood before the shimmering embers, fascinated by the quivering coals. An idea of a new kind of game grew and took root in my mind. Why not throw something into the fire and watch it burn? I looked about. There was only my picture book and my mother would beat me if I burned that. Then what? I hunted around until I saw the broom leaning in a closet. That's it . . . Who would bother about a few straws if I burned them? I pulled out the broom and tore out a batch of straws and tossed them into the fire and watched them smoke, turn black, blaze, and finally become white wisps of ghosts that vanished. Burning straws was a teasing kind of fun and I took more of them from the broom and cast them into the fire. My brother came to my side, his eyes drawn by the blazing straws.

"Don't do that," he said.

"How come?" I asked.

"You'll burn the whole broom," he said.

"You hush," I said.

Reading Skill

Evaluate Reread the text highlighted in green. What is your opinion of what the narrator does?

_____

_____

_____

_____

English Coach

Sheet of yellow is an example of figurative language. Figurative language uses words to imply ideas indirectly, not literally. There was not really a yellow sheet in the room; the author is describing the harsh light from the fire. Continue reading the rest of the paragraph and underline another example of figurative language.

"I'll tell," he said.

"And I'll hit you," I said.

My idea was growing, blooming. Now I was wondering just how the long fluffy white curtains would look if I lit a bunch of straws and held it under them. Would I try it? Sure. I pulled several straws from the broom and held them to the fire until they blazed; I rushed to the window and brought the flame in touch with the hems of the curtains. My brother shook his head.

"Naw," he said.

He spoke too late. Red circles were eating into the white cloth; then a flare of flames shot out. Startled, I backed away. The fire soared to the ceiling and I trembled with fright. Soon a sheet of yellow lit the room. I was terrified; I wanted to scream but was afraid. I looked around for my brother; he was gone. One half of the room was now ablaze. Smoke was choking me and the fire was licking at my face, making me gasp.

Have you ever seen a fire in person or on TV? How would you describe it?

I made for the kitchen; smoke was surging there too. Soon my mother would smell that smoke and see the fire and come and beat me. I had done something wrong, something which I could not hide or **deny.** Yes, I would run away and never come back. I ran out of the kitchen and into the back yard. Where could I go? Yes, under the house! Nobody would find me there. I crawled under the house and crept into a dark hollow of a brick chimney and balled myself into a tight knot. My mother must not find me and whip me for what I had done. Anyway, it was all an accident; I had not really intended to set the house afire. I had just wanted to see how the curtains would look when they burned. And neither did it occur to me that I was hiding under a burning house.

Presently footsteps pounded on the floor above me. Then I heard screams. Later the gongs of fire wagons and the clopping hoofs of horses came from the direction of the street. Yes, there was really a fire, a fire like the one I had seen one day burn a house down to the ground, leaving only a chimney standing black. I was stiff with terror. The thunder of sound above me shook the chimney to which I clung. The screams came louder. I saw the image of my grandmother lying helplessly upon her bed and there were yellow flames in her black hair. Was my mother afire? Would my brother burn? Perhaps everybody in the house would burn! Why had I not thought of those things before I fired the curtains? I yearned to become invisible, to stop living. The commotion above me increased and I began to cry. It seemed that I had been hiding for ages, and when the stomping and the screaming died down I felt lonely, cast forever out of life. Voices sounded near-by and I shivered.

"Richard!" my mother was calling frantically.

Word Power

deny (di nī´) v. to refuse to admit something; to say something is untrue

Connect to the Text

Reread the boxed text. Think about a time when you wanted to run away and never come back. What happened to make you feel this way? What did you do?

_____

_____

_____

_____

_____

Reading Skill

Evaluate Reread the highlighted text. The narrator is regretting his actions. In your opinion, could he have predicted the results of his actions? Should he be hiding under the burning house thinking about this? Why or why not?

_____

_____

_____

_____

_____

_____

Reading Skill
Draw Conclusions

Reread the highlighted text. Think about the clues the narrator has given about his mother's likely reaction to this incident. What is the **best** conclusion you can draw about why the narrator stays hidden? Check the correct response.

- ☐ His mother does not see him so he is safe from punishment for the moment.
- ☐ He doesn't know there is really a fire; he is just playing hide-and-seek.
- ☐ He is curious to see what the fire looks like from underneath the house.

I saw her legs and the hem of her dress moving swiftly about the back yard. Her wails were full of an agony whose intensity told me that my punishment would be measured by its depth. Then I saw her **taut** face peering under the edge of the house. She had found me! I held my breath and waited to hear her command me to come to her. Her face went away; no, she had not seen me huddled in the dark nook of the chimney. I tucked my head into my arms and my teeth chattered.

"Richard!"

The distress I sensed in her voice was as sharp and painful as the lash of a whip on my flesh.

"Richard! The house is on fire. Oh, find my child!"

Yes the house was afire, but I was determined not to leave my place of safety. Finally I saw another face peering under the edge of the house; it was my father's. His eyes must have become accustomed to the shadows, for he was now pointing at me.

"There he is!"

"Naw!" I screamed.

"Come here, boy!"

"Naw!"

"The house is on fire!"

"Leave me 'lone!"

He crawled to me and caught hold of one of my legs. I hugged the edge of the brick chimney with all of my strength. My father yanked my leg and I clawed at the chimney harder.

"Come outta there, you little fool!"

"Turn me loose!"

Word Power

taut (tôt) *adj.* stretched tight; tense or showing strain

I could not withstand the tugging at my leg and my fingers relaxed. It was over. I would be beaten. I did not care any more. I knew what was coming. He dragged me into the back yard and the instant his hand left me I jumped to my feet and broke into a wild run trying to **elude** the people who surrounded me, heading for the street. I was caught before I had gone ten paces.

From that moment on things became tangled for me. Out of the weeping and the shouting and the wild talk, I learned that no one had died in the fire. My brother, it seemed, had finally overcome enough of his panic to warn my mother, but not before more than half the house had been destroyed. Using the mattress as a

Did You Know?

A *stretcher* is used by medical professionals to carry injured patients from one place to another. The patient is placed on the stretcher and then carried by two people, one at the head and one at the feet.

. . . .

stretcher, Grandpa and an uncle had lifted Granny from her bed and had rushed her to the safety of a neighbor's house. My long absence and silence had made everyone think, for a while, that I had **perished** in the blaze.

"You almost scared us to death," my mother muttered as she stripped the leaves from a tree limb to prepare it for my back.

I was lashed so hard and long that I lost consciousness. I was beaten out of my senses and later I found myself in bed, screaming, determined to run away, tussling with my mother and father who were trying to keep me still. I was lost in a fog of fear. A doctor was called—I was afterwards told—and he ordered that I be kept abed, that I be kept quiet, that my very life depended upon it.

Word Power

elude (i lo͞od ′) *v.* to avoid; escape the grasp of
perished (per′ ishd) *v.* ceased to exist; died

Comprehension Check

Reread the boxed text. What does the narrator do after his father drags him into the back yard?

_____

_____

_____

_____

Reading Skill

Evaluate Reread the highlighted text. Then evaluate the mother's reaction to the situation. What is your opinion of her actions toward her son? What might she have done differently?

_____

_____

_____

_____

_____

_____

_____

_____

Literary Element

Autobiography Richard Wright has written about an event that happened when he was four years old. Why do you think it was important for him to include this event in his autobiography?

_____

_____

_____

_____

_____

_____

_____

_____

My body seemed on fire and I could not sleep. Packs of ice were put on my forehead to keep down the fever. Whenever I tried to sleep I would see huge wobbly white bags, like the full udders of cows, suspended from the ceiling above me.

Later, as I grew worse, I could see the bags in the daytime with my eyes open and I was gripped by the fear that they were going to fall and drench me with some horrible liquid. Day and night I begged my mother and father to take the bags away, pointing to them, shaking with terror because no one saw them but me. Exhaustion would make me drift toward sleep and then I would scream until I was wide awake again; I was afraid to sleep. Time finally bore me away from the dangerous bags and I got well. But for a long time I was chastened whenever I remembered that my mother had come close to killing me.

Portrait of Willie Gee, 1904. Robert Henri. Oil on canvas, 31 ¼ x 26 ¼ in. Newark Museum, NJ.

Does the boy in this painting look like what you imagine the narrator might look like? How is he similar? How is he different?

_____

Respond to Literature

Black Boy

A Comprehension Check

Answer the following questions in the spaces provided.

1. Why are the narrator and his brother warned to stay quiet? _____

   _____

2. Where does the narrator hide when the house catches on fire? _____

   _____

   _____

B Reading Skills

Answer the following questions in the spaces provided.

1. **Draw Conclusions** Think about the events that lead up to the house catching on fire. What conclusions can you draw about why the narrator

   sets the fire? _____

   _____

   _____

   _____

2. **Evaluate** Think about the way the author describes the events in the story. Do you think his descriptions are interesting and well told? Why or

   why not? _____

   _____

   _____

C Word Power

Complete each sentence below, using one of the words in the box.

yearningly	placidly	deny
taut	elude	perished

1. We sat _____, not wanting to disturb the girl shooting the free-throw.

2. Many soldiers _____ in the terrible battle.

3. I looked _____ at the cake, but I knew I couldn't have a piece until after dinner.

4. She tried to _____ the dog, but it ran up to her and licked her face.

5. Pierre could not _____ that he had missed his curfew because his mother saw him come home late.

6. After I had run five miles, my muscles felt stiff and _____.

D Literary Element: Autobiography

Read the passages below from *Black Boy*. As you read, think about the characteristics of an autobiography. Then answer the questions that follow.

> One winter morning in the long-ago, four-year-old days of my life I found myself standing before a fireplace, warming my hands over a mound of glowing coals, listening to the wind whistle past the house outside.[1]
>
> An idea of a new kind of game grew and took root in my mind.[2] Why not throw something into the fire and watch it burn?[3] I looked about.[4] There was only my picture book and my mother would beat me if I burned that.[5]

1. Which words in sentence 1 help you understand that the writer of *Black Boy* is telling his own story? _____

   _____

   _____

   _____

2. An autobiography often contains events from the author's childhood. In sentences 2–5, how does the author illustrate his young age at the time of the event? _____

   _____

   _____

   _____

   _____

E Comic Strip

Look at the four frames of the comic strip below. Read the speech balloons for Richard's brother and parents. Add words to Richard's thought balloons to show what he might be thinking. Draw more details and color in the frames if you wish.

Assessment

Fill in the circle next to each correct answer.

1. When the narrator starts playing with fire, what is his brother's reaction?
    - ○ A. He begs him to let him play along.
    - ○ B. He tells him not to do it.
    - ○ C. He says that it looks like fun.
    - ○ D. He runs and tells his mother right away.

2. Based on the details in the selection, what is the **best** conclusion you can draw about why the author starts the fire?
    - ○ A. He wants to burn the whole house down.
    - ○ B. He is only trying to make the house warmer.
    - ○ C. He is young, bored, and angry at being left alone.
    - ○ D. He is mean and wants to hurt his family.

3. Based on the details the author gives, what is the **best** conclusion you can draw about how he feels after the fire starts?
    - ○ A. terrified and guilty
    - ○ B. proud and impressed
    - ○ C. scared but excited
    - ○ D. surprised but happy

4. Which of the following sentences from the selection **best** illustrates that it is an autobiography?
    - ○ A. His eyes must have become accustomed to the shadows.
    - ○ B. In the next room Granny lay ill.
    - ○ C. Burning straws was a teasing kind of fun.
    - ○ D. I found myself standing before a fireplace, warming my hands.

5. Which of the following words means "in a calm way"?
    - ○ A. yearningly
    - ○ B. placidly
    - ○ C. taut
    - ○ D. elude

Get Ready to Read!

NIGHT

Meet Elie Wiesel

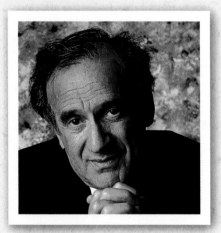

Elie Wiesel (el′ē wē sel′) was born in Romania in 1928. At age 15, he and his family were imprisoned in concentration camps. Although Wiesel survived, most of his family died. After the war, Wiesel worked as a journalist in Paris before moving to the United States. He has devoted his life to speaking out against human rights violations. He won the Nobel Peace Prize in 1986. *Night* was published in English in 1960.

What You Know

What do you know about the Holocaust, when millions of Jews and other European civilians were killed during World War II?

Reason to Read

Read to share the author's horrors as he tries to survive in a Nazi concentration camp.

Background Info

During World War II, Nazi leader Adolph Hitler ruled Germany. He declared Roma, Jewish, and Slavic people, and other groups of people "undesirable." Hitler stripped these people of their citizenship. He ordered them to be locked up in crowded, forced-labor concentration camps where they were starved, tortured, and killed.

Several prison camps in Germany and Poland became "death camps." Enormous numbers of murders took place at "death camps" such as Buchenwald in Germany and Auschwitz in Poland. The concentration camps were run by members of the SS. The letters *SS* came from the German word *Schutzstaffel,* or "protection staff." SS troops were in charge of killing prisoners throughout Europe. Many of the victims' bodies were burned in big furnaces called crematories. The Nazis killed about six million people. Half of the victims were Jewish.

In this excerpt, the author describes events from his own life. The events take place in 1944, after he and his father had been sent to Buna (bōō′ nə), a forced-labor camp in Poland.

Word Power

anguish (ang′ gwish) *n.* great suffering or pain; agony; p. 280
Both parents waited in *anguish* as the police searched for their missing child.

reprieve (ri prēv′) *n.* a chance to escape pain or danger; p. 281
The mild day gave everyone a *reprieve* from the bitterly cold winter.

interminable (in tur′ mi nə bəl) *adj.* endless; seeming to be without an end; p. 283
The audience grew bored listening to one *interminable* speech after another.

emaciated (i mā′ shē āt′ id) *adj.* extremely thin; p. 284
This *emaciated* kitten needs to put on weight.

avidly (av′ id lē) *adv.* eagerly; with great enthusiasm; p. 284
Sports fans *avidly* look forward to every game.

meager (mē′ gər) *adj.* not enough; too little; p. 285
My lunch was so *meager* that I still felt hungry after eating it.

din (din) *n.* loud, continuous noise; p. 287
All the workers wore earplugs to protect their hearing in the *din* of the factory.

**Answer the following questions that contain the new words above.
Write your answers in the spaces provided.**

1. If you ate a *meager* meal, would you have eaten a large or small meal? _____

2. What might cause *anguish,* a lost pet or a lost pencil? _____

3. If you see an *emaciated* dog, does it need food or a new toy? _____

4. If you heard the *din* of your neighbor's New Year's Eve party, would it be noise that continued for a long time, or a short, quick shriek?

   _____

5. If you were *avidly* watching TV, would you be interested or bored? _____

6. What is more likely to be *interminable,* a long wait or a great movie?

   _____

7. If you had a *reprieve* from a test, would you get a break or would you be told to

   continue working? _____

NIGHT

Elie Wiesel
Translated by Stella Rodway

Background Info

The boxed words on this page relate to the Nazi prison camps. All prisoners were tattooed with a number on the left forearm. Each person was known by his or her number, not by name. The bodies of dead prisoners were burned in a furnace called a crematory. Some prisoners served as Kapos (kä´ pōz) and were put in charge of other prisoners in a building.

English Coach

Veterans can be people who have served in the armed forces. Here, *veterans* are people who have been in the camp the longest and have the most experience living in this situation. If you were a *veteran* at something, such as basketball or playing an instrument, would you be experienced or inexperienced?

The SS gave us a fine New Year's gift.

We had just come back from work. As soon as we had passed through the door of the camp, we sensed something different in the air. Roll call did not take so long as usual. The evening soup was given out with great speed and swallowed down at once in **anguish.**

I was no longer in the same block as my father. I had been transferred to another unit, the building one, where, twelve hours a day, I had to drag heavy blocks of stone about. The head of my new block was a German Jew, small of stature, with piercing eyes. He told us that evening that no one would be allowed to go out after the evening soup. And soon a terrible word was circulating—selection.

We knew what that meant. An SS man would examine us. Whenever he found a weak one, a *musulman* as we called them, he would write his number down: good for the crematory.

After soup, we gathered together between the beds. The veterans said:

"You're lucky to have been brought here so late. This camp is paradise today, compared with what it was like two years ago. Buna was a real hell then. There was no water, no blankets, less soup and bread. At night we slept almost naked, and it was below thirty degrees. The corpses were collected in hundreds every day. The work was hard. Today, this is a little paradise. The Kapos had orders to kill a certain number of prisoners every day. And every week—selection. A merciless selection. . . . Yes, you're lucky."

Word Power

anguish (ang´ gwish) *n.* great suffering or pain; agony

"Stop it! Be quiet!" I begged. "You can tell your stories tomorrow or on some other day."

They burst out laughing. They were not veterans for nothing.

"Are you scared? So were we scared. And there was plenty to be scared of in those days."

The old men stayed in their corner, dumb, motionless, haunted. Some were praying.

An hour's delay. In an hour, we should know the verdict—death or a **reprieve.**

And my father? Suddenly I remembered him. How would he pass the selection? He had aged so much. . . .

The head of our block had never been outside concentration camps since 1933. He had already been through all the slaughterhouses, all the factories of death. At about nine o'clock, he took up his position in our midst:

> *"Achtung!"*

There was instant silence.

"Listen carefully to what I am going to say." (For the first time, I heard his voice quiver.) "In a few moments the selection will begin. You must get completely undressed. Then one by one you go before the SS doctors. I hope you will all succeed in getting through. But you must help your own chances. Before you go into the next room, move about in some way so that you give yourselves a little color. Don't walk slowly, run! Run as if the devil were after you! Don't look at the SS. Run, straight in front of you!"

Background Info

The German word *Achtung!* (äKH toong´) means "Attention!"

Reading Skill
Draw Conclusions
Reread the text highlighted in green. What conclusion can you draw about why the men are told to run? Check the correct response.
☐ Running is an exercise that will make them stronger.
☐ Moving around and running will help them pass the time.
☐ Having color and running will make them appear healthier.

Word Power
reprieve (ri prēv´) *n.* a chance to escape pain or danger

My Workspace

Connect to the Text

Reread the boxed text. Have you ever been in a situation in which you were told "don't be afraid"? What was it that made you afraid? How did you react?

_____

_____

_____

_____

_____

He broke off for a moment, then added:

"And, the essential thing, don't be afraid!"

Here was a piece of advice we should have liked very much to be able to follow.

I got undressed, leaving my clothes on the bed. There was no danger of anyone stealing them this evening.

Tibi and Yossi, who had changed their unit at the same time as I had, came up to me and said:

"Let's keep together. We shall be stronger."

Yossi was murmuring something between his teeth. He must have been praying. I had never realized that Yossi was a believer. I had even always thought the reverse. Tibi was silent, very pale. All the prisoners in the block stood naked between the beds. This must be how one stands at the last judgment.

"They're coming!"

Anywhere in Europe 1933–1945. Gertrude Jacobson. Acyrlic and steel barbed wire on board, 34 x 44 x 4 in. Collection of Yad Vashem Museum of Art, Jerusalem.

What do the title and the barbed wire contribute to the artist's message? How does this excerpt from *Night* convey what it might be like to be a person in this painting?

There were three SS officers standing round the notorious Dr. Mengele, who had received us at Birkenau. The head of the block, with an attempt at a smile, asked us:

"Ready?"

Yes, we were ready. So were the SS doctors. Dr. Mengele was holding a list in his hand: our numbers. He made a sign to the head of the block: "We can begin!" As if this were a game!

The first to go by were the "officials" of the block: *Stubenaelteste,* Kapos, foremen, all in perfect physical condition of course! Then came the ordinary prisoners' turn. Dr. Mengele took stock of them from head to foot. Every now and then, he wrote a number down. One single thought filled my mind: not to let my number be taken; not to show my left arm.

There were only Tibi and Yossi in front of me. They passed. I had time to notice that Mengele had not written their numbers down. Someone pushed me. It was my turn. I ran without looking back. My head was spinning: you're too thin, you're weak, you're too thin, you're good for the furnace. . . . The race seemed **interminable.** I thought I had been running for years. . . . You're too thin, you're too weak. . . . At last I had arrived exhausted. When I regained my breath, I questioned Yossi and Tibi:

"Was I written down?"

"No," said Yossi. He added, smiling: "In any case, he couldn't have written you down, you were running too fast. . . . "

I began to laugh. I was glad. I would have liked to kiss him. At that moment, what did the others matter! I hadn't been written down.

Word Power

interminable (in tur′ mi nə bəl) *adj.* endless; seeming to be without an end

Background Info

Dr. Josef Mengele (meng′ ə lə) was among the worst of the Nazi war criminals. Dr. Mengele performed gruesome experiments on prisoners. He also selected nearly half a million prisoners for death in the Auschwitz (oush′ vits) gas chambers. Birkenau (bûr′ kə nou) was one section of the Auschwitz camps.

Literary Element

Autobiography An autobiography is the story of a person's life, written by that person. One reason people like to read autobiographies is to learn about historic events the writer has lived through. Reread the highlighted passage. What event is being described? Check the correct response.

☐ Dr. Mengele is selecting weaker prisoners to send to the crematory.

☐ The "officials" of the block were in perfect physical condition.

☐ Kapos are people who are in charge of the prison.

Those whose numbers had been noted stood apart, abandoned by the whole world. Some were weeping in silence.

The SS officers went away. The head of the block appeared, his face reflecting the general weariness.

"Everything went off all right. Don't worry. Nothing is going to happen to anyone. To anyone."

Again he tried to smile. A poor, **emaciated,** dried-up Jew questioned him **avidly** in a trembling voice:

"But . . . but, Blockaelteste, they did write me down!"

The head of the block let his anger break out. What! Did someone refuse to believe him!

"What's the matter now? Am I telling lies then? I tell you once and for all, nothing's going to happen to you! To anyone! You're wallowing in your own despair, you fool!"

The bell rang, a signal that the selection had been completed throughout the camp.

With all my might I began to run to Block 36. I met my father on the way. He came up to me:

"Well? So you passed?"

"Yes. And you?"

"Me too."

How we breathed again, now! My father had brought me a present—half a ration of bread obtained in exchange for a piece of rubber, found at the warehouse, which would do to sole a shoe.

The bell. Already we must separate, go to bed. Everything was regulated by the bell. It gave me orders, and I automatically obeyed them. I hated it. Whenever I dreamed of a better world, I could only imagine a universe with no bells.

Reading Skill

Evaluate Reread the paragraph highlighted in green. Why do you think the head of the block speaks this way? What effect do you think the words have on the prisoners?

_____

_____

_____

_____

Literary Element

Autobiography Reread the sentence highlighted in blue. Wiesel recalls dreaming of a better world. Why might he have included this memory in this autobiography?

_____

_____

_____

_____

Word Power

emaciated (i mā′ shē āt′ id) *adj.* extremely thin

avidly (av′ id lē) *adv.* eagerly; with great enthusiasm

Several days had elapsed. We no longer thought about the selection. We went to work as usual, loading heavy stones into railway wagons. Rations had become more **meager:** this was the only change.

We had risen before dawn, as on every day. We had received the black coffee, the ration of bread. We were about to set out for the yard as usual. The head of the block arrived, running.

"Silence for a moment. I have a list of numbers here. I'm going to read them to you. Those whose numbers I call won't be going to work this morning; they'll stay behind in the camp."

And, in a soft voice, he read out about ten numbers. We had understood. These were numbers chosen at the selection. Dr. Mengele had not forgotten.

The head of the block went toward his room. Ten prisoners surrounded him, hanging onto his clothes:

"Save us! You promised . . .! We want to go to the yard. We're strong enough to work. We're good workers. We can . . . we will . . ."

He tried to calm them, to reassure them about their fate, to explain to them that the fact that they were staying behind in the camp did not mean much, had no tragic significance.

"After all, I stay here myself every day," he added.

It was a somewhat feeble argument. He realized it, and without another word went and shut himself up in his room.

The bell had just rung.

"Form up!"

Word Power

meager (mē´ gər) *adj.* not enough; too little

Reading Skill

Draw Conclusions
Reread the first passage highlighted in green. What conclusion can you draw about what will happen to the men whose numbers are called?

_____

_____

_____

_____

Reading Skill

Evaluate Reread the second passage highlighted in green. Do you think the head of the block is doing a good job handling this situation?

_____

_____

_____

_____

_____

_____

_____

285

Connect to the Text

Reread the boxed sentence. When have you tried to comfort someone even though you may have been suffering yourself?

_____

_____

_____

_____

_____

English Coach

An *inheritance* is a valuable possession that is given to someone when the previous owner dies. If you received an inheritance, would you purchase it, or would it be given to you?

_____

_____

It scarcely mattered now that the work was hard. The essential thing was to be as far away as possible from the block, from the center of hell.

I saw my father running toward me. I became frightened all of a sudden.

"What's the matter?"

Out of breath, he could hardly open his mouth.

"Me, too . . . me, too . . .! They told me to stay behind in the camp."

They had written down his number without his being aware of it.

"What will happen?" I asked in anguish.

But it was he who tried to reassure me.

"It isn't certain yet. There's still a chance of escape. They're going to do another selection today . . . a decisive selection."

I was silent.

He felt that his time was short. He spoke quickly. He would have liked to say so many things. His speech grew confused; his voice choked. He knew that I would have to go in a few moments. He would have to stay behind alone, so very alone.

"Look, take this knife," he said to me. "I don't need it any longer. It might be useful to you. And take this spoon as well. Don't sell them. Quickly! Go on. Take what I'm giving you!"

The inheritance.

"Don't talk like that, Father." (I felt that I would break into sobs.) "I don't want you to say that. Keep the spoon and knife. You need them as much as I do. We shall see each other again this evening, after work."

He looked at me with his tired eyes, veiled with despair. He went on:

"I'm asking this of you. . . . Take them. Do as I ask, my son. We have no time. . . . Do as your father asks."

Our Kapo yelled that we should start. The unit set out toward the camp gate. Left, right! I bit my lips. My father had stayed by the block, leaning against the wall. Then he began to run, to catch up with us. Perhaps he had forgotten something he wanted to say to me. . . . But we were marching too quickly. . . . Left, right!

We were already at the gate. They counted us, to the **din** of military music. We were outside.

The whole day, I wandered about as if sleep-walking.

Now and then Tibi and Yossi would throw me a brotherly word. The Kapo, too, tried to reassure me. He had given me easier work today. I felt sick at heart. How well they were treating me! Like an orphan! I thought: even now, my father is still helping me.

I did not know myself what I wanted—for the day to pass quickly or not. I was afraid of finding myself alone that night. How good it would be to die here!

At last we began the return journey. How I longed for orders to run!

The military march. The gate. The camp.

I ran to block 36.

Were there still miracles on this earth? He was alive. He had escaped the second selection. He had been able to prove that he was still useful. . . . I gave him back his knife and spoon.

Word Power

din (din) *n.* loud, continuous noise

Reading Skill

Evaluate Reread the text highlighted in green. The father calls the narrator "my son" and says "Do as your father asks." How do these words add meaning to the story? Check the correct response.

☐ They emphasize the father-son relationship.

☐ The formal words show the father and son are not close.

☐ They show the father is not serious about the gift.

Literary Element

Autobiography Reread the text highlighted in blue. Wiesel recalls the day that he thought he had become an orphan. Describe how he felt that day.

_____

_____

_____

_____

_____

_____

_____

Respond to Literature

NIGHT

A Comprehension Check

Answer the following questions in the spaces provided.

1. What was a "selection" in a Nazi concentration camp? _____

_____

2. What happens to the father at the end of this excerpt? _____

_____

_____

B Reading Skills

Answer the following questions in the spaces provided.

1. **Draw Conclusions** What conclusion can you draw about the head of the block as he prepares the prisoners for the selection?

_____

_____

2. **Draw Conclusions** What conclusion can you draw about why the father wants to give his knife and spoon to his son? _____

_____

3. **Evaluate** Wiesel wrote, "Those whose numbers had been noted stood apart, abandoned by whole world." Do you think this sentence effectively describes how these men might have been feeling? Explain.

_____

_____

C Word Power

Complete each sentence below, using one of the words in the box.

anguish	reprieve	interminable
emaciated	avidly	meager	din

1. Clothing hung loosely over the _____ bodies of the starving people.

2. The week of work seemed _____, but Friday afternoon finally arrived.

3. The children listened _____ as the storyteller described the magical land.

4. After eating a huge dinner at Mama's Restaurant, we went on a diet and ate _____ meals for three days.

5. For people who live next to the highway, the _____ of traffic never ends.

6. A quick game of basketball was a welcome _____ from hours of studying.

7. The family cried in _____ as they watched their house burn.

D Literary Element: Autobiography

As you read the passage from *Night*, think about how Wiesel shows his own thoughts and feelings. Then answer the questions that follow.

The bell rang, a signal that the selection had been completed throughout the camp.[1]

With all my might I began to run to Block 36.[2] I met my father on the way.[3] He came up to me:[4]

"Well? So you passed?"[5]

"Yes. And you?"[6]

"Me too."[7]

How we breathed again, now![8] My father had brought me a present—half a ration of bread obtained in exchange for a piece of rubber, found at the warehouse, which would do to sole a shoe.[9]

1. How do sentences 5–8 show that Wiesel remembers how tense he felt, and then how relieved he felt? _____

_____

_____

2. In sentence 9, Wiesel remembers exactly what his father gave him and how his father got it. In your opinion, why are those details important to him?

_____

_____

_____

E Emotion Graph

The author of *Night* faces some terrible moments as well as moments of great relief. Complete the statements below. Then make a line graph in the box at the bottom of the page. Plot the letters on the graph to show "highs" and "lows" in the author's experience. Connect the letters. A and D have already been done for you.

A. As the New Year begins, all the prisoners get ready for a selection.

B. The author runs past _____

_____

C. The author learns that he has _____

_____

D. The author runs to see his father. He learns that his father has passed too.

E. Several days later, the head of the block announces the numbers. The author learns that his father must _____

_____

F. The author spends a whole day _____

_____

G. The author finds that his father _____

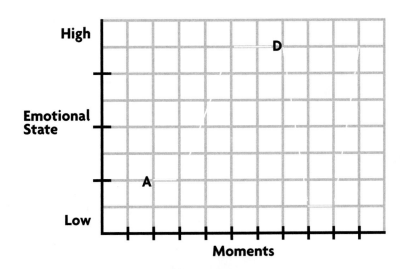

Assessment

Fill in the circle next to each correct answer.

1. What work does the author do in the camp?
   - ○ A. running errands
   - ○ B. building fences
   - ○ C. repairing shoes
   - ○ D. dragging heavy stones

2. When the head of the block gives instructions for the selection, what conclusion can you draw about why his voice quivers?
   - ○ A. He is old.
   - ○ B. He cannot hide his strong feelings.
   - ○ C. He wants everyone to listen carefully.
   - ○ D. He is very angry.

3. How can you tell that this work is autobiographical?
   - ○ A. The narrator and the author are the same person.
   - ○ B. The author imagines dialogue and events.
   - ○ C. The author did research to write about a famous person.
   - ○ D. Only some of the events are true.

4. What is the author's main feeling when he marches out to work and sees his father left behind at the camp?
   - ○ A. unconcern
   - ○ B. despair
   - ○ C. disinterest
   - ○ D. tired

5. Which of the following words means "extreme suffering"?
   - ○ A. reprieve
   - ○ B. meager
   - ○ C. anguish
   - ○ D. din

UNIT 5

Wrap-up

Compare and Contrast

Black Boy and *Night* are **autobiographical** writings. In each selection, the author writes about a terrible experience he lived through. Although the times and places of their experiences are different, both authors are deeply affected by the events.

Complete the boxes below. In the left box, tell how the stories are alike. In the right box, tell how they are different. Consider the following points in your comparison:

- the settings
- each boy's age
- their relationships with their parents
- their situations
- their feelings

An example in each column has been done for you.

Alike	Different
• Both authors are young boys.	• Richard is very scared of his mother and tries to hide from her. Elie loves his father and is scared he will be killed by the SS.

Glossary

A

abruptly (ə brupt´ lē) *adv.* suddenly; without warning; p. 200

abundance (ə bun´ dəns) *n.* a great amount; p. 175

abyss (ə bis´) *n.* an extremely deep pit; p. 5

acrid (ak´ rid) *adj.* sharp, bitter, or irritating to smell or taste; p. 110

agony (ag´ ə nē) *n.* intense pain or suffering; p. 4

anguish (ang´ gwish) *n.* great suffering or pain; agony; p. 280

anniversary (an´ ə vur´ sə rē) *n.* the yearly date on which a past event happened; p. 75

anthology (an thol´ ə jē) *n.* a collection of poems, stories, or other writing, in a single book; p. 238

apex (ā´ peks) *n.* the highest point; p. 129

avidly (av´ id lē) *adv.* eagerly; with great enthusiasm; p. 284

B

baffled (baf´ əld) *v.* confused; p. 61

boldly (bōld´ lē) *adv.* in a way that shows no respect; arrogantly; p. 199

C

careen (kə rēn´) *v.* to tilt or sway while moving, as if out of control; p. 87

cascade (kas kād´) *n.* a waterfall; a series of small waterfalls; p. 37

clammy (klam´ ē) *adj.* cold and sticky; sweaty; p. 5

collateral (kə lat´ ər əl) *n.* money or property that is given to a lender as a pledge that a loan will be repaid; p. 255

companions (kəm pan´ yənz) *n.* people who accompany others; p. 174

complied (kəm plīd´) *v.* obeyed; agreed to do something; p. 51

conscious (kon´ shəs) *adj.* aware; p. 75

consciousness (kon´ shəs nis) *n.* the state of being awake and aware of one's surroundings; p. 118

consoling (kən sō´ ling) *v.* comforting or cheering someone who is sad or hurt; p. 230

cower (kou´ ər) *v.* to crouch down in fear; p. 108

craved (krāvd) *v.* wanted very badly; p. 42

D

deny (di nī´) *v.* to refuse to admit something; to say something is untrue; p. 269

deserted (di zurt´ id) *v.* left someone alone in time of need or danger; p. 212

despair (di spār´) *v.* to lose all hope; p. 153

din (din) *n.* loud, continuous noise; p. 287

discourage (dis kur´ ij) *v.* to try to persuade someone not to do something; p. 87

discreet (dis krēt´) *adj.* showing good judgment; cautious; p. 21

disregarding (dis´ri gärd´ ing) *v.* treating without respect or attention; p. 72

distraught (dis trôt´) *adj.* very upset; p. 26

E

elated (i lā´ tid) a*dj.* filled with joy; p. 251

elation (i lā´ shən) *n.* a feeling of great joy; p. 25

eloquence (el´ ə kwəns) *n.* an expressive or strong way of speaking; p. 257

elude (i lo͞od´) *v.* to avoid; escape the grasp of; p. 271

Glossary

emaciated (i mā′ shē āt′ id) *adj.* extremely thin; p. 284

enthralled (en thrôld′) *adj.* spellbound; fascinated; p. 23

excruciating (iks krōō′ shē ā′ ting) *adj.* extremely painful; p. 228

exhilarated (ig zil′ ə rāt′ id) *adj.* cheerful, lively, or excited; refreshed; p. 255

F

faltered (fôl′ tərd) *v.* stumbled or paused in an awkward way; p. 37

fates (fāts) *n.* outcomes that have been determined to happen and over which human beings have no control; p. 194

futilely (fū′ til ē) *adv.* uselessly; without hope; p. 128

G

gravely (grāv′ lē) *adv.* seriously; with a sense of importance; p. 55

grieve (grēv) *v.* to feel great sadness; p. 162

H

hideous (hid′ ē əs) *adj.* very ugly; p. 6

horizontally (hôr′ ə zon′ tə lē) *adv.* in a position that is parallel to the horizon; p. 242

I

imposing (im pō′ zing) *adj.* impressive in appearance or manner; p. 254

improvised (im′ prə vīzd′) *v.* acted without a plan; made something up along the way; p. 58

incomprehensible (in′ kom pri hen′ sə bəl) *adj.* impossible to understand; p. 54

indestructible (in′ di struk′ tə bəl) *adj.* not able to be destroyed; p. 110

inevitably (i nev′ ə tə blē) *adv.* certainly; predictably; p. 128

infatuated (in fach′ ōō ā′ təd) *adj.* in love or attracted in a foolish way; p. 22

interminable (in tur′ mi nə bəl) *adj.* endless; seeming to be without an end; p. 283

intervened (in′ tər vēnd′) *v.* played a role in changing an event; interfered; p. 213

invalid (in′ və lid) *n.* a person who is sick or disabled; p. 85

investment (in vest′ mənt) *n.* spending in the present for a gain in the future; p. 241

K

kin (kin) *n.* relatives; family members; p. 150

L

laboriously (lə bôr′ ē əs lē) *adv.* done with hard work or a lot of effort; p. 40

lanky (lang′ kē) *adj.* ungracefully thin and tall; p. 106

leisure (lē′ zhər) *n.* free time that is not spent doing a job or other work; p. 242

loll (lol) *v.* to act or move in a lazy and relaxed way; p. 88

M

mammoth (mam′ əth) *adj.* extremely large; p. 39

meager (mē′ gər) *adj.* not enough; too little; p. 285

mercy (mur′ sē) *n.* compassion or forgiveness; p. 97

Glossary

merged (murjd) *v.* joined together; p. 4

mocks (moks) *v.* makes fun of; shows no respect for; p. 150

mortality (môr tal´ ə tē) *n.* the condition of being sure to die; p. 229

N

nostalgia (nos tal´ jə) *n.* a sentimental longing for the past; p. 240

P

panorama (pan´ ə ram´ ə) *n.* a complete view of an area from every direction; p. 132

parched (pärcht) *adj.* extremely dry; p. 229

perils (per´ əlz) *n.* dangers; risks; p. 197

periphery (pə rif´ ər ē) *n.* the surrounding area; outskirts; p. 51

perished (per´ ishd) *v.* ceased to exist; died; p. 271

perspective (pər spek´ tiv) *n.* point of view; p. 127

philandering (fi lan´ dər ing) *adj.* carrying on a love affair with someone who is not one's spouse; p. 239

placidly (plas´ id lē) *adv.* in a serene, peaceful way; calmly; p. 266

potential (pə ten´ shəl) *n.* the ability to grow or develop; p. 130

precariously (pri kār´ ē əs lē) *adv.* dangerously; insecurely; p. 95

profound (prə found´) *adj.* significant; deep; intense; p. 18

R

reinforcements (rē´ in fôrs´ mənts) *n.* fighters and weapons added for a battle; p. 210

relented (ri lent´ əd) *v.* gave in; p. 52

replenished (ri plen´ isht) *v.* made full or complete again; p. 174

reprieve (ri prēv´) *n.* a chance to escape pain or danger; p. 281

resolving (ri zolv´ ing) *v.* making a strong decision; p. 6

retrieving (ri trēv´ ing) *v.* taking or getting something back; p. 209

retrospect (ret´ rə spekt´) *n.* the act of looking back or thinking about the past; p. 239

reverently (rev´ ər ənt lē) *adv.* in a way that shows honor and love; p. 135

rile (rīl) *v.* to make upset; p. 157

ruthless (rōōth´ lis) *adj.* without pity or mercy; cruel; p. 214

S

saunter (sôn´ tər) *v.* to walk slowly and easily; to stroll; p. 132

savages (sav´ ij əz) *n.* people who are brutal and cruel; people who live in a basic, uncivilized way; p. 175

seize (sēz) *v.* to grab and hold suddenly; p. 193

severance (sev´ ər əns) *n.* the act of cutting off or apart; p. 226

shrine (shrīn) *n.* a place to offer prayers or to honor someone; p. 153

skeptically (skep´ ti kəl lē) *adv.* doubtfully; in an unconvinced manner; p. 112

slaughter (slô´ tər) *n.* the killing of many people or animals; p. 207

solace (sol´ is) *n.* relief from sorrow or disappointment; comfort; p. 27

Glossary

spite (spīt) *n.* a mean feeling toward someone; p. 98

strategy (strat′ ə jē) *n.* a plan of action; p. 181

sullenly (sul′ ən lē) *adv.* in a bad-tempered, sulky, or gloomy way; p. 88

surged (surjd) *v.* grew higher and stronger like a wave; p. 184

sympathetic (sim′ pə thet′ ik) *adj.* sharing the feelings of another or expressing pity; p. 76

T

taut (tôt) *adj.* stretched tight; tense or showing strain; p. 270

tediously (tē′ dē əs lē) *adv.* in a bored way; in a boring and tiresome way; p. 226

twilight (twī′ līt′) *n.* soft, hazy light reflected from the sun just after sunset; p. 76

V

ventured (ven′ chərd) *v.* risked; dared to do something or go somewhere; p. 115

vigilant (vij′ ə lənt) *adj.* careful and looking out for trouble; p. 22

vigorous (vig′ ər əs) *adj.* strong and active; p. 75

W

weary (wēr′ ē) *adj.* very tired; p. 197

Y

yearningly (yur′ ning lē) *adv.* with strong and deep desire; longingly; p. 266

My Personal Dictionary

ACKNOWLEDGMENTS

LITERATURE

UNIT 1

Adapted from "American History" from *The Latin Deli: Prose and Poetry,* by Judith Ortiz Cofer. Copyright © 1993 by Judith Ortiz Cofer. Adapted and reprinted by permission of The University of Georgia Press.

Adapted from "The Horned Toad," by Gerald Haslam. Adapted and reprinted by permission of the author.

UNIT 2

Adaptation of "Soul-Catcher," by Louis Owens. Adapted and reprinted by permission of Polly Owens.

Adapted from "Sweet Potato Pie" by Eugenia Collier. Adapted and reprinted by permission of the author.

UNIT 3

From *An Adapted Classic: Romeo and Juliet by William Shakespeare,* © 1996 by Pearson Education, Inc., publishing as Globe Fearon, an imprint of Pearson Learning Group. Used by permission.

UNIT 4

From *An Adapted Classic: The Odyssey of Homer* adapted by Henry I. Christ, © 1992 by Pearson Education, Inc., publishing as Globe Fearon, an imprint of Pearson Learning Group. Used by permission.

UNIT 5

Adapted from "Field Trip" by Naomi Shihab Nye. Adapted and reprinted by permission of the author.

"Only Daughter" by Sandra Cisneros. Copyright © 1990 by Sandra Cisneros. First published in *Glamour,* November 1990. Recorded by permission of Susan Bergholz Literary Services, New York. All rights reserved.

"Of Dry Goods and Black Bow Ties" by Yoshiko Uchida. Courtesy of the Bancroft Library, University of California, Berkeley.

From *Black Boy* by Richard Wright. Copyright © 1937, 1942, 1944, 1945 by Richard Wright; renewed © 1973 by Ellen Wright. Reprinted by permission of HarperCollins Publishers.

Excerpt from *Night* by Elie Wiesel, translated by Stella Rodway. Copyright © 1960 by MacGibbon & Kee. Copyright renewed © 1988 by The Collins Publishing Group. Reprinted by permission of Hill and Wang, a division of Farrar, Straus and Giroux, LLC.

IMAGE CREDITS: